1-4-57

Marriage and Family Relationships

THE MACMILLAN COMPANY
NEW YORK · CHICAGO
DALLAS · ATLANTA · SAN FRANCISCO

MACMILLAN AND CO., LIMITED
LONDON · BOMBAY · CALCUTTA
MADRAS · MELBOURNE

THE MACMILLAN COMPANY
OF CANADA, LIMITED
TORONTO

MARRIAGE AND FAMILY RELATIONSHIPS

REVISED EDITION

ROBERT GEIB FOSTER

THE UNIVERSITY OF KANSAS
AND THE MENNINGER FOUNDATION

THE MACMILLAN COMPANY : NEW YORK

PREFACE TO THE REVISED EDITION

Decision to publish a revised edition of this book is due to the hearty reception it received from many teachers, students, and young men and women throughout the country. At the time it was written it seemed to have met an important need. Young men and women of marriageable age were overseas fighting World War II, and their brothers, sisters, mothers, fathers, sweethearts, brides, and children were in this country each doing his bit on the home front to win the war and to bring the world back to sanity and to (they believed) a lasting peace.

Since that time many things have changed. More marriages and divorces have occurred in any single year than in our previous history. Hundreds of thousands of young men and women have re-entered school, married in many cases, and established their own homes. The urge to return home and to have a home of their own seemed to be their one paramount desire. The world had indeed been at the brink of a precipice, and they all looked forward to the coming of a new era. It is the conditions, problems, and circumstances of this new era to which this revised edition is addressed.

While young people continue to marry and have families, parents struggle with the problems of bringing up their children, and adults are beset with all of the same family decisions they might have had in any period of history; while young people court each other, get engaged and grow into maturity, the stresses and strains of living seem not to have lessened, although they may be somewhat different in nature than those of war itself. Young people are asking, "What of the Future?" just as young people have always asked this question. The essential and basic problems of growing up, getting married and living one's family life successfully are no different than formerly, but the circumstances of living are different for the young, and still baffling to their elders. The solution to a way of living peacefully and in harmony with our family, our associates, and with other countries, seems not to have been found. Science has given man the tools of destruction on the one hand, and the knowledge for saving and healing human life on the other. The conflict between these self-destructive and self-preservative tendencies in mankind constitutes the basic problem which the next generations must solve. The choice must be made between Love and Hate. Love leads to constructive acts and accomplishments, whereas Hate leads to self- and world-destruction.

It is hoped, therefore, that what has been done in the revision of this volume will be helpful to young people in solving this major conflict in man and between men. It is hoped that some progress may be made by those who read and take seriously what is contained in the following pages. Only through family experience and the rearing of new generations of children, who can love and invest emotional energy in something outside of themselves, can our family relationships be happy and our civilization improved.

I am indebted to my wife, Luella M. Foster, instructor in Child Development at the University of Kansas, for reading the entire manuscript and especially for re-writing the chapters on Finances and Home Management.

To my many students I owe a debt of appreciation for their helpful suggestions, and finally, I shall always be grateful to publishers, and to my publisher in particular, for their careful and helpful guidance throughout this task of revision.

ROBERT GEIB FOSTER

Lawrence, Kansas

PREFACE TO THE FIRST EDITION

Many good books have been written about every phase of marriage and family life. There is available an abundance of statistical and factual information on the subject which it is not the intention of this volume to repeat. The main purpose, therefore, of this addition to the field is to emphasize the personality and relationship phases of marriage and family life, referring the student to other standard sources for much of the straight, factual information which already has been well formulated and presented by other authors.

No involved research studies nor tedious statistics have been included, although references are made to the more recent and better known studies. The author has drawn for much of this text upon his knowledge of research and his years of experience as a parent, teacher, and counselor. He has also leaned heavily upon the excellent works of others. If credit has not been given in any instance, it has been due to the lack of knowledge of the source.

Although there are many persons to whom he is indebted the author wishes especially to thank his wife, Luella M. Foster, for reading the entire manuscript and contributing the content of Chapter XIII.

To friends and colleagues who have given of their time and professional advice in the preparation of the manuscript the author's obligations are boundless. Miss Opal Powell, formerly of the Merrill-Palmer School staff, read the entire manuscript and made many helpful suggestions which have been included in the final writing. Her practical knowledge of the field and her critical suggestions have been of inestimable value. To the young people who contributed their own early married experiences in wartime, there is due a debt of thanks which cannot for obvious reasons be acknowledged to them personally. Appreciation is due Mrs. Dorothy Hippler who typed the manuscript and offered many helpful suggestions from her own experience as a young married woman, and to Mrs. Maybelle Stevens for her artistic contributions which have greatly added to the attractiveness of the volume. Finally, the author cannot fail to acknowledge his appreciation to the publishers for their helpful advice and, through them, to the readers of the manuscript who made many invaluable suggestions.

ROBERT GEIB FOSTER

CONTENTS

APPENDIX

INTRODUCTION—A PREVIEW

> The world has always been at the brink of a precipice and at the beginning of a new era. The very essence of life lies in its continuous and intermittent changes between security and insecurity. When these pulsations cease, decadence and death are upon man and his society.—ROBERT G. FOSTER.

The Importance of Family Life Today

We have just begun to recognize the futility of placing too much confidence in the kind of personal and social security that is based upon material things. We fought a war, in part at least, for control of natural resources, but in large measure we fought it because man has not yet learned how to understand himself and his fellow man, nor how to work, plan, and live peacefully and cooperatively. Man's life and development have been conditioned by many influences which have made him fearful, hostile, resentful, dishonest, and insecure. Everything seems to be a threat to his security. The predominant technique he has learned for meeting opposition is to fight, and once the fight is on, he then must punish, repress, and humiliate the conquered, thus forming the basis for more resistance, hostility, and smoldering fury within the human breast.

Where does all of this begin? Where does it lead? What can be done about it? Will people ever learn how to develop "friendliness patterns" instead of "hostility patterns?" To what extent do these patterns originate in family life?

As men and women reach the age of biological maturity, they naturally begin looking for a mate. Mating was hurried up during and following the war. This is both good and bad. It is good for healthy, intelligent young people to

marry and begin rearing a family while they are young and
pliable.   It is bad if they marry too young or too hastily,
with the result that, as with large numbers of young people,
they are disillusioned about marriage and family life.   This
type of marriage inevitably ends in separation and heartache.

There were 1,800,000 marriages during 1942.   This was
the largest number of marriages ever recorded in this country
in a single year up until that time.   Husbands left for army
duty almost immediately after the ceremony, and their wives
who remained at home were in many cases gainfully employed and living with their own or their husbands' families.
Marriage was carried on largely by correspondence and under
conditions of greater stress and strain than usual.

Today conditions are somewhat different.   Most men and
women are in civilian life.   Many of those who were overseas
are taking advantage of continued education at the expense
of their government.   The married couples in college and
those who marry in college are one of the new phenomena of
our time.   There were 2,291,045 marriages, reported in 1946.
Many are college marriages.   Husbands study and many
times work to supplement their G.I. pay, and wives assist
their husbands both at home and often in some kind of
supplemental gainful employment, if they too are not finishing their education.   "Marriages are made in College"
could almost be an accepted truism, were it not for the fact
that most marriages occur among young people who never
go to college.

It is hoped that the information and philosophy contained
in this volume will be an aid to many young people looking
forward to marriage, and to young husbands and wives in
initiating and carrying on successfully their most important
life work — marriage, the ultimate establishment of a home,
and the rearing of a happy family.

Learning About Family Life

Many sciences must have a special laboratory equipped
with expensive paraphernalia before the student can acquire

a practical knowledge of the field. This is not true of the social sciences. The individual himself, his family, and his observations and experiences with people and things constitute a rich source of knowledge about human relationships. His own experiences with people and his own family life are one source of knowledge. His observations and studies of the family life of others is a second source of knowledge. A study of research work, literature, including the drama, philosophy, religion, and other fields affords a third source of information. All of these are ways by which a person may enrich his own knowledge and understanding of marriage and family relationships. One of the purposes of this book is to act as a guide for anyone who wishes to learn about and improve his own ability to marry successfully and live his married life happily. A book such as this can only tell him about family life, suggest other reading in the field, and acquaint him with experiences which will help him tie up his reading with his own knowledge on the subject. By this process one may gain some insight into how human relationships actually operate.

Aims of the Present Volume

A book cannot yet be written which will answer the questions every individual may have about his own particular life. We do not yet know enough to do this. But there is much more written than the average person knows about or tries to put into practice. And if we read all we could about marriage and family relationships we would be only half educated. We need to provide a proper balance in our study between reading and the observation of actual relationship situations. This book is not primarily a textbook, a reference book, nor a study guide, but rather a combination of all three. It says to the reader, "Let us look at ourselves and other human beings and try as best we can to understand their basic needs, their attempts to satisfy these needs, and their behavior, especially in relationship to the opposite sex; let us look at marriage in order to see what decisions and experiences family life involves; let us look at our 'culture' to see what the influences in our environment are and how they accentuate or minimize the problems which married people have to meet. Then let us turn to research findings and examine the significance of our observations."

Because living one's life as a married person is the expectancy as well as the experience of most young people, the author has tried to present what he has to say in an informal style and has covered a wide range of situations. It is written from the personal rather than the sociological point of view. Since there is such a variety of individual differences among people and in the specific nature of the situations they have to meet, only a general, guiding philosophy and certain facts and general principles can be offered for the reader's consideration. He should not feel that there is any one, invariable way of managing his personal or family life. The specific pattern will vary with each couple, although the successful methods will fall within the confines of the principles given.

Some families seem to be highly successful. Others seem to be in conflict most of the time. More study has been devoted to the problems of marriage than to its successes. What every person should do if he is interested in a successful marriage is attempt to find out why some families are successful, and then try to apply these principles and practices to his own life. We learn why families fail by studying failures, but we do not always know why families succeed unless we study successful ones too.

This is the aim of the present book: to guide students to an understanding of themselves, of the relationships involved in dating, courtship, and engagement, and the management of a variety of situations after marriage which the author believes may contribute more to success than to failure. The volume is addressed to all who want to know about marriage and family relationships, to young people in and outside of college who are dating, courting, or engaged, and to the young married couples who are meeting for the first time the many, new, shared experiences of married life.

References

No attempt has been made to provide an exhaustive bibliography. The basic supplementary readings have been confined to approximately fifty books which constitute a well rounded library for the person with either an academic or a personal interest in the subject. All references are given in Appendix A.

Questions and Exercises

Appendix B contains questions and exercises which may be used as each chapter is studied. Specific answers to some questions may not always be found in the chapter, and in some cases they may be questions which have no clear-cut yes or no answer.

In Appendix C will be found classified, according to Parts I, II, III, and IV of the text, questions from college freshmen about marriage and family life. These will be useful as a basis for class or panel discussion, or for individual student reports.

How to Use This Book

This volume is intended as a guide to the study of marriage and family relationships in our society. It does not always explain what you observe. It cannot tell you what to do about every situation you might happen to encounter. The supplementary references, conference with your teacher, or some other competent person, may help you here. Most personal problems, the student will soon learn, are problems which he will have to work out for himself, just as others will also learn that they have to work out their own problems. Books, experiences, observation of others, parents, teachers, ministers, doctors, and other counselors are all aids in helping the student to settle in his own mind how he feels about a particular situation.

Since the author believes that successful families depend largely upon the kinds of individuals who marry and become husbands, wives, and parents, Part I discusses personal development in relation to marriage. The first task, therefore, is to try to better understand one's self and others by observation and study of what is known about human beings in these usual premarriage and family situations.

Part II introduces the student to a specific consideration of some of the situations experienced during dating, courtship, and engagement and presents some of the known facts about these situations.

Part III is a discussion of marriage, particularly for the young married couple, although much of the philosophy contained therein is applicable to any stage of family development.

Part IV considers social and economic influences as they are affected by family life, and how family life is affected by these major societal conditions.

Part I

Personal Development in Relation to Marriage

For you see, Callicles, our discussion is concerned with a matter in which even a man of slight intelligence must take the profoundest interest — namely, what course of life is best?

—— Adapted from Socrates, in Plato's *Gorgias*.

CHAPTER I

UNDERSTANDING ONE'S SELF AND OTHERS

One day, a young woman in one of my classes came into the office and said she was worried because she thought she was unattractive. She believed she was homely, not as well or as smartly dressed as the other students, and she wanted always to stay in the background of a group. She hated to recite in class. She avoided many social situations because of her attitude about herself. I had thought she was one of the most attractive young women in the entire assembly.

It is not uncommon, however, for individuals to feel quite differently about themselves than others may feel toward them. This little example is just one more instance illustrating the fact that the most baffling, yet fascinating, object of study to man is himself.

From earliest childhood we begin to sense how people feel and act toward us and how we feel and react to them. Every contact with another person involves the possibility of the relationship becoming a friendly one or one in which there is mild to violent hostility. Learning to understand ourselves better, to sense the reasons for the reactions of others toward us, and to acquire facility in the art of getting along with other people is the first basic prerequisite for successful living.

The business of understanding one's own feelings and behavior is a lifetime job. But it is a never-ending intriguing process of growth if one acquires early a kind of objective, mature ability to let himself become attuned to the sensitive workings of his soul. The importance of studying a book of

this kind lies in the fact that it should be the means of starting the individual on the road to understanding and accomplishment.

The nature of the answers to a child's earliest questions
may easily form the basis for his later attitudes toward and
behavior with other human beings. Let us, therefore, examine ourselves and see if we can have a better understanding of some of the factors which have contributed to making
us the kinds of persons we are.

Looking at Ourselves

One of our earliest experiences is that of seeing ourselves in
the mirror. A baby responds to his image and reflection in
only a simple and elemental way. As he grows older, he dis-
covers his physical self and begins to ask questions about
the parts of his body and their functions. Then there ensues,
over a period of several years, a more or less casual acceptance of himself, until, all of a sudden, the "self" becomes
the center of attention once more. The young adolescent
girl, for example, begins to show evidences of extreme
modesty and a desire to isolate herself for short periods of
privacy. She wants to look at herself, make herself up,
admire herself, and feel the admiration of others. She wants
family members to knock before entering her room, and she
is very sensitive to being teased. She needs understanding
and help in achieving her purpose — that of growing from
childhood into young womanhood, and attaining a feeling of
security in her estimate of herself and of what others think
of her.

A boy shows similar signs of maturing in his boyish way.
Both boys and girls, with girls maturing about two years
ahead of boys, are learning and forming attitudes about
themselves and about each other from infancy through
adolescence.

So, whether or not our parents have set out to influence
our attitudes and behavior patterns in certain specific ways,
we inevitably acquire a set of attitudes and behavior charac-

teristics in the course of our development. At birth we do not distinguish between ourselves and our mothers, but gradually, as we learn, we acquire a sense of "I" or "me" as a person distinct from others. Whatever idea of "one's self" one has, comes to one through his father, mother, brothers, sisters, teachers, and friends. Later one sees "one's self" as the girl on the front page, attractive or unattractive, social or unsocial, or the boy who is the bully or chosen leader, the insecure and fearful person, or the one who has confidence in himself and is unafraid to meet the realities of everyday living. These come to be the attributes, taken as a whole, which characterize John Smith or Mary Jones as unique personalities.

The Physical Self

Understanding one's physical self is our most concrete and tangible problem. One cannot with certainty separate the hereditary from the environmental aspects of growth and development. We know that such characteristics as body type, eye color, hair color, and skin color are transmitted from parents to children, as well as other similarities in facial contour, handedness, color blindness, diabetes, and certain types of allergies, feeble-mindedness, deafness, blindness, and insanity. There are, however, many other physical characteristics and diseases about which little is known as to the certainty of their hereditary nature.

The first step, therefore, in understanding one's physical self, is to learn something about the facts of heredity — the way in which those facts may affect one's self-estimate, one's self-confidence and aggressiveness, or one's timidity and reticence. We are concerned with other heredity factors only in so far as they have a bearing upon whether a person should or should not marry, and, if he marries, to what extent he should have children.

There are ways in which we come to feel inferior or inadequate because of many preconceptions which we may have acquired with reference to our hereditary family background.

While there are certain factors tied up with one's hereditary background that may have a marked influence upon the future course of a person's life, in general the great majority of individuals probably have few factors in their life history which should prevent them from leading a relatively successful and happy existence.

There is a basic fact about human beings which should be recognized. It is that of variability. It is the one fact which makes the study of human life intriguing. For human beings are not like the lower forms of animal life and are not limited in their physical characteristics and behaviors by a narrow, instinctive pattern. One need only look at the life history of the bacteria or observe the activities of the common farm animals to realize the limits within which their lives are patterned along lines of an instinctive nature.

Actual body structure and function is another important part of human life with which one must, sooner or later, become acquainted, particularly those parts which have to do with nutrition, reproduction, and adaptation to environment. In this area also one needs to recognize the fact of individual variability. There is no standard rule or norm which applies to all human beings alike. Each person needs to study and understand his own system in order to recognize his own personal capacity for optimum performance in each area of life.

There are also, from the time of conception, differences in chromosome composition between men and women. Male and female are different in every cell of their bodies. There are differences in metabolic rate, in glandular secretion and function, in body structure, and the organization of their reproductive organs to perform their respective functions. In women the metabolic rate is usually lower, the heart rate faster, and the blood temperature warmer than that of men. The internal glandular secretion of the male stimulates growth of beard, deepening of chest, physical stature, and the normal sex characteristics of the male, while in the female these secretions produce the female characteristics in body form and structure and the reproductive characteristics of her sex.

These structural differences are noticeable throughout development but become marked at the onset of puberty. There are many social and emotional concomitants which go along with this physical development, and which, as we shall see later, may definitely affect the establishment of friendly relationships with the opposite sex. They may lead to normal and satisfactory mating and marriage, or the development of other patterns which lead to unsatisfactory mating or possible celibacy.

The Emotional Self

One may, by the time one is through high school, have learned most of the facts about his physical self. The emotional self, so closely interrelated with the physical, is even more complex and difficult to understand. Everyone, no doubt, realizes that infants at birth vary greatly in their capacity for development and learning. It is generally believed that at birth we possess only the bare potentialities for the development of future patterns of emotional behavior. Like organic functions, emotional responses, whatever they may be, largely provide the basis upon which social responses are developed.

It is well, therefore, in any attempt to understand one's emotional self, to proceed from two points of view — first, by asking ourselves the question, "What kind of an individual was I at birth?" and, second, "What kind of conditioning have I had in the course of my development?"

There are fundamental differences, as have been shown by the studies of many child psychologists, in the basic capacities and characteristics of individuals at birth. Dr. James S. Plant (1),* for example, in his analysis of the structure of personality, concludes that we all differ with respect to certain elements at birth which he calls, first, alertness, which

* Numbers in parentheses refer to books and articles listed in Appendix E at end of this volume.

means our degree of sensitivity to our external environment; second, complexity, that is, the extent to which we are either simple or complex in the organization and integration of our organic and mental equipment; third, the degree to which we are pliable, adjustable, or adaptable to the conditions of life; fourth, our temperaments or the extent to which, with relative ease, we make various orientations to the outer world; and, fifth, cadence, or the degree to which we are resistive to change, including also the rate of development or maturity in the course of our development.

This is only one of many possible interpretations of basic conditions at birth which are highly variable as between individuals and constitute the inherent characteristics upon which we build our subsequent social and emotional attitudes, sentiments, and behaviors.

Apparently, the majority of emotional feelings and sentiments are learned. The process by which this learning is acquired we will call conditioning; this, reduced to simplest terms, merely means the way in which we are cared for and managed throughout the early years of our lives. It is during this period that we begin establishing for ourselves certain behavior characteristics which may be described as friendly or hostile in our relationship to people. It is during this period of conditioning that we develop such characteristics as shyness, timidity, caution in our approach to human situations, or characteristics of aggressiveness and boldness.

There are many kinds of emotional states which the individual recognizes. Fear, love, and anger are important ones. While the entire process of emotional development deserves careful and intensive study by every student, it is not possible, in this instance, to go into much detail. Two emotions, which are common and which seem to be the cause of many varieties of human frustration and maladjustment, will be briefly discussed.

Fear is one of the earliest forms of behavior exhibited in infants when they sense a loss of support, or when they are startled by loud noises. As is indicated above, all of our fears are due, for the most part, to early conditioning, that is, they are acquired through experience rather than inherited. As they grow older, they become afraid of many material things and human associations — fear of the dark, of sharp knives, water, insects, fire, and so on. We may acquire fears of reciting in class, of any person who is in a position of authority, of social functions, of meeting strangers, or of people who are fat or sarcastic, as well as the fear of remote circumstances such as poverty, death, or failure.

Since fear is one of the universal emotions which affect people's behavior, it should be eliminated from our lives as far as possible. Most of it could have been avoided or soon eliminated in the early years of our life by proper parental guidance. Fear is useful in some ways as a protective device against injury or destruction but is more often disastrous because its modes of expression are not conducive to effective learning and good adjustment.

Anger is another emotion which often gets us into difficulty. Young children scream and beat the floor, become rigid, kick, scratch, and cry; adolescents pace the floor, talk, sulk, and fight, and adults express their wrath by many of these same forms, as well as by verbal outbursts.

The causes of anger are many and varied. With young children it is usually brought about through interference with their playthings, through being thwarted in their activities, and in relation to eating, dressing, and going to the toilet. During adolescence, anger arises mostly from social situations, from failure of environmental objects to function well, and from events which are unavoidable. The adult is angered by social slights and by the inadequate functioning of material objects.

Love and hate, of which jealousy is often a part, are other forms of emotional response which the individual must learn to handle. Our entire attitude toward love and affection, toward recognition and approval, toward all the other things which mean acceptance, friendliness, and personal status is acquired early in life. It is shown by the many ways in which we meet and associate with people and by our ability to deal with situations that involve both success and failure. Love and hate are closely tied up with the basic need for security and with the way in which we have been trained to meet reality, that is, the situations in our environment which must be dealt with from day to day. If we can analyze ourselves and understand our anger, fear, love, hate, and the many other specific kinds of emotional feelings we have and learn to redirect our emotion along the lines of constructive outlet toward the ideal of what we call emotional maturity, we will then have acquired one of the basic and fundamental assets for success and happiness in married life, as well as in all other human relationships.

The Social Self

The social self is more or less our conception of ourselves, the estimate we have of ourselves, and the feeling we have about what others think of us as members of social groups and society at large. Here, again, our early conditioning is important in that we learn, from the years of birth to maturity, various techniques for meeting and associating with people in what are commonly called social situations. Depending upon how we are raised, we may acquire either attitudes and characteristics of friendliness or attitudes and characteristics of defensiveness, of hostility, or withdrawal from meeting the normal social demands of community life. We are not born social beings. It is interesting to note, in this connection, the large number of people who, as adults, feel shy, are timid, and feel insecure in relation to normal, everyday social functions. Thousands of us are shy and afraid to meet strangers, avoid participating in social functions because we have acquired, in the course of our social development, many fears or feelings of insecurity, or, perhaps, have never learned, because of our family background, many of the social graces and techniques which make it easy for us to take part in social life with a sense of ease, confidence, and security. This is, perhaps, one of the most easily modified of our "selves." The basic inferiorities, however, which are deeply associated with our emotional feelings, may be more difficult to handle. Growing up and maturing and arriving at a better understanding of one's self, and being, thereby, better able to live a more mature life, is a process in which we must all engage throughout the entire course of our lifetime. The degree of our success will be determined by our will to grow in understanding and our persistent efforts toward changing our attitudes and behavior.

The Intellectual Self

There are some aspects of one's mental capacity which are not subject to a great deal of modification. A person may be born with a mental capacity which is below normal, and only through special education can he acquire the facility which will enable him to meet life in a reasonably self-sufficient manner. Most of the persons, however, who read these pages will have little to worry about in terms of their inherent mental capacity. The main problem is that of finding one's place in life and utilizing one's intellectual equipment to fullest capacity. It is easy to acquire a sense of inferiority with reference to our ability in intellectual pursuits. We may be told early in life that we are "dumb" and actually believe it, when, as a matter of fact, we may have an intelligence quotient of 120. Many people are afraid to try to find out what their actual intellectual capacity is, while many others are intellectually lazy. Sensing our strengths and weaknesses may guide us to improve our limitations and to capitalize upon our greatest assets. It should be re-emphasized again that there is great variability among human beings in respect to their intellectual equipment. We are often misled, by superficial manifestations of another person's intellectual characteristics, into feeling either that we are inferior and inadequate, or that the other person is brilliant or dull. Quickness of intellectual response or deliberateness of intellectual response may both be manifestations of individuals who have comparable intelligence. Quantity of intelligence is one factor in judging one's intellectual self, and quality of intelligence is equally important. This qualitative difference may be observed in two students of equal intelligence, but whose approach to learning is qualitatively quite different.

The Spiritual Self

We do not consider spiritual values as being within the realm of scientific inquiry, and yet no man can live successfully in any culture unless he lives by certain values which he acquires throughout the course of his development in that culture. Every society defines for its members certain values which are held to be acceptable or not acceptable, and, within the framework of these definitions, we must make our decisions and live our lives.

Beyond the strictly cultural and ethical values in life, every person needs some basic philosophy which will give him a sense of being related to the universe as a whole, to its evolution, past and future, and to those imponderables of life and death, such as man's origin and the destiny of man's "soul" after death. This phase of one's self is what might be termed one's spiritual self. Understanding, or at least achieving for one's self a reasonably well defined ethical and spiritual set of values, is an important basis of successful living. These may not be, and actually are not, the same for everyone, but the fact of actual difference is less important than the fact of recognition of a need for something which each individual holds for himself to be his basic ethical and spiritual values.

We have attempted to look at ourselves in terms of the physical, the emotional, the social, the intellectual, and the spiritual person. You may prefer to organize these categories in some other fashion. But regardless of the way in which it is done, the first step toward human understanding and, thus, being able to live and work in man-made situations lies in understanding, in so far as possible, the various aspects of one's complex self. It is evident that these various phases

of the total person are not separable but are highly integrated
and function together in terms of a total personality. This
total personality, in turn, is functioning at all times in relation to a complex social life, involving contacts with innu-
merable interrelationships.

Conditioning Factors

By the time we have reached early adulthood, we are
physically mature, we have a certain rather fixed intellectual
capacity, we have achieved a certain degree of emotional and
social maturity, and we have acquired a certain set of ethical
and spiritual values by which we make decisions and judgments in meeting the day-to-day experiences of life. It is
not only important that we understand ourselves at a particular time, but also that we recognize some of the factors
responsible for our being the kind of people we are at the
particular time we undertake to look at ourselves.

Our family is the first, and probably the most important,
set of relationships in determining our personality and cultural attitudes. We are exposed to family relationships during those years of life when our basic habits, attitudes,
sentiments, and feelings are most subject to impression.
Each of our families attempts to make out of us what it feels
our society expects it to make of us, plus what that individual
family may hold to be important in terms of behavior and
ideals. The family, as a matter of fact, is a dictator for many
years, and we, as children, are dependent upon the intelligence, understanding, insight, and direction of those who
control our early environment. We develop sentiments of
friendliness, of kindness, of altruism, of industry, and of
honesty, or we develop sentiments which are the antitheses
of these, depending upon the standards of our parents and
the manner in which they manage and direct our early
development.

Nurture may also be a determining factor, particularly as
it has a bearing upon our physical and emotional development. The kind of food which we are given in our earliest

years and the nature of our habits of eating, sleeping, playing, eliminating, and so on, will condition our later feelings
and attitudes toward and about ourselves, as well as give
us the kind of physical and mental energy, stamina, and
health which will make it possible for us to function at a
high level of efficiency rather than a low one.

The kind of community in which we live conditions many
of our attitudes and feelings, both about ourselves and other
human beings. We may be born in a neighborhood of high
economic status or in one in which poverty is prevalent.
We may attend schools where there are many other children
of comparable social, economic, and cultural background or
schools where there is a greater degree of heterogeneity
among our associates. We may grow up in a community
where there is intense prejudice against certain races or
religions and, thus, carry into adult life emotions and attitudes about human endeavor quite different from those of
other individuals who have been reared in a different kind
of environment. We may have been reared in a particular
religious faith which may color our attitude toward society,
government, social participation, science, and intellectual
endeavor, and so on. Thus, many factors in neighborhood
and community and in the accidental social and economic
level into which one is born may be elements to be considered
in understanding one's self and how one came to be as one is.

The particular culture in which we live is by no means the
least important of the conditioning factors. It happens that
most of us live within the confines of the United States of
America. This, in turn, means that we have been exposed
to certain cultural standards or sanctions and restrictions
with reference to our behavior and moral conduct. We have
evolved certain folkways, mores, laws, and institutions
which, more or less, express and define for us the proper
channels by which we are to satisfy our basic drives and
needs. While the extent to which cultural influence affects
our lives varies and increases from infancy to adult life, and
although there are variations in the degree to which different

individuals are affected in the same manner, one must always attempt to understand one's self in terms of the cultural patterns to which he has been exposed.

The Personality

Probably the most practical and useful definition of personality is the one formulated some years ago by Professor Mark May (2) of the Yale Institute of Human Relations. His definition includes the total external manifestations and internal feelings of the individual. He looks at personality from two points of view. The first concerns that part of the individual which is exposed to human observation. This he calls social stimulus value. This is what other people see. Our size (tall, short, fat, thin), color (blond, brunette, or redhead), behavior (loud, quiet, aggressive, or shy), our mannerisms, our voices, facial expression, and observable behavior determine in large measure the way other individuals respond to us. In other words, we are the stimulus constantly evoking certain responses from the different people we meet.

But this is only part of our personality. While we are seeing others, and they are reacting to the kind of stimulus we present, we are also reacting to them, either in the way we feel or in concrete, observable responses. We have certain feelings about ourselves, about what others think of us, and how other individuals impress us as to physical characteristics and manner. How we feel inside is what might be called the response value side of our personality. Taken together, these two aspects of ourselves make up what we may consider to be our total personality.

Most of our physical characteristics we acquired from our parental ancestry, but most of the manifestations we show in terms of behavior and feelings about life are conditioned throughout the course of our development. We are, thus, the product of both heredity and environment, and any attempt to differentiate discretely between hereditary and environmental factors is almost futile. The practical and important procedure in attempting to understand ourselves is to recognize, in so far as possible, what our basic capacities, tendencies, and characteristics are at birth, the ways in which we have been trained and molded into the culture of which we are a part, and how we behave and feel in our day-to-day relationships with other people. From this point of view, to say we are personalities is more accurate than to say we have personalities.

Looking at Others

Observing others is another way of better understanding ourselves. There are two ways of looking at other people. One way is to stand on a street corner, sit in a public gathering, or go to the races. In this way we can observe human beings under all kinds of conditions. But this casual observation of people may become more meaningful if we also study what has been learned about them from scientific observation. The studies of the characteristics of infants at birth, the growth and development of preschool and school age children, the characteristics of early and later adolescence, and of adults both young and old, provide us with ample information for acquiring a much better understanding of human beings than we now have.

The careful observation of the behavior of others can be a source of much learning and insight into human motivation and relationships. We can only see, however, the external manifestations of personality expressions by this behavioristic method. For example, we do not know by observation alone why a mother spanks her child, nor why a person weeps in church. For the complete picture, we have to get additional observations of a different kind. These consist, for the most part, of the response or feeling values of the individual himself. We learn about these, not by observation, but through the written or spoken testimony of the person. He may write an autobiography which describes his feelings; or he may consult a psychologist, and from the psychologist's findings — which record the person's problems, feelings, and history — we are supplied with more data, which will add to our insight into human nature.

But casual observation and analysis of this kind are still not enough. It is necessary to rely upon the work of skilled scientists for data which get at the origins of behavior and show the causal relationships between individual action or feelings and the past experiences in the life of the person.

As we have said previously, we feel differently about different people, because they act as different kinds of stimuli to us, and because of previous experiences we may have had with other human beings with similar characteristics.

The Case of Mary Jane Smith

Let us now examine the report of a college student, who tried to say on paper what kind of person she thought she was, and what things she considered to be associated with her development, to see what we can learn about human relationships by this means.

"WHY I AM WHAT I AM," BY MARY JANE SMITH

"The first thing I think of in connection with my inner personality is my general feeling of inferiority. I have been bothered by this feeling ever since I can remember, even though I realize how silly it is. I invariably feel inferior to strangers, no matter who they are or what their age. I am afraid and keep in the background when I am in a strange group, although once I get acquainted, I take an active part in group activities and discussions. Furthermore, when I only have one stranger to deal with, I seldom have any difficulty in getting acquainted, and on a train or bus I sometimes take the initiative in starting a conversation with the person who happens to be in the same seat.

"People who have a lot of money or who are very good-looking make me feel even more uncomfortable than others, until I get to know them.

"I dislike formality of any sort, and I hate ceremonies. I feel so self-conscious and nervous when I am in front of a group, that I would prefer scrubbing floors.

"Although I have many acquaintances, I only have one or two intimate friends at a time. Yet, every time I go to a new place or enter a new group, I cultivate a really pleasant friendship with someone.

"I lack self-confidence and feel as if I were about the 'dumbest' person I know. I doubt my ability to do new things, although once I get started doing something, I usually become interested and do it well.

"When I am with people I know and like, I don't feel inferior. I forget myself and have a lot of fun, and anyone seeing me in a group with which I am familiar might think that I was a decided extrovert.

"My leisure time is usually spent in reading, unless one of my friends gets me to go out. I never take the initiative in suggesting to my friends that we go somewhere but sit back and wait for them to ask me. As I write this, I wonder why they ever bothered. I don't very often invite my friends to my home and never have parties or anything. This is not because I am ashamed of my home, but because I just don't think of it.

"I am not particularly religious, but I used to enjoy going to Sunday School, because I felt at ease there and enjoyed the social situation.

"I never have gotten more than mildly interested in politics and always keep my ideas about them to myself. I hate arguments and always try to avoid them, if possible.

"I am not particularly interested in sports and only participate in them when one of my friends drags me along. I enjoy going to the movies, but I don't go very often, because I can't afford it. I stay home rather than go alone.

"I am inclined to be submissive in social situations and follow the leader, as long as I trust the leader and his or her ideas are not in opposition to my morals and ideas in general.

"I don't have any feeling of dislike against any race or anyone whose religion is different from mine. I only dislike individuals.

"I have a normal interest in the opposite sex and have gone 'steady' several times rather than going with a lot of different boys at once. If I had my choice of marriage or a career, I would choose marriage, provided the man measured up to my ideas of what I want.

"This, in general, is the way I feel about myself. Following are some of the factors in my family background that have, perhaps, made me the way I am:

"I am the youngest of three children, and both my parents are living. My brother and sister are nine and eight years older than I am, respectively. My father, until recently, was a janitor, and I have always been ashamed of this fact. Although the family income is small, my mother is a wonderful manager, and we have lived as comfortably as most middle-class families. We own our home in a city of about 30,000, and I was born and have always lived in this same house. Although the house is small, it is pleasant, and I like it.

"One of the reasons for my feelings of inferiority, besides the one mentioned above, might be the fact that, since everyone else in my home was so much older, I felt that nothing I said was important. Even now I don't talk very much at home. My father worked nights and slept days, so we always had to be quiet in the daytime. I usually went to my friend's house to play, so we could be in a place where we could make some noise. I imagine this is one of the reasons why I never got the habit of inviting children to my home and never entertained. Another reason for this is, probably, the fact that my parents did not belong to any social groups or clubs and did not do any entertaining.

"I think one of the most important influences of my life has been the fact that almost ever since I was born I have had a chum. This girl is five weeks younger than I am, and I suppose in the beginning our parents brought us together so much that we just thought it was the natural thing. She did not live in our immediate neighborhood but was within walking distance, so we played together almost every day. I played some with the children who lived nearer, but she was always my particular friend. Her main influence on me has been her personality. She has always been larger and stronger than I am and has always taken the lead. I never bothered to think up things to do, because she had so much imagination and ingenuity that I didn't have to. I have found out since we have grown up that she has a Stanford Binet IQ of 146, so it is no wonder that she took the lead. When we were about three, we started going to kindergarten, and two other little girls began to play with us. I was the smallest and always got tired the quickest when we were playing. As we got older, our group increased to six and, later, to about ten, and my friend was always the leader. Throughout all this time, we were still chums and played with each other more than we played with the others.

"Although my friend excelled in so many ways, she hated school and never read as much as I did. I did at least as well, and sometimes better, in my school work than she did. She did not attend college, so when I did, I finally had to develop a will of my own. We still get together on Saturdays, and we are still the best of friends.

"Another reason for my backwardness in social situations is the fact that I have always thought of myself as being homely, and I am always conscious of this when I meet new people, or when I am standing in front of a group. I remember an incident in my childhood that may have something to do with my feeling self-conscious. I was sitting in the dining room looking at the funnies, one day, when I began to wonder whether or not I was 'pretty.' I asked my mother, and she, not wanting me to be conceited, answered me with a very emphatic 'No!' I was terribly hurt, and I think I have felt homely ever since.

"Another factor that probably had some influence on me was the fact that my older sister was very smart in school. When I was in high school she was pulling down a lot of honors in college. I managed to get on the 'Honor Roll' in high school half the time, but that was nothing to what she was doing, so my natural conclusion was that I must be 'dumb.' When I finally got in college, I was amazed when I did even better than she had. I began to get a little confidence in myself, but I still have a long way to go in that direction.

"I don't know exactly where I got my attitudes and beliefs, but I can guess at some of the reasons. I think the reason I don't have any race or religious prejudices is the fact that I attended large public schools, where there were students of different races, colors, and religions. They were accepted as part of the group, and since I liked them, I didn't see any reason for hating the races from which they came.

"My mother is Protestant, and my father was originally Catholic, was Protestant when he was married, and is Catholic again. We children have been brought up as Protestants, but religion is sort of a sore subject between my father and mother, so we keep still about it. This may have something to do with my not being especially religious.

"My mother is much more intelligent than my father, and I have always talked to her rather than to him. I have often felt that I didn't even have the kind of a father that the other kids did and wished that I had.

"My mother and father have nothing in common, and, although outward conflict hasn't been very much a part of my home life, I have always felt that my parents weren't like other parents because they never did things together. I feel as if I had only one parent — my mother. Although there is a lot more to be said about the reasons for my being the way I am, I think this picture of my family background reveals some of the main factors involved."

As we read Mary Jane's description of herself, the first thing that attracts our attention is her statement that she has a marked feeling of inferiority. It has existed as far back as she can remember, and she says she knows how silly it is. Is it silly? Let us see.

Here is a girl who, in the first place, lived on "the wrong side of the tracks." She felt all through her early development that her family did not have the same social status as that of many of the families of her friends. Her father was a janitor in a small town. In addition, her family was poor and had to skimp to make ends meet, and she could not have many of the things other girls had. At the age when all girls want to feel that they are attractive, normal, and approved, she was told by her mother, in answer to her inquiry if she were pretty, emphatically "no." Also, her family life was a nonsocial one. Because of circumstances, she could not bring other girls into her home, and she had little social experience, because her home was not the kind where friends were invited to dinner, to parties, or just for an evening of neighborliness. Does it seem that her feeling of inferiority was silly, or a natural consequence of her earlier experiences?

We see also that Mary Jane felt inferior to strangers, and that it was hard for her to get acquainted with people. She especially disliked formality, ceremonies, and group participation. These feelings are accentuated if the people she is with are people with money or high social position. Here, again, we can see the connection between her family experiences, or rather her want of certain kinds of social experience, and why she thinks that she "lacks self-confidence and feels that she is the 'dumbest' person in the world."

We see in this report the evidence of the kind of patterns of friendliness which Mary Jane Smith acquired in the course of her development. We see her as a person, not hostile, but afraid of people, because she is afraid of herself, and because she has had little experience in the social techniques of getting along with people. Her main friendship was with a girl friend, and she clung to this association because it gave her a sense of security — she did not have to go through the agony of making new friends, and, thus, she was able to protect herself against being hurt because of her basic feelings of insecurity.

There are thousands of other people in the world like Mary Jane Smith. They are shy, timid, and feel inferior. They have many vague fears, insecurities, and timidities. Their external behavior is constantly exposing the fact that they have not acquired the normal kind of self-sufficiency and confidence which would make life more satisfying and challenging for them. They avoid, evade, and run away from the very kind of experiences they most long for. They need help in overcoming their feelings and experience in participation, so that they are able to let their normal desire for friendliness become their basic pattern of life. On the other hand, other individuals grow up under circumstances similar to those just cited and show few, if any, of the characteristics of Mary Jane Smith. How do you account for this difference in the way in which individuals vary in their response to what would, on the surface, seem to be similar circumstances?

Do you know anyone who feels anything like Mary Jane? How do you think these inner feelings affect her external behavior and the number and kind of friends she has? In what ways do you think her early development has determined the kind of young man she will marry? In what ways does her preparation for marriage begin during infancy and early childhood? Can you begin to understand why some people have many and others few friends, and, consequently, why some have many dates and marry, while others have none and never marry or marry the wrong person? In what ways has your personality been influenced by factors in your early family experience? What do you think Mary Jane could do toward overcoming her problems? What experiences would you have her seek? How ready are you to make this type of analysis for yourself?

Summary

Looking at ourselves and others, studying behavior and mannerisms, as well as reports of life and experience, are ways of better understanding ourselves and all human relationships. This is especially true if we acquire the habit of continually asking ourselves the question, "Why?" Why does the other person act as he does, or why do I feel and act as I do in a particular situation? What lies back of the other person's actions and my own feelings or behavior? When another person is abrupt, sharp, apparently hostile, or angry, we cannot always be sure that criticism or retaliatory actions are in order unless we know why he acts the way he does — what factors and conditions have led to his frustration, conflict, or emotional outburst. To understand an individual's action, it is necessary to look behind his overt expressions and find out what has thwarted or blocked him in achieving his goal or in satisfying some basic physical, social, emotional, or other need. All of this is particularly true in relation to marriage. There will be many occasions when one or the other person is fatigued or has had reverses in the day's work or a social disappointment, which may make him less cordial or friendly and more easily irritated. These moods, temperamental spells, or outbursts are often not directed at the thing that caused the frustration but at whoever happens to be near at the time. They are a way of blowing off steam and getting rid of the frustration rather than meaningful attempts to be purposely hostile or unkind. Understanding helps one to meet life's emergencies. The more we come to understand ourselves, and the more we study the behavior and feelings of others, the better able we will be to meet the daily events of marriage and family relationships successfully.

CHAPTER II

BASIC NEEDS AND HUMAN BEHAVIOR

Some years ago, Professor W. I. Thomas (3) established what he thought were the basic needs of human beings. First, he put the need for *security* — not just economic security but social and affectional security. This is one of the earliest needs we have. Our family, upon whom, as children, we are dependent for years, should provide us with love and affection, give us a sense of being wanted and a feeling of security in this complex world. When our family fails in this, we tend to look to others for a substitute kind of affectional security. We are often unhappy either at not finding it, or at being taken advantage of by those who mistake our external strivings for affection and accept them at their face value, without seeing, behind our actions, our basic need for a deeper kind of affectional security than "petting" or infatuation can give.

Second, there is the need for recognition, to be important and to feel accepted by others. This is a socially derived need. Everyone likes to be thought well of and to have approval for what he does. When recognition is too freely given, a pampered and spoiled child may be the result; but when approval is never forthcoming, one may tend to strive for it in ways which alienate his friends and associates rather than bind them closer to him.

Third, we have the need for *response*, to be in close enough rapport with others, to feel that they respond to and understand us. We often find this need satisfied by our parents, and, as we grow older, by close friends and the person we marry. In a world in which events change so rapidly, in which security is only a temporary condition, and problems are constantly to be met, we need these intimate, human relationships to give us a greater sense of security and encouragement.

Fourth, there is a need for new experience, change, new problems to solve, new worlds to conquer, and new stimuli to tickle the senses. New experience broadens our comprehension, adds to our feeling of confidence and gives us, if successfully engaged in, new motivation to move ahead to other challenging and worth-while fields.

All of the items in this classification of human needs are basic to the full development of human personality. A lack in fulfillment, to a marked degree, of any one of these affects the individual's attitude toward himself and his association with others. It is not an all inclusive list, however, but largely one which emphasizes social and emotional needs.

Another and more recent classification of human needs is made by Professor Daniel A. Prescott (4):

"The structure and dynamic processes of the human organism imply the need for certain things, for certain conditions, and for certain activities of the body, if physical and mental health are to be maintained. The structure and processes of society imply certain knowledges, skills, and functional relationships as necessary to the individual, if he is to be effective and adjusted. As he grows up, the experiences of life are sure to raise questions in the mind of each individual about his personal role and about the meaning of life; therefore, each one needs to arrive at a satisfactory mental organization or assimilation of his experiences. Thus, the structure of the organism, the processes of society, and the nature of a person's experiences contrive to give rise to a series of needs, of quasi-needs, and of operational concepts which must be met if wholesome personality development is to be achieved.

"These needs are the basis of permanent adjustment problems which all of us face. They are more or less continuously with us. Our behavior is patterned in accordance with what experience has shown us to be the most satisfactory means of working them out, but, as conditions around us vary and change, we are continuously under the necessity of modifying our behavior. These needs become sources of unpleasant effect, and even of serious personality maladjustments, if they are not met adequately. Furthermore, our society is rich in circumstances which deny to individuals the fulfillment of one or several of these needs and quasi-needs for periods of varying lengths — this is what has happened to the thousands of maladjusted school children. There is a serious disharmony between the needs which they feel to be vital to themselves and the experiences of life as they meet them.

"These categories of need can be called: (1) physiological, when describing needs that spring primarily out of structure and dynamic bio-chemical equilibria; (2) social or status needs, when describing the relationships that it is essential to establish with other persons in our culture; and (3) ego or integrative needs, when describing needs for experience and for the organization and symbolization of experience through which the individual will discover his role in life and learn to play it in such an effective manner as to develop a sense of worthy selfhood."

Our physiological needs include, first, the preservation of the essential demands of the body for air, food and liquids, and such clothing and shelter as will permit the proper maintenance of temperature; second, a rhythm of activity and rest; third, sexual activity.

Our social needs grow out of the fact that life must be lived in contact with other people; they include such things as affection, a sense of belonging, and a feeling of likeness to others.

Our ego and integrative needs include a belief in ourselves, contact with reality, a harmonious relationship with reality, a sense of balance with respect to the meaning and significance of the various aspects of the common life, economic, religious, social, political, etc., increasing ability in self-direction, a fair balance between the meaning and achievement of success and failure, and the attainment of a degree of self-confident individuality.

Such a classification as that just referred to gives us a convenient and scientific basis for understanding human beings. The physiological needs are easy to understand, because we all have been hungry, cold, or thirsty; we have found ourselves needing physical activity, because for a time we have led a sedentary life, along with over-indulgence in high calorie foods; and, long before we are eighteen, we have learned that sex is a normal part of life, what its functions are, and that the biological drives arising from the fact that we are "sex," male or female, must find healthful and socially approved ways of expression. The social needs are much the same as those given by Thomas. These, taken together with what Prescott calls the ego-integrative (self-organization and sufficiency) needs, are of basic importance to mature, self-sufficient functioning in everyday life and are the ones which are most sensitive to good or bad education, from infancy to maturity.

The task of understanding human needs, motivations, and relationships seems staggering when we consider the fact that there are over 130,000,000 persons in the United States of different racial and nationality backgrounds, hereditary characteristics, social and economic status, religious affiliation, educational training and political beliefs, about equally divided between the sexes, of all degrees of age from infancy to senility, most of whom are actually living in some form of natural family group. But the needs expressed by Prescott and others seem to be basic, regardless of color, creed, or political belief, economic status or social position, sex or age.

The Individual Expression of Needs

From an individual point of view, we begin, from earliest infancy, to learn ways of satisfying our needs. When we are not fed on time, we cry, and some mothers let us cry until they are ready to feed us, other mothers have a schedule based upon a study of our feeding rhythm, while still others run to our crib with the bottle every time we make a sound. These beginnings in human relationships between mother and child are also the beginnings in us of learned ways of getting what we want or need. The same is true of the young child when he first engages in social contacts with other children his own age. If, when Johnny comes over from next door, mother runs out and brings us in every time she hears one of us crying, we are, again, learning something of human relations, i.e., that mothers protect us against every little experience, whether or not it is wise for her to do so. When we are in the early adolescent stage, some of our parents repress and suppress our activities to the extent that we are hardly able to look at the opposite sex without being reproved. We are shadowed and managed to the point of confusion. Some of us revolt at this kind of treatment and begin going out on the sly, telling lies about what we did or where we are going, and still others of us leave home completely. Some of us may submit to this unwise domination and become socially crippled personalities for life, in that we can never make a decision for ourselves, can never find the courage to marry, and may suffer great emotional crises at the loss of either, or both, of our parents. On the other hand, we may be allowed, by wise guidance, to satisfy our need for association with other young people and, in the course of time, make a normal and happy marriage for ourselves.

Our physical needs are, for the most part, easily satisfied in our earlier years, until we reach the time of life when wants and needs tend to become one and the same thing. Then we are constantly striving to satisfy wants that are stimulated by advertising and salesmanship, by what other persons have that we do not, and by many other reasons. Out of these efforts to satisfy our physical wants and needs, we often find that compromises have to be made. Here, again, we must look to our learned behavior to understand why one person has a temper tantrum when he cannot get the particular pair of shoes he wants, whereas another merely says, "Well, I am sorry you haven't them," and goes on his way to look elsewhere.

Thus, we are constantly learning ways of satisfying basic human needs and drives from early infancy throughout adult life. As infants, we learn to live in an outside world, to co-ordinate our bodily functions, and to behave in harmony with those around us. During childhood we learn to accept emotionally the ways of our family and social environment, to meet the problems of daily life, to accept the fact of our particular sex, and to continue learning about the world and people. As we grow into, and through, adolescence our needs expand. We not only continue to meet previously encountered needs, but also those of becoming independent of our family, making vocational choices, choosing a mate, assuming responsibility for our personal behavior, and organizing our ideas about values which constitute the core of our philosophy of life. From early adulthood to old age, we continue striving to satisfy our basic needs.

The Societal Expression of Needs

When we look at society at large, we see that because man has had certain basic needs he has, through the development of folkways, mores, laws, and institutions, attempted to work out an organization of society, designed to meet common, human needs. Looking at man's basic needs from the point of view of society at large, we find that in a culture such as ours in the United States there are four fundamental kinds of organization of life which have developed in response to human needs.

The first of these is that maze of economic and industrial organization of man's life, with attendant legal statutes, developed in the interest of self-maintenance. Our adjustment to our natural resources has always been, and will, no doubt, always be, one of the basic problems to which we must make some form of adaptation. What the natural resources are, their quantity and quality, and the genius with which we are able to utilize them for our advantage, form the starting point for an understanding of most other forms of organization in any society. Every individual and every nation is confronted with the problem of dealing with the realities of the economics of self-maintenance, and some philosophy of human relationships is implicit in the manner of dealing with the problem.

One of the important economic functions which our family performs for us is that of introducing us to the ideology and technique of living in the kind of economic organization we have. Although the function is not the same as that of the family a few generations ago, it is equally as difficult a one to perform.

The adjustment between men and their natural resources gives rise, also, to a struggle among men. As a result, there arises need for a second kind of organization which may be called regulative and protective, or governmental. Here are regulated the crucial problems of the rights of particular men and groups of men within the total life of the people, with respect to their share of the common dividend and protection of rightful owners against unjust aggression.

In the United States, this form of government is called democracy. Its fundamental aims are well stated in the Declaration of Independence:

"We hold . . . that all men are created equal; that they are endowed by their Creator with certain inalienable rights; that among these are life, liberty and the pursuit of happiness; that to secure these rights governments are instituted among men, deriving their just powers from the consent of the governed; that, whenever any form of government becomes destructive to these ends, it is the right of the people to alter or to abolish it, and to institute a new government, laying its foundation on such principles, and organizing its powers in such form, as to them shall seem most likely to effect their safety and happiness."

Quite apart in some respects, but very closely allied with the problem of self-maintenance and government, there exists among all groups of human beings the feeling of insecurity in this universe, of the mystery in which man lives; accordingly, there has always arisen some form of religious ideology. In some societies it has been dominant in the political and economic life of the people. In others, while continuing to be dominant in the life of the individual, it has become more or less removed from the political and economic organization of society. In the United States, there is no one dominant form of religion. One may satisfy this need according to the dictates of his own conscience, and the separation of church and state is absolute. There may be competition among religious groups and much conflict in the minds of individuals as to which, if any, religious philosophy to adopt, but there is little, or no, vital relationship between the state, religion, and our economic system.

The fourth basic organization of life within our culture is brought about by the fact of bisexuality. Because of bisexuality, there have developed folkways, mores, the institution of marriage, and many customs involving sanctions and restrictions regarding the way in which the sexes are associated from earliest childhood to old age. We regulate the sexes in their relationships before marriage; we decide who shall marry; we prescribe their conduct after marriage, the causes for which, and ways by which, the union may be terminated, and ways of dealing with widowhood, celibacy, and similar problems. The one, outstanding, persistent fact, which has been true throughout history and is true of all contemporary societies, is that human conduct is, and has always been, subject to certain cultural regulations. Whatever our individual needs, they must be satisfied within the framework of the sanctions and restrictions of the particular culture in which we live.

From the foregoing, it is clear that we are confronted with two major problems. The first is the understanding of our basic needs, urges, and drives, and the second is the organization of our life to fit into the larger social group pattern of sanctions and restrictions. Fitting into the larger social group pattern requires that we learn to inhibit some of our desires and give full vent to others, under social rule and sanction. To study just basic needs alone would be inadequate. We must also understand "society," "culture," to understand fully why and how some of our conflicts and frustrations arise. We must learn to adjust to these cultural expectations or become a social deviate, among whom are classed eccentrics, delinquents, criminals, and many of the mentally unfit.

Throughout this process of growing and living, we must, in the attempt to satisfy our basic elemental needs, make decisions, as best we can, which are most nearly in line with society's expectations of us. There is no escape. If we do not like the rules of the U. S. A., we can migrate to Samoa or to Russia or to the Andes; but unless we live as a recluse, we will find rules, different from our own, to be sure, but regulations within which we must organize our life.

Properly interpreted, stabilized cultural patterns help us to live a stabilized life, whereas instability within a society promotes personal and family disorganization, frustration, conflict, and even panic and revolution, particularly where a free, democratic process is not available to help us work out a stabilized and democratically established set of cultural patterns and regulations of human conduct.

In summary, then, we may say that there are numerous factors which affect human relationships:

1. Our basic physical, mental, and emotional constitution.
2. Our individual needs, and the degree to which those needs are being satisfied or thwarted.
3. The habits and attitudes which we have acquired in the course of our development, e.g., how the learning process has proceeded.
4. The fact that we happen to have been born of a particular family, race, religion, social or economic position, in a particular region of the country, and in rural or urban setting. Each of these elements transmits to us certain attitudes about ourselves and our relation to the rest of human society and also conditions the attitudes and behavior of the rest of society toward us.
5. The predominating ideas of the culture as a whole, and the type of social organization under which we live.

Making Adjustments

Because we are constantly making adjustments in an attempt to satisfy our individual needs and conform to society's regulation of our behavior, it is desirable to learn something of the ways in which human behavior expresses the fulfillment of our needs or the thwarting of our attempts to satisfy our needs. The first adjustments we make are to basic, physiological needs and drives. At birth, we enter a world of temperature variations, loud noises, glaring lights, hard, material objects, and a variety of human beings. Our original equipment is largely that of sensitivity, and multiform activity, with a capacity for growth and for learning and adaptability. We begin to learn that wants are not always immediately satisfied and must often be altered or inhibited completely. The adjustments we make, therefore, are dependent upon the nature of our original equipment at birth, the way in which we learn to meet the situations of everyday life and to handle our basic, physiological drives, the strength of our drives, and the motivations and effort we have put forth in trying to satisfy them.

The adjustment we make to life situations is learned. We may learn from experience by trial and error, or because someone has guided in certain specific ways the random attempts we made to satisfy our needs. In the course of our development, we acquire habits which tend to become the usual or characteristic ways in which we approach and attempt to meet new situations. Some of these learned ways may prove to be successful and constructive, while others may prove to be destructive and unsatisfactory. By constructive, we mean beneficial to our physical, social, and emotional stability and contributing to, or giving evidence of, maturity in our behavior.

Ways of Meeting Situations

The quality of the learning and the goal which we seek are matters subject to both cultural definition and education. We are expected to behave according to the moral code and social standards of our culture. In the course of development, we may, because of circumstances or experience, become antisocial and criminal in our tendencies. We may, because of severe, harsh discipline, form early patterns of hostility toward other human beings and society, or we may, because of wiser guidance, acquire friendliness ways and socially beneficial habits and attitudes. Good adjustment, therefore, is an ethical concept and subject to those criteria of good or bad which our society, our community, our friends, and our families hold to be good and acceptable.

For adults, then, whether the situation to be met be an environmental obstacle, a personal defect, a social situation, or a conflict over antagonistic motives, varied efforts are usually made in attempting an adjustment. Success in adjustment depends, in large measure, upon the individual's ability to continue varying his responses until success is achieved. Poor adjustment is often due to lack of motivation or because of emotional situations created by the baffling situation. A good adjustment is one which satisfies the needs of the individual. It may be a socially desirable or undesirable response. One purpose of education is to help us to understand both our behavior and that of others and to utilize personally and socially desirable ways of making adjustments to all kinds of life situations.

Running Away

Running away is one of the common forms of adjustment we find people making. This kind of behavior is desirable where the situation may endanger the health, life, or morals of the person. One would naturally avoid living in an area infected by malaria or where conditions of sanitation were likely to promote disease and ill health. One would ordinarily tend to flee from a burning house or from an area where rioting was in progress. These are forms of running away or avoidance behavior which protect us from injury or death. On the other hand, there are forms of running away which are used to avoid responsibility or to avoid consequences of a situation that frightens us. These are signs of social or emotional immaturity which can, to some degree, and should be modified.

Examples of running away behavior may be viewed in

our everyday experiences. The very short person often compensates for his stature by aggressiveness. He really feels inferior and inadequate, and so he tries to make up for his feelings by these kinds of actions. The girl who is insecure may attach herself to the teacher or a prominent person, and, thus, through identification, help to build up her sense of importance. Projection is blaming someone else for our failure or the failure of a situation. All of the above are kinds of defense mechanisms we use to save face, avoid criticism or blame, or to put ourselves in a better light.

One way of withdrawing or running away from a situation is by being negativistic. We strike back, say no, disagree constantly, and refuse to cooperate. Because we are afraid and insecure, we protect ourselves by hurting others through negative responses, so that they will not hurt us. Another form of running away is through phantasy or daydreaming. We spend time wishing ourselves beautiful, important, rich, or something else, without putting any real effort into trying to achieve our ambition. This is a kind of inability to face reality. Seclusiveness and timidity need no example. Shy, timid individuals avoid all kinds of situations because they are overly aware of themselves. They are afraid someone will think they are queer, or that they will not act correctly at a party, or that they will be a failure at whatever task they undertake. This kind of behavior is often associated with overly strict discipline or standards, which brings about a fear of criticism or self-criticism as a result of failure. Retrogression is adjustment by returning to infantile or childish forms of behavior. The adult temper tantrum is a good example. Adjustment by the use of ailments is very common. A student is expected to take a final examination; he acquires a severe headache and general indisposition and avoids meeting the disagreeable situation by staying away. His feigned illness, often very real in its symptoms, has been used to escape from meeting an intolerable and difficult situation.

Rationalization is perhaps the most common form of

evasion. We are afraid of the water, and so we turn down all invitations to go swimming with the "gang." We manufacture beautiful excuses or justifications for not being able to go. What makes this form of running away bad is that we come to believe our rationalizations and allow this form of mental evasion to become a fixed habit pattern. We thereby build up a protective way of always shielding ourselves from facing and accepting our true needs and difficulties.

Another most commonly used form of adjustment is worry and anxiety. A sorority tea is planned, and you are chairman of the committee. You worry and fret yourself into a sick headache before the time for the tea has arrived. Worry is the commonest form of emotional dissipation. It blocks accomplishment and frustrates normal, physiological functions.

Attacking Situations

There are both wise and unwise techniques which may be learned when trying to tackle life problems.

The least valuable forms of attack are nagging, bullying, and temper tantrums. These, for the most part, are childish ways of meeting a situation. We only exhibit to others our emotional instability when we use them. They may be the ways by which, throughout life, we have gotten what we wanted, and, if they are long standing mechanisms of response, they will be all the harder to change.

The more mature person attacks a situation by first giving some thought to it. He will figure out a solution, try it out and then try another if the first fails. His attack is more reasoned and controlled than that of the immature person, who kicks and screams at the screen door when it sticks a little in wet weather. There are many situations that can be solved by this direct and intelligent approach. The intelligent person proceeds to do what he has decided to do, whether it is to build a culvert over a ditch, oil a gate so that it does not squeak, or fix a windowpane that has been broken.

Altering Our Own Attitudes

There are other situations that cannot be changed unless we change our own attitude toward the problem.

Take the case, for example, of the college freshman who wishes to get married. This is a situation which may involve parental desires, lack of means of support, immaturity of age, and giving up one's education. The values for and against such action have to be carefully evaluated. One has to ask one's self what the pleasures or advantages are if one marries under these circumstances, and what the pleasures or advantages are if one does not choose to marry.

Or a young woman may have married a man who likes to have wine served with his dinner, but she herself has been brought up to abhor the thought of having liquor in the home. She has the alternative of having her husband eating elsewhere, trying to change his desire for wine at mealtimes, or of altering her own feelings about the situation. If an issue is made of the matter, he may prefer to eat with "the boys" and do his social drinking away from home, whereas, if she changes her attitude, he may be more likely to do a minimum of drinking. Any compromise or adjustment involves a certain amount of pain for the one who makes the greatest sacrifice in his behavior or beliefs.

Or we may have had our heart set on going to a particular university and, due to financial reverses, find it impossible. In this case, circumstances have created a situation which we cannot easily alter. We must decide to go to a different school or get a job until we can go to the college of first choice. In making this adjustment, we may find ourselves utilizing many of the behavior mechanisms previously discussed, such as rationalization, projection, and so on, or we may approach the problem intelligently.

It should be pointed out, however, that being blocked or thwarted in the pursuit of a certain goal leads to frustration which must be allowed some form of release. Anger outbursts, blaming others for our disappointments, drinking to drown our troubles, or withdrawing from society may be the ways we use, or we may face the situation by praying about our troubles, taking a walk around the block, talking the matter over with a friend, or going out and playing a game of golf. It depends upon the patterns of response to frustration we have learned. Doing something about the situation is better for personal integration and mental hygiene and is, at the same time, more socially acceptable.

Balance in Living

By acquiring satisfying and constructive ways of meeting frustration, we are more likely, through force of habit, to make better adjustments. This acquiring of good habit patterns for satisfying our physical, social, and other basic needs is the way we arrive at what is called maturity. Physical maturity means the attainment of as nearly optimum physical stature and proportions as possible, the ability to function normally in one's physical activities, and the practice of desirable habits of physical care. Mental or intellectual maturity consists for the most part of daily performances that are in accordance with one's mental development. Alertness, curiosity and the acquiring of new knowledge from day to day, which facilitate one's successes, are characteristics of the mentally mature person.

Emotional and social maturity imply that one acts and behaves in a manner which is in accord with his age. Poise, stability in facing disappointments, persistence in accomplishing one's goals, friendly social relationships and many other characteristics are found in the mature person.

The attainment of maturity and good adjustment ways of living is a process which wise persons strive for at all ages of development. Acquiring many interests and outlets at each stage of our development is an advantage in helping us achieve maturity and happiness. Music, art, hobbies, friends, social interests, the theater, gardening, nature study, crafts, one's work, writing, and a hundred other interests offer a wide field from which to choose one's activities. They provide fun and enlightenment at all times and are useful outlets for emotional hurt in times of crisis. For example, the college student who is dependent upon the friendship of a single person, or who tends to withdraw from coeducational social contacts is perpetuating a pattern which, in time of need, will prove to be a liability. These kinds of patterns are like building a bridge with only one prop under it. When a storm comes, out goes the prop and away goes the bridge. Balance in living is the best insurance we can have for meeting the many inevitable problems which life is sure to bring.

If not already apparent, however, it will be seen later that success or failure in marriage depends upon the habit, attitude, and adjustment ways which individuals learn in the process of growing up, and upon their ability to make an adequate adaptation of these patterns of life to their relationships with each other, as young people, before marriage, as husband and wife, as parents, and in the many situations which arise in marriage.

CHAPTER III

THE EVOLUTION OF FRIENDLINESS PATTERNS IN RELATION TO MARRIAGE

Modern research is discovering that individuals who have a wide variety of friends throughout the course of their development tend to marry better mates and live more happily than those who lead a more isolated kind of existence. This means that we have made the normal transitions from infancy to maturity more successfully and happily than others. It means that we have had nearly twenty years of practice in the fine art of meeting, adjusting, and adapting ourselves to other people. We have practiced and learned much of human relationships by experience. Our basic learning of social habit patterns has followed all the rules of good education, i.e., we have satisfactorily acquired both attitudes — a philosophy and habits of working, playing, and associating with other human beings. True character development — real democracy — has been at work.

Early Stages of Development

Close observers of infancy are accustomed to think of our first four years as falling into three periods. The first of these is when our main contacts are with the outside world through our mother. Eating and sleeping are our main preoccupations. Our bodily functions are carried on almost automatically. Then, around the end of the first year or beginning of the second, we begin to take an interest in our normal bodily functions. This is an important period. We find that we can use these functions to annoy our parents and get our own way. While this is not the first time that we come in conflict with our environment, since we may not make an early adjustment to feeding, it is the time at which we are likely to be thwarted or punished for what, to us, seems a natural act. It is possible that such traits as stubbornness and self-assertiveness or extreme submissiveness will begin to appear. During this time, from birth to the middle or end of our second year, we are gaining our first real knowledge of what other humans are like, whether they are friendly or hostile. It is the origin of our first friendliness or hostility patterns. If we are forced, scolded, shamed, or punished too much, we are likely to develop a negative and hostile attitude. If our handling is kind, understanding, firm, and consistent, we are more likely to develop reciprocal attitudes. The best patterns of affectional relationship result from lack of anxiety, anger, or concern and from consistent habit training.

The last stage of this earliest development pattern is when we discover our genital region. Before this stage is over, we will have thoroughly explored our bodies and asked many questions about our origin and the difference between ourselves and the other sex. Here again, over-concern or too strict discipline may focus too much attention upon this normal period of development which will ordinarily give way to growing interests along other lines.

The world is becoming a friendly and interesting place, or it is becoming a disagreeable and hostile environment. This entire stage through the fourth year is one in which we are concerned largely with ourselves. We are engaged in getting acquainted with our own body as a means of becoming at home in the world and of becoming aware of ourselves as persons, distinct from other persons.

We have seen earlier that one of the basic needs of every human being is love — affection — affectional security. The fulfillment or thwarting of this begins when we first suckle our mother's breast and is particularly important during our early years. Our first love experiences are bound up with our bodily needs and the way in which our mother is associated with these needs, with affection or indifference or hostility or over-protective anxiety. Thus, our first love object or friend object is our mother. It is easy to see the importance of the kind of love or friendliness pattern the mother has with the father, other children, or relatives. One of the basic factors, important in the prediction of success in marriage,

is that the couple have had a wholesome, affectional relationship with their respective parents. Thus, again, we see that at this early stage real preparation for success or failure in later marriage is, in part, in the making for us.

Another pattern that is developing is a certain degree of attachment to one or the other of our parents. As boys, we may identify ourselves so completely with our mother as to become too effeminate, or, if too closely with the father, we may develop prolonged interest in members of our own sex, which may affect our later adjustment to those of the opposite sex.

By the time we enter school, we have laid the foundations of our future personality. We are, in fact, already a real, independent personality in our own right. We are constantly experiencing the same needs as the adult and are finding ourselves being thwarted as well as achieving success in fulfilling our needs.

Later Stages of Development

By the time we have reached the grades in school, we have passed through the second stage of development. It is one of self-centeredness and self-admiration. While our attachment to our mother is still important, our interests are centered largely upon ourselves. Characteristics of selfishness, individualism, show-offishness, attention getting, and a consciousness of ourselves as boy or girl begin to appear. This stage lasts only a short time, and we normally pass into that period of life when segregated interests in our own sex are important. Boys' "gangs," girls' clubs, secret societies, sports, games, and the apparent rejection of the opposite sex are characteristic of our age.

The friendship importance of this stage is apparent. As boys, we learn to be boys, and, as girls, we learn to be girls and to get along with our own sex. It both precedes and laps over into the turbulent changes of the physical and emotional onset of puberty and adolescence, which rapidly differentiates us from the opposite sex by the very fact of the difference in the nature and rapidity of this development in boys and girls.

Our little-girl friendships develop into "crushes," and, as boys, we may attach ourselves to pals and buddies. Throughout a good part of adolescence, these friendships continue and are a normal part of our preparation for adult life. This "homosexual" stage centers around puberty and early adolescence, and friendships with both boys and girls are on a romantic and sentimental level. These "crushes" and "homosexual" friendships are intense, but both lack the depth of mature, adult love and are short lived. They are fraught with jealousy and possessiveness and are easily forgotten as we pass on to new friendships.

Many times real harm is done to us by the attitudes which adults show toward our early homosexual and beginning heterosexual "crushes." Out of these normal experiences, with the bestowing and receiving of affection and compan-

ionship from our own sex, come not only many lasting friendships, but they satisfy needs for intimate response obtained in no other way. They are aids to us in breaking down some of our dependence upon our parents while we are developing self-confidence and making the slow, but necessary, transition to a normal, adult, heterosexual interest. The entire drama of growing into young manhood and young womanhood is complicated by the development of primary sex characteristics and the fact that girls begin to develop about two years ahead of boys. As junior-high-school girls, we become the friendship object of the senior-high-school boy, while our erstwhile "twin brother" of the same age continues his "homosexual" interests, with only casual concern for girls.

By the time we reach the age at which most people marry, we should have acquired the characteristics of a young adult. Chiefly, these include the development of a normal love interest in the opposite sex of our own age and the selection of a mate; emancipation from dependence upon our parents, which includes reliance upon ourselves and the planning of our own future; the ability to meet life situations with reasonable emotional and social maturity; being economically self-sufficient and having developed a reasonably good start at formulating for ourselves a working philosophy of life.

When Bill Jones, age twenty-four, cannot give up his mother to marry the girl of his choice, and when attractive Mary Smith is so timid and afraid of men that she has never had a date at the age of twenty-three, we see evidence of faulty development. We see cases which indicate that early friendliness patterns and attitudes have been misdirected. They not only are thwarted in achieving their desire for marriage and a family, but every aspect of their lives will be colored by their choice, or, rather, their inability to make a choice in line with what is ordinarily the usual and typical performance of other young adults of their own age.

Thus, the attainment of the heterosexual goal means physical and intellectual maturity and the beginning of the achievement of that more difficult state — emotional maturity. This involves leaving behind our childish and adolescent desires and ways of satisfying them and the gradual acceptance of adult responsibility, extending both to our individual associations and mates and to society. Many people do not attain this goal. Others attain it only temporarily and are frustrated and fall back to earlier levels. The majority who attain mature relationships in certain aspects of their lives may not be able to do so in others.

The evolution of friendliness patterns has been discussed only through the chronological age of adolescence. By that time we are expected to have acquired some degree of maturity, and we are supposedly ready to assume the responsibilities of adult life, of which selecting a mate, marriage, and the establishment of a home and family is one. What seems to be true for most of us is that we pass through a pattern of growth and development more or less similar to the one previously described. But, from the end of adolescence, each of us then seems to struggle with life, utilizing the basic and acquired patterns we have developed up until this time as tools by which we make our adjustments and adaptations. We seem to be always in the process of achieving maturity.

These early patterns have, for each of us, led to certain emotional attachments, behavior characteristics, and response feelings toward and about life, including ourselves. At the beginning of maturity, they act, in some cases, as aids to human associations and, in others, as handicaps.

Mate Selection in Relation to Personality

Library shelves are filled with books, each emphasizing, in its own good way, the sexual, economic, historical, anthropological, spiritual, educational, or other aspects of daily living as the important cornerstones upon which marriage is based. But I am convinced that finding the right mate, getting along well with that mate, and success in fulfilling parental responsibility are basically personality problems.

Physical attraction is never in and of itself a satisfactory basis for permanent and successful marriage. It is much more important that we consider the possibility of continuance of affection, respect, and understanding and those other attributes which make for day-to-day relationships of a friendly, cooperative, and understanding nature. Man's physical appearance and functions change rapidly with time, but the more basic qualities which underlie stable patterns of friendliness are things which endure throughout the entirety of one's lifetime. A friendship is no transient affair but the product of early formed shared appreciations, interests, and activities. For friendships to continue through all of the physical changes which take place in man's development, they must be built upon a much firmer basis than mere physical attraction.

The development of relationships of friendliness may involve only single individuals with whom we have a firm and life-long companionship, or they may involve a larger number of persons with varied interests from our own. Since our appreciations change throughout the years, it is desirable that we acquire, early in life, the ability to develop friendships with several people, as well as more intense friendships with one or two people. Very often an individual will make the statement that he has no friends in the community, not realizing that those persons who have many friends are friendly persons and have the capacity essential to being a good friend. The extent of our friendship and the richness of it, however, may be enlarged by our having acquired a wide range of interests which gives us a better basis of common understanding of other people. Often a person, who is a close friend during one period of our life, may become only a casual friend, because the basis of our relationship has centered largely around some specific, passing interest, such as, for example, stamp collecting, dancing, or photography.

Perhaps even more important than these single interests is the fact that individuals develop, among themselves, certain lines of communication which make it possible for each to sense and understand the actions and motives of the other. The basis of communication between any two individuals lies in those overt expressions of mannerism, voice, and action which the other person learns to interpret as friendly or hostile. These gestures and mannerisms by which we convey to the world some clue to our own private, inner feelings may not be a true record of what we actually are. It is easy for us to misconstrue another person's apparent preoccupation and absent-mindedness or indifference. If we recall the case of Mary Jane Smith, we find that her basic feeling of inferiority may have, in many ways, conveyed to other people that she was aloof or snobbish. But we know that what she was actually doing was running away from people in social situations, not because she disliked them or felt she was better than they, but because she was afraid and had not learned self-confidence in the matter of social behavior.

Another important quality of friendship, which we see evolved in the process of growing up, is shown in the degree of dependence or over-protection which one person may exhibit in relation to another. This kind of friendly relationship may be called possessiveness. It is possible that in the course of our life we may have been starved for recognition, approval, and affection, so that when we reach our high-school or college days we are constantly seeking for those things which we have had little of in our past experience. The nature of all of our relationships with our peers will be affected by the efforts we put forth to gain their approval. On the other hand, we may have grown up in a family where we were completely engulfed in constant love and affection. In this case, upon leaving home, we desire it so greatly that we attempt to engulf others with the kind of possessive friendliness which may tend either to drive them away from us or create in them a feeling of being smothered by our well-meaning attentions. In cases of this sort, we are not really being a friend to the other person, but we are needing the love and affection of someone else so badly that it is ourselves we are concerned about rather than the other individual.

Capacity for Giving and Accepting Affection

Friendliness, as well as love, involves the capacity for giving as well as the capacity for accepting. It is not uncommon to find individuals, both of whom are old enough to marry or, in many cases, may already have married, who are tremendously in need of affectional response from each other but unable to give the very thing which is needed. It may seem strange that two individuals, each wanting love and affection, are unable to provide each other with the very thing which they need the most. In cases of this kind, we see individuals who have all of their lives been on the receiving end of recognition, approval, and affection but who, in their experience, have never learned how to give of these same experiences. All of this means that there has to be a maturity or balance in the quality of the friendliness which we evolve if we are to pass through childhood into the later stages of our development and find suitable friends of our own and the opposite sex with whom we can share experiences, on both a personal and impersonal basis, without frightening the other person away by our apparent abnormal need for dependence upon him nor losing him as a friend because of our own apparent lack of cordiality.

We may also see exhibited in individuals the antithesis of this behavior in that they are constantly running away from and rejecting any friendly approach on the part of another person. The underlying cause of this may be their great need and desire for affectional security which they have never had in the course of their lifetime or, at least, have never had to their satisfaction.

From the time we enter elementary school until we reach the age of maturity, we see evidences of both friendly and unfriendly relationship patterns in our home life, in our associations with those of our own age, in the selection of a mate, and after marriage itself. All of these activities between our associates and ourselves are concrete evidence of friendliness patterns or hostility patterns in the making.

Let us look at the cases of two children of elementary school age and see what kinds of attitudes toward other human beings they are developing as a result of their experience with their families and, in the latter case, teachers.

Johnny Jones is a six-year-old whose father is a very intellectual person, but who also is very excitable and very much concerned over the fact that Johnny has a speech difficulty. Johnny stammers a great deal, particularly when his parents have company and, at times, when they want him to be a nice, mannerly little boy. His mother is also a very excitable person who talks rapidly and is very much worried and concerned over her son's speech impediment. The parents have done almost everything, so they say, to cure Johnny of his bad habit. They prompt him, they sit him in a chair and smack his hand when he makes a mistake, they have taken him to a great many doctors to see if there is some physical difficulty, but Johnny gets worse rather than better. Johnny has an eight-year-old brother who has no speech difficulty, and who is doing unusually well in school. The parents are continually pointing out to the six-year-old the things his older brother does and the way in which he does them and are constantly pushing Johnny to achieve a standard of behavior and conduct like that of his brother. As a result of this pressure, anxiety, and tenseness in the family situation, Johnny is developing many kinds of behavior which we might call resentful and hostile. He is learning that other people are not nice, friendly, helpful, sympathetic individuals, but rather that they are severe, harsh, and lacking in understanding. In this situation, we have the beginnings of a pattern of hostility toward human relationships which make it difficult for Johnny to live a happy and cooperative life in his relationship with other human beings in whatever situation he may find himself.

This case concerns a little boy eight years of age whose father had gone to war and whose mother was so busy with a job that she had little time to devote to her son. After seven years of stability and security within the family, things had to be changed for him. He no longer saw his *Daddy* coming home in the evening to play with him, and his mother no longer had the amount of time to devote to his questions and interests that she used to have. Billy had to get up earlier in order to be fed, dressed, and left with a neighbor so that mother could get to work on time and Billy could get to school with the neighbor's children. After school, Billy had to go home with the neighbor children and stay there until six o'clock, when mother returned from work. Just as the neighbor family was sitting down to dinner, Billy had to be taken home where he waited for dinner to be prepared, and then, in order that he would get enough sleep, he was hurried off to bed so that he could get up early the next morning, have breakfast, and start the routine again. Billy was exhibiting many kinds of behavior problems at school. His actions were not in conformity with school standards, and he had developed a kind of indifference toward discipline which exasperated the teacher.

"He even was so bad one day that, when the class stood to salute the flag, he said, 'Heil Hitler' instead," reported the teacher.

This created a good deal of comment in the class. The teacher promptly took Billy to task for saying such a thing and sent him to the principal's office, whereupon the principal told Billy that if he did it again she would have to call the F.B.I.

The case of Billy is another illustration of the way in which even an eight-year-old reacts to changes in his environment and added stress and strain to which he is having difficulty making a normal adjustment. It also illustrates the fact that Billy is learning about people. He is learning to feel that his father and mother no longer have time for him and beginning to think that he is rejected and neglected. He is also learning that schoolteachers do not understand little boys, and that they are severe and threatening in their attitudes and actions. He is learning to feel certain ways about authority and about security and about all of his relationships with those with whom he would like to have a closer, warmer, and more affectionate association.

If we look in upon the relationships of boys and girls who have reached the later years of their elementary school career, we see boys teasing girls, and girls teasing boys. We find boys isolating themselves into groups of boys, and girls being more interested in each other than in the opposite sex. We find that boys, in the eyes of girls, for the time being, are unmannered, hostile little creatures, and that girls, in the eyes of boys, are "sissies." These relationships, however, in contrast to those previously recited, are a part of the normal development which we all pass through and will very quickly change to that heterosexual interest which leads to dating and, later on, engagement and marriage.

Continuation of Conditioning

If we look at the things that happen to us during our four years of high-school experience, we are certain that there is a continuation of that conditioning which further adds to our feeling of friendliness, fear, or hostility toward other human beings. High-school boys and girls are constantly asking questions like these: "What can I do to keep my mother from nagging me morning, noon, and night?" "Whom should I obey when my parents do not agree?" "Why am I allowed to say things and do as I like when the family is alone and then get scolded for those same things when we have guests?" "Why do my sister and I constantly quarrel with each other?" "Why won't my parents allow me to have dates with boys?" and "How can I change the mind of a boy who always wants to get 'fresh' on a date, without hurting his feelings?"

It is evident from these questions, which could be multiplied tenfold, that, throughout the past history of these young people up to the time they finish high school, their lives with their parents and associations with their friends have resulted in a puzzled attitude toward the establishment of friendly relationships. All of these experiences are reflected more or less in their overt behavior and relationship to other people.

Let us look at the questions from young people of college age who are engaged and contemplating marriage. One young woman asks, for example, what constructive attitude might be taken toward a prospective mother-in-law who is friendly, but who holds her son's affection by taking all her problems to him. Here is a case where, no doubt, the mother's over-protective attitude toward her son and his development of dependence upon her may be so strong that he can never actually emancipate himself.

Another college freshman asks the question, "How can a child help a parent to readjust, to find new interests as the child grows more independent of the family?" These kinds of feelings are primarily feelings of attachment to and affection for one's family. They show, at the same time, a need to grow up and become self-sufficient and independent of the protection and security which one has enjoyed for a long period of years. This is one of the normal problems which confront every young person when he leaves home for the first time to attend college, to go into the army, or to embark upon a career. A similar type of question is asked by a young woman who wants to know what to do because her family has become so dependent upon her as a means of support that she is in conflict over her desire to marry and her loyalty to support her family. These are not easy questions to answer, but they do, again, show us how inevitably our experiences during the first eighteen years of life affect all of our feelings, attitudes, and relationships with other human beings and may contribute to feelings of hostility or resentment at being unable to achieve for ourselves certain goals or ambitions or contribute to our finding happiness in the achievement of our ideals.

A last example is that of a young married couple who are in conflict over how to divide their leisure time between their respective families when the mother of an only son cries if 75 per cent of their time is not spent with her. Little comment is needed to point out the way in which the relationship of this mother and son is affecting his relationship to his wife and his personal adjustment and relationship to other people.

The early and continuous development of friendliness patterns, which give us the ability to meet and live with other people successfully, are significant from the standpoint of establishing initially satisfactory relationships with those of the opposite sex. That they are important in the development of a normal courtship which leads to engagement and the possibility of a successful marriage would seem to be an indisputable point.

The maturity of one's human association patterns is an important index of his possible success in marriage, in his chosen occupation, in his participation in civic and public affairs, and in all the rest of his daily living.

Maturity in Relation to Mate Selection

In relation to chronological age, research has established certain standards of performance for individuals of different age levels. Whereas the child one year old weighs about 20 pounds and is 25 to 35 inches tall, creeps, pulls himself up to a standing position, can use his hands well, has begun to do things with blocks and ball, can say one or two words, is weaned from the bottle, can usually control his bowels, the same child at three is very active. He weighs about 26 pounds, is from 28 to 40 inches tall, runs, jumps, balances himself well, likes rhythmic play, can ride a tricycle, can string beads, likes to draw and paste pictures, can pretend a line of blocks is a train, likes to hear and try to repeat nursery rhymes, is imitating many things he sees, can talk full sentences, can feed himself, help with dressing and undressing, brush his teeth, and no longer wets the bed.

Physical maturity has, first of all, certain criteria. The above examples illustrate maturity at two age levels. The person of eighteen or over also has certain characteristics of physical maturity. Some boys and girls are physically more mature at fourteen than others at sixteen or seventeen. This factor is important in relation to dating and mate selection. A first evidence of maturity is the age of puberty. This ranges from about ten years of age to as late as eighteen in some boys and girls, with the average usually between twelve and sixteen. The sex organs begin to mature rapidly, and secondary characteristics are noticeable. The boy's voice change begins to appear, his muscles increase in size, pubic hair appears, his beard becomes shavable; whereas in the girl menstruation begins, her breasts enlarge, her figure fills out, the pelvis broadens, pubic hair appears, and usually from one to three years after first menstruation she becomes fertile and able to bear children.

Mental age or intellectual maturity is important for two reasons. The mating of the mentally deficient tends to lower the quality of the population. The quality of intelligence is an important factor in determining the individual's capacity for growth and adjustment in every sphere of his life.

Social maturity more often than not goes hand in hand with emotional maturity. It is particularly important in relation to marriage. Many fine, physically and mentally above average young men have never married because they were socially immature. Their lack of having acquired social friendliness patterns thwarted their development, made them insecure, fearful of social contacts with the opposite sex. They avoided the opposite sex during adolescence and continued to find greater security either alone or with their own sex. This may have resulted from fear and shyness, lack of knowledge of and about the opposite sex, or rigid and unwise parental control of their relations with others during childhood and, particularly, during adolescence.

Social and emotional maturity, which is reflected in our everyday association with others, is one of the most important aspects of our development. There are many criteria for maturity, but none seems to be very practical and easy of interpretation. We may say, for example, that a mature person has a reasonably objective point of view about himself and other people. To achieve this, however, is not easy, nor is it easy to define for ourselves what we mean by objective in this sense. To say that one is mature who is able to profit by his own experience and the experience of others may be easier to follow, as well as saying that we have some knowledge of social life and what the requirements are for living in the kind of society of which we are a part. The mature person might also say that he is one who makes concessions to others but, at the same time, does not become too dependent upon them, and that he is a person who faces every situation with a minimum of frustration and a maximum of poise. He may also be an individual who can fulfill his economic role in life, thus becoming relatively independent of his parents or other sources of economic support; he can accept responsibility for his own actions and is not overly dependent upon flattery, praise, and compliments and does not take offense too easily at what he deems to be slights. The mature person may also have the ability to weigh immediate versus ultimate value and make decisions accordingly. No one person can achieve perfection; just as there is no such thing as 100 per cent efficiency in the operation of an engine, so we should not expect 100 per cent efficiency in personal living, in marriage, or in other human relationships. We need not feel discouraged because we find many situations in which we feel that we do not fully measure up to our expectations. We need only to attempt to understand our own capacity and ability and undertake to improve those qualities in which we feel ourselves to be the least mature and successful.

If one is as physically mature for his age as he can be and practices living in such a way as to foster continued physical health; if one recognizes his intellectual capacity, accepts himself for what he may be able to accomplish; if one understands his social needs and works at the task of strengthening his deficiencies; and if one knows about wherein his emotional maturity or immaturity is an asset or a liability and is trying to make continued improvement, he is a ready candidate for marriage. It is important to note that he need not necessarily have arrived at perfection, but rather at an understanding and acceptance of himself, an awareness of his needs, and a desire for improvement. When any two individuals of this caliber meet and have the other qualifications basic to mating for them, a good start on a successful marriage has been made.

Summary

Up to this point an attempt has been made to show something of the origin of human behavior patterns and to point out how, at every turn of our life, we are gradually but inevitably acquiring habits, attitudes, and basic patterns which are forming the basis for the kind of friendliness patterns we will carry through life with us.

We have also attempted to point out the fact that, as personalities, we function in terms of our total, integrated self, and not in parts. There is no legitimate separation of the biological from the social, emotional, intellectual, or spiritual self. We have seen that, at birth, we have a certain basic personality structure which is variable among individuals, and which forms the basis for our future development. We have seen that everyone has certain basic and acquired human needs which, when not satisfied, lead to forms of adjustment which are detrimental to the best interests of the individual and society. We have seen how all of life experiences contribute to the formation, in each of us, of certain patterns of adjustment, which make it inevitable that we become the kind of functioning adults we are. Whether we are friendly, have many associates, participate in life actively and confidently, succeed in finding a mate, establishing a home and raising a family, or whether we are hostile, unfriendly, and antisocial is determined by the course of the development of our patterns of adjustment early in life. Finally, we have tried to emphasize the importance of personality development and the acquiring of friendliness patterns as basic to later success in mating and marriage adjustment.

We shall, from now on, be thinking almost entirely about ourselves, our relationships, and our ways of meeting the wide range of problems which in the course of living everyone must meet, successfully or unsuccessfully. The immediate problem is one of considering how mate selection takes place, the factors which seem to make a good match, some of the problems which arise during courtship, engagement, and planning for marriage. This phase of our study of marriage and family relationships is especially important, since success or failure is so dependent upon the kind of mating which takes place at the outset. Many unsuccessful marriages might not develop if the factors suggested in the following chapters were carefully applied to one's selection of a marriage partner.

Part II

The Immediate Prelude to Marriage

"Love not as do the flesh imprisoned men
Whose dreams are of a bitter bought
    caress,
Or even of a maiden's tenderness
Whom they love only that she loves again.
For it is but thyself thou lovest then,
Or what thy thoughts would glory to
    possess;
But love thou nothing thou wouldst love
    the less
If henceforth ever hidden from thy ken."

— Santayana, George, *Poems*, p. 8,
    lines 1–8, Sonnet VI. Charles
    Scribner's Sons, New York,
    1923.

CHAPTER IV

DATING AND COURTSHIP

In our American culture, dating, beginning at about twelve to fourteen years of age with girls and fourteen to sixteen years of age with boys, is as normal a part of growing up as the onset of puberty. The vast majority of young people associate with the opposite sex from preschool years through adult life. The period of intense interest of boys and girls in each other is just an extension of their play activities which take a particular form and come under more closely supervised social control. Our keepers of public morals keep closer tab on our social behavior at this period. Dating and courting are essentially social in their character at the outset. The problems which arise and often carry over into the period approaching engagement are essentially the same. The anxieties, frustrations, and problems are those which we find associated with the undertaking of any new experience. In order to understand our feeling of concern when we go out for the first time and the other insecurities and self-consciousness we may feel, it is necessary to recognize the fact that these feelings are normal for everyone and are related to the kinds of social experiences and emotional development we have had. The new element in the situation is not so much one of being conscious of sex per se, as of being self-conscious of the other sex and naive in our experience with that sex at a grown-up level. We are made more aware of our developing interests and activities with boys or girls by increased parental concern over whom we go with and where we go, by the active interest of younger brothers and sisters in what is happening, who, in their own stage of

61

development, tease and try to stay in the limelight generally, and by the passing remarks of teachers and others as they see these budding romances in the making.

Being popular with one's own and the opposite sex begins in high school and continues indefinitely. It probably is more acutely sensed at the ages from fifteen to twenty-four than later. The difficulty attached to being popular lies in the fact that popularity is the result of one's behavior, attitudes, standards, etc., and not always something one goes out for, as one goes out to "make" the tennis or swimming team. When most people try to be popular, it is a sign of deeper seated needs for recognition, approval, and affection. These are usually not satisfied by the more superficial position of gaining popularity, because the person, when put in the spot light of so-called popularity, feels just as insecure and wants just as much to get out of the situation as he did previously. Ways of achieving a sense of security with our peers or with older persons are by being interested in what others do or say rather than by being too much concerned about ourselves, being ready and willing to help in whatever needs to be done, trying to see the good rather than that which annoys us in another person's expressions or behavior, realizing that we run others down only because we feel inferior and need, in this way, to build ourselves up, and utilizing all the simple ways of keeping ourselves clean and attractive in manner and appearance. All of these things can be done by the poor or the rich.

The personality problems, which many times keep us from achieving satisfying social relationships, are less easily remedied than the external causes of our not belonging to, or being accepted by, certain groups of our peers or not being accepted by others as companions and friends. These characteristics of timidity, fear, over-aggressiveness, negativism, and so on, result from the kinds of friendliness patterns and feelings we have acquired and practiced for years. The serious personality problems which keep us from dating, from dating in a particular group, or from other social relationships may need to be given help by an analysis of the origin of these feelings and the use of sound, psychological techniques for correcting them.

Dating and Courtship Problems

Dating and courtship, then, involve facing many kinds of questions and decisions for which many of us have not been adequately prepared, either at home or in school. The decisions necessitate both a knowledge of facts and a set of values or basic philosophy — standards and ideals — against which to weigh decisions.

Questions of fact that arise can usually be easily answered. For example, it is not difficult to tell the number of recorded marriages for any single year, what babies usually weigh at birth, or what are the effects of untreated venereal disease.

Questions involving value judgments, however, usually require some knowledge of facts as well as a basic set of standards in order to answer them for one's self. While there may be indications that a positive or negative answer is best from what social experience teaches, the individual must often make his decision in terms of an acquired set of values of his own. During the period of dating, courtship, and engagement, many such questions arise which the individual has to learn to decide for himself. We learn to make decisions for ourselves by gradually being given responsibility and allowed to make decisions for which we are expected to accept responsibility. If we are older and have never had to make them, it will be difficult, and we need both a strong incentive and the help of a good friend or counselor. We cannot go through life always leaning upon some external authority to make our decisions for us. To be able to make independent decisions in terms of one's own philosophy of life is one criterion of maturity.

While we are at home, it is often more difficult to become as mature and self-sufficient as when we leave home for college, employment, or marriage, which take us into a self-controlled environment. Our parents are interested in our safety and welfare, and many times we acquire the habit of leaning upon them for all of our decisions in matters which we should have acquired the judgment and self-confidence to decide. There has always been a difference of opinion between the older and the younger generation on matters of conduct, freedom of action, and one's relation to the authority of the family in matters of everyday living. This conflict of the generations is most marked in cases where parents so restrict and dominate our development that, long after our adolescent years, we are only able to meet life situations in an infantile manner. This conflict is especially marked in our culture, where there is so much emphasis on change. We expect our parents to grow out of date and to be of no further value to us, just as we do our car or a pair of shoes. This is in marked contrast to the family system found among the Chinese people.

What, then, are some of these needs and problems which confront us as we reach the age of active dating, courting, and becoming engaged? The actual age may vary. Some young people may have had dozens of dates with dozens of boys by the time they are eighteen, whereas others may never have had a date. Regardless of the time the new set of experiences begins, the same problems and feelings attendant upon undertaking any new experience will be felt. The problems which confront us at this time are those centering around social etiquette and form, personal standards, social and recreational needs, personality development, the growth of the body, and family and home relationships.

We learn certain social forms in our family. We all, however, must learn how to meet, associate with, and enjoy our social relationships with the opposite sex or withdraw, as many do, from all social contacts because they are afraid or insecure and do not know how to act. The mastery of social etiquette and proper form can be acquired, if we really want to learn them, from our family experience, from observing what others do, by asking friends, by reading good books and articles on the subject, and by participating in social affairs.

As far as dating and courting relationships go, questions of what to wear, the proper things to do, whether to accept gifts from a boy, what to do when you disapprove of the conduct of the boy you are with, and many others, will have to be decided on each occasion. When we are at home, these matters are proper subject for discussion with our parents and friends, and, when we are away from home, we then must rely upon our own judgment and the advice of others whose judgment we trust.

It is understandable that many young people want someone else to tell them what to do in many social situations. Even if this could be done, it would not be a satisfactory solution. Herein lies the crux of the matter of maturity. A mature individual is one who, among other things, has emerged from parental supervision, who relies upon the security he can give himself, and who is able to plan his own time and make his own decisions. From an emotional point of view this means learning to face things that are unpleasant, to react to emotional situations objectively, and to eliminate childish fears. From a social point of view this means the ability to get along with others, to take part — in the work of a group of one's own peers, and to be free from such dependence upon one's social group that one thinks constantly of what others are going to say or think about one's behavior, etc. In the last analysis, becoming a mature person means the acquisition of a set of general principles of conduct for one's self, and the ability to find more satisfaction in loving others than one finds being loved.

Personal standards of conduct are closely related to both social form and our philosophy of life or values. On matters of this kind we cannot always count upon facts alone to help us answer the question. Almost everyone who has reached college age has had to answer for himself such questions as the following: Should a girl smoke and drink when she is out with a boy? How can she change a boy's mind if he wants to neck and she does not? How much intimacy is considered proper and what, in general, is considered proper conduct on a date as to places one goes, how late one stays out, and what one does in the way of "petting"?

One of the chief purposes of dating and courting is to become acquainted with several persons of the opposite sex so as better ultimately to select a suitable marriage partner. One learns most about the opposite sex by associating with them and not from books or lectures. Lectures and discussion may supplement and help us to clarify our philosophy and attitudes toward and about our own, as well as the other, sex.

One of the reasons why so many young men and women of eighteen and over raise questions such as those previously listed, is that in our society there are many taboos and restrictions placed on the association of the sexes for several years past the time of biological maturity. This means that, where men and women usually postpone marriage until their early to middle twenties, they may find themselves, during long months of constant association, tempted to yield to the biological nature of the human organism in spite of social restrictions. We have to realize that we live in a society where the rules set up and evolved out of years of experience must, in general, be abided by. There are, of course, individuals who violate the mores, and who, on the surface, seem to suffer little damage. With the kind of early home training our society provides, reinforced by the social attitude of the church, the community at large, and the law, it is probably most desirable to respect and learn to live within these conventions.

As to whether couples should "pet" or not, this is an academic question. Everyone who grows up, becomes engaged, and marries, has or does "pet." But it is necessary to define what we mean by "petting" and the extent to which "petting" goes. "Petting," "necking," "wolfing," and other such terms are heard among young people and have various meanings. For our discussion let us ignore these terms, as such, and talk about the degree to which friendships, during the time of dating, courtship, and engagement, need to develop into more intimate feelings and experiences for the welfare of the individual and the success of his marriage.

Normal Dating Relationships

The most usual forms of expression among couples are smiling, holding of the girl's arm by the boy, opening the car door, and performing other simple acts of social etiquette. A couple may hold hands and, as their casual friendship deepens into a more substantial one, put their arms around each other, kiss each other good night, and show similar expressions of the sincerity of their friendship. By the time a young person has entered college, he may have experienced this much of deepening friendship with a member of the opposite sex, while others may not. As one becomes definitely older and enough interested in one person to become engaged to him, physical contacts may become more frequent and emotionally satisfying. The couple feel that they are in love, and this is just one of many ways of expressing one's love for another person. While it is true that a small proportion of engaged couples may go so far as to consummate their marriage before the ceremony, in general this is not true and has many of the risks and disadvantages of promiscuous, heavy "petting." Studies show that the couples who rate the highest in marital happiness are those who, in general, have been more conservative in their intimacies before marriage.

Intimacies of Courtship

Intimacies during courtship and engagement may become more difficult to avoid the longer marriage has to be postponed, because each person becomes emotionally more closely identified and dependent upon the other, and because their physical contacts may take up a major part of their leisure time together in comparison to other forms of social and recreational activities. We have to realize that the only concern of our biological urge is to procreate and replenish the species, whereas our social pattern emphasizes the desirability of controlling these impulses until after marriage.

That at eighteen we are biologically ready to be so stimulated and to produce children is common knowledge, but satisfying the biological need for such premarital contacts has never been advocated. The popularity which results from engaging in socially disapproved relationships in order to become popular is only temporary and does not prove to be continuous and lasting. There seem to be many more disadvantages than advantages, in our culture, in engaging in too great intimacies during courtship. These disadvantages are well known to everyone.

There is first of all the danger of pregnancy, which, if it occurs, will necessitate marriage to someone who is not, perhaps, the person one would wish to marry or having an illegitimate child. Some may think of contraceptives or abortions as an escape from possible pregnancy. The first is no absolute guarantee against conception, and the latter is dangerous and illegal when done under the conditions necessitated by the above circumstances.

Possible infection from venereal diseases should not be overlooked as a hazard. While gonorrhea may be largely controlled by the use of certain kinds of contraceptives, syphilis, the more serious of the two, may be contracted by other means. They both are serious in their physical effect and may contribute to anxiety, feelings of guilt, and more complex emotional disturbances.

Risk of discovery is always a factor to be considered. Because we are engaging in secret behavior, there cannot be the same feeling of confidence and lack of fear comparable to normal conditions. There almost always results, particularly for the girl, a sense of guilt following these affairs, which often results, also, in feelings of resentment toward the boy and a fear that others may know of her misconduct and general social unworthiness.

Such relations are not a preparation for marriage. Sex experience is a creative expression of love between two individuals, and promiscuous relations before marriage, carried on under the usual unsatisfactory conditions, do not provide one with the same pattern which the security of marriage offers. The man, more often than the girl, loses interest and may look for new fields to conquer. The person who seeks complete intimacy, usually the man, is thinking mostly of his own satisfaction rather than the welfare of the girl in the situation. Marriage is based upon each person's being concerned with the other person's rights and his own responsibilities rather than being concerned with his own rights and the other person's responsibilities.

The human, basic need for biological fulfillment is thwarted because childbearing cannot result with social approval, and the physical release becomes more important than the basic expression of love.

We often need to feel a sense of continued, affectional security and response and mistake sex per se as giving us just that. When we need to be loved and to have something to love, sex expression may be one form of expressing that love, but, without the basic qualities of deep affection, sex, as the beginning point in friendship, can rarely lead to the deeper attachments and sentiments.

Our personal standards must give us the basis for deciding upon these as well as many other problems. We have to consider both our personal satisfactions, desires, and needs as an element on the one hand, and the social customs we have to live with on the other hand.

Importance of Many Interests

If we find adequate outlets for our social and recreational needs, we will have gone a long way in acquiring habits and tastes which offer opportunity for dating and courtship activities which are socially acceptable, personally satisfying, and which reduce the time and emotional need for purely physical contact and release. All kinds of sports, travel, adventure, games, dancing, parties, etc., when actively participated in, provide us with fun and social opportunities with others of our own interests and age. This does not mean that personal and intimate feelings are to be repressed or avoided. It only means that they are, according to experience and the soundest knowledge available, best controlled until after they can be engaged in wholeheartedly with social approval, security, and a feeling of their being right. Sex expression, engaged in on this basis, does not leave a sense of personal frustration which usually results when it is engaged in as a social style, a college prank, or to aid war morale.

The Role of the Family in Courtship

The family is legally responsible for our support until we are of age, and the community holds our parents responsible for our conduct, protection, education, health, and morals. These are some of the reasons for what seems to be parental concern over many activities in our earlier dating relationships. Some parents are overly cautious and strict, thus causing us to "sneak" out on dates and engage in social activities under conditions that are not desirable. Others are so little concerned about where we go or what we do, that trouble often arises. In most cases, parents are interested and concerned; they want to help us, but their apparent interference is more often due to ignorance of young people's needs than a desire to be old-fashioned or mean. The remedy for many of these problems is for us to talk over our point of view with our parents and for our parents to discuss their views with us. Often we complain that our parents use the technique of forbidding us to do something without explaining why they object to our activities. Some of the problems in this area are indicated by the following questions: "If parents do not understand and, therefore, disapprove of some of the modern ideas, what can we do about it?" "Should parents be told where we are going with our dates, and who our companions have been?" "Should a mother interfere with her daughter's private affairs, such as whom she should and should not go out with?" "Should not a girl almost nineteen be allowed to have a little say about her personal activities?" "Is it always a good idea for us to confide in our parents — tell them everything?"

Our questions on the facts of life should be answered continuously from early childhood until we are married. This is essentially a job for our parents. Where parents are themselves uninformed or shy, they should be given help by parent education opportunities. Churches, youth organizations, settlement houses, libraries, and other organizations in the community contribute to this fund of information for young men and women. The school, of course, in its biology, sociology, home economics, physical and health education classes should make a great contribution. In view of the observable differences between men and women which occur at the same time, interest in dating and courting are important, and there is every reason to accept as normal our interest in these physical changes. Questions about menstruation, reproduction, the reproductive structure of the sexes, and other similar questions should be expected, and we should attempt to satisfy ourselves on these matters at home, at school, or through other reliable sources.

The social purpose of dating and courtship is to allow for a final choice of one person as a marriage partner, after having sampled the field of available persons rather extensively. This leads to engagement, which has a personal and social function peculiar to itself.

CHAPTER V

MATE SELECTION

Dating is not done with any conscious motive, such as marriage, in mind. Social and personal factors are predominant. A boy sees a girl, she appeals to him, he arranges to get acquainted and then makes a date. It may be a single date, or this one chance meeting may ripen into friendship, engagement, and matrimony. Such is the fortuitous nature of selective mating. The conditioning factor has largely been propinquity. On the other hand, back of this are factors often unconsciously operative in the mind of the individual.

Process of Mate Selection

It should be remembered, however, that one is always forced, if he makes a choice, to choose between his ideal, the type of person he needs, and the type of person he is likely to be able to get in the marriage market at the time. This, of course, varies in different parts of the country and at different times. The sex ratio of men to women may be one of excess women to men in one area, and here men have a wider choice, whereas women are thrown into keener competition. Under these conditions, the man is more likely to pick what he thinks is his ideal, and the girl may have to sacrifice some points she has considered important in an ideal mate, remain single, or seek elsewhere. If there is an excess of men over women, the men are more likely to have to take what the market offers, and the woman is more likely to choose more nearly what she considers her ideal.

On the other hand, a Protestant college girl of English descent may go out to a small town or rural school to teach. The majority of young men have only a high-school education and are predominantly Irish. In such a case, she may have to accept the attentions of a man of less education, although not necessarily of less intelligence, of different nationality and, possibly, religion from herself. She may be thrown into conflict if she dates and finds a person who seems to meet her needs emotionally but has radically different religious background. It is out of these chance associations of young men and women, at school, in social life, and on the job, that arise many difficult decisions during courtship and engagement.

Most men arrive at maturity expecting to marry and seriously looking for a wife. This process of looking has usually been preceded by a long period of observing, sampling, and finally making a decision. While there are many elements of chance involved, the process is not unlike buying a suit or a dress. If one finds a wide assortment to choose from, begins shopping early, and looks around a bit, one is more likely than not to finish the shopping tour with a garment of good quality, which was purchased within his means, and which is attractive and suited to his physical and personal qualities. But this last will only result if the shopper has some knowledge of quality, costs, type, and style suited to his own coloring and physique. In mate selecting, likewise, the importance of having some knowledge of what one wants and the qualities essential to good mating for one's self is necessary. The man or woman who is out to marry anything that is male or female is likely to get just that. The same is true if the sole and primary motive is money, social status, or sex satisfaction alone.

While acquaintance is determined in the first place by race, neighborhood, family, social or economic status, school or college, religion, etc., it is also determined by a man's or woman's conscious effort to cultivate the right kind of friendliness patterns with those of the opposite sex.

The process, therefore, by which we arrive at the choice of a mate is somewhat like this. Because we belong to a particular race, nationality, family, religious group, or live in a particular community and go to a particular school, we are likely to meet certain people who become first our casual associates, then our friends, and one of these friendships may lead to engagement and marriage. Throughout the years, while we are in the early stage of going with members of the opposite sex, we tend to try out a succession of individuals, thus becoming better acquainted with several members of the opposite sex. Thus, also, we acquire a certain degree of confidence in ourselves as we mature in our ability to meet with and carry on more sustained dating relationships. These first affairs tend to develop along the line of group dating and double-dating.

As the mating process continues, we may experiment with individual dating and allow ourselves to go "steady" at an age considerably younger than we might contemplate the possibility of marriage. Throughout this entire period we continuously experiment with ways of getting and holding the interest of the other person. We are apt to be quite insecure and are not, as yet, either interested in, or willing to reveal too deeply, our own emotional feelings. This is followed by a gradual unfolding of ourselves to the other person to a limited extent, always allowing ourselves the opportunity for retreat, if necessary, and we spend our time in small talk and often belie our real motives by pretending to be a man or woman hater, with no intention of ever marrying. We are likely, at this stage, to engage in casual intimacies which involve, perhaps, no more than holding hands, kissing, or what might be termed very light "necking." After having gone through these stages of development in our relationship with one of the opposite sex, we gradually acquire enough experience and contact with others to have arrived perhaps at the point where we can accept, as well as give, a greater degree of intimacy and sympathetic understanding, and the emotional ties between ourselves and another individual may become closer and more deeply established.

When we finally meet someone who satisfies, in most respects, our social criteria of race, religion, social status, and so on, and who seems to satisfy our emotional needs, we then begin to reveal ourselves little by little in terms of our inner thoughts, feelings, desires, and ambitions. At first we are very careful not to reveal our basic needs while exploring each other's mutual interests, partly because we are not aware of the fact that there is a growing inter-dependence between ourselves and another person which is the result of the fulfilling, by each, of certain deep-seated needs that we may have. In the later stages of the process of selecting a mate, a mature and wholesome love affair may develop which reveals both the deepest feelings of mutual need and frank and sympathetic understanding of the needs of each other. There may result a tremendous increase in our social activities, in our occupational effectiveness, and in our physical health and vigor, due to the added motivation which results from having achieved a common incentive that grows out of engagement that looks forward to marriage. In this final consummation of friendship into a mature engagement and potential marriage, each has arrived at the point where he has less anxiety concerning himself and has acquired a predominant loyalty and paramount interest in the other person which, in each case, is reflected by those attitudes and sentiments we call appreciation, tolerance, and sympathetic understanding. We have now arrived, in the process of assortive mating, at a state of emotional readiness for those responsibilities which marriage entails.

Family Relationships That Affect Mating

In the preceding pages an attempt has been made to present some of the processes involved in the beginnings of mate selection and its development from these initial beginnings into a successful engagement and potential marriage. After studying several hundred young married couples, two professors at the University of Chicago (5) developed the first scientific attempt at the determination of those factors which were basic to predicting possible success or failure in marriage. It is significant that their findings reveal factors which are almost entirely associated with our developmental relationships in our own family. The first nine of the ten factors listed as being significant were, whether the individuals contemplating marriage came from homes in which their parents were happily married; was each individual happy as a child in his own home relationships; was he in conflict or in accord with his mother; did each have a reasonably strong attachment for both mother and father; to what extent was there much conflict between the father in the family and each individual; to what extent was each person's home discipline firm but not severe and harsh; to what extent were each individual's parents frank on matters of sex; to what extent was each person punished infrequently and mildly; and, finally, what were the attitudes toward sex before marriage and, especially, were those attitudes free from disgust and aversion.

All of these factors, which were found to be important in predicting success or failure in the marriage of any couple, are intimately related to our very earliest relationships to both our mother and father. They indicate the degree to which we have found stable security in our family relationships and the kind of adjustment we have learned to make to authority. These two attitudes of individuals, that is, toward security and authority, are fundamentally basic to one's adjustment in any close or intimate relationship with another individual.

The last set of items under point ten which seemed to have greatly contributed to predictable success or failure had to do with the extent to which the individual was a socialized person, particularly the extent to which he was given good education, had a reasonable contact and participation experience in relationship activities and social organizations, had a variety of friends of both sexes, and had acquired respect for the social rules and conventions of our culture. While these are not primarily relationships that involve only one's family, they are, to a large extent, relationships and developmental experiences for which the family is largely responsible. These might be said to contribute to our general attitude toward facing reality, that is, the experiences of the outside world. In so far as our developmental family life contributed to our ability to meet these beneficial situations, as well as others which might be called less socially acceptable than beneficial to the individual, we can assume that the large responsibility for our adjustment in these areas is also primarily related to our family.

Some of the characteristics of unhappily married women showed evidence of emotional tenseness, deep-seated feelings of inferiority often accompanied by aggressive attitudes rather than timidity, an inclination to be irritable and dictatorial, a tendency to be aggressive in business and over-anxious in social life, to be more concerned about being important than being liked, and a tendency to be ego-centric and little interested in benevolent and welfare activities except as these offered opportunities for personal recognition. They were impatient and fitful workers, disliked cautious and methodical people and the type of work that requires painstaking effort. In politics, religion, and social ethics they were often more radical than the happily married group.

Husbands of marriages which were the least happy tended to be moody and somewhat neurotic, were prone to feelings of social inferiority for which they often compensated with domineering attitudes, particularly when they were in positions of superiority, often compensated for their feelings of inferiority by withdrawal into daydreams and phantasies in which they pictured themselves in supreme command of every situation, seemed to be more sporadic in their work habits and more often than not expressed irreligious attitudes and were more inclined to a radical attitude toward sex morals and politics. These unhappily married men and women had acquired characteristics of hostility and other destructive tendencies largely as a result of their training from infancy to maturity.

On the other hand, let us contrast some of the characteristics of the men and women who came from the more happily married portion of this important research study. The women, as a group, were characterized by kindly attitudes toward others, did not easily take offense and were not unduly concerned about the opinions of others toward them, did not look upon social relationships as rivalry situations, were cooperative, did not object to subordinate roles, were not annoyed by advice from others, enjoyed activities that brought educational or pleasurable opportunities to other people and liked to do things for the dependent and underprivileged, were methodical and painstaking in their work, careful in regard to money, expressed attitudes which implied self-assurance and an optimistic outlook on life, and tended to be conservative and conventional in religion, morals and politics.

In comparison with the unhappily married men the happy group tended to show superior initiative, a tendency to take responsibility, and a willingness to give close attention to detail in their daily work. They were more thrifty in their financial affairs and conservative in their attitudes toward religion, sex morals, and other social conventions. Their most characteristic reaction to others was that of cooperation, which was reflected in their relationship to their business superiors with whom they worked well and in their attitude toward women, which reflected an equalitarian standard. They tended to have a benevolent attitude toward inferiors and the underprivileged and to be unselfish and unselfconscious in their approach to their associates.

This evidence all seems to indicate an important correlation between the early development of physical, social, and emotional maturity and one's success in dating, mating, and adjustment in marriage. In reading over lists of characteristics, however, such as those mentioned above, one needs to be careful not to identify too much with individual items.

It is the total composite pattern of behavior which characterizes a person that is important and not single traits, because one may have a sense of inferiority or any other of the single characteristics given for the unhappy group and still be predominantly a type of person whose chances of success might be very high because success in human relationships, particularly marriage, is not only a matter of individual characteristics but also the kind of person one marries and the characteristics which that person possesses. In other words, it is important that this paired relationship of two personalities be kept in mind, because to the extent that each individual supplements and reinforces the other and, in the long run, is able to satisfy the basic needs of the other person, to that extent will his relationship tend to be a successful and lasting one.

Subjective Aspects of Mate Selection

A good many writers have asked students to list those qualities which they would expect in a person whom they might wish to marry. These kinds of subjective lists are only indicative in general of the ideal character which individuals think they would like a person whom they might marry to have. They are only valuable in so far as they stimulate our thinking in terms of those things which are important both for us and the other person. One such list, for example, compiled by the writer, asked 162 boys, sixteen to twenty-four years of age, three questions: "If you marry what are the things your prospective wife has a right to expect of you?" "What are the things you feel you have a right to expect of her?" "What are some of the factors which you think are important to both of you in terms of compatibility and the establishment of happy relationships?" In answer to the first question, this group, as well as others who had been asked similar questions, felt that a wife should first of all have a right to expect her husband to be interested in her affairs and problems, to be affectionate, to provide a convenient home and adequate income, to participate in family life, allow time for pleasure and social life together, be morally upright, share in planning of economical expenditures, and cooperate in the activities of home and community life. These factors are, of course, all important in carrying on any permanent relationship with another person and are qualities which might be important to consider as far as attitudes and general characteristics are concerned during the period of getting acquainted prior to engagement and marriage.

When 226 young women, sixteen to twenty-four years of age in this group, as well as others who have been asked the same question, considered what a prospective husband had a right to expect of them, their answers were almost the same as those given by the young men. They all indicated such items as being a good homemaker, an economical manager, being neat and attractive in appearance, cooperative, affectionate, interested in their husbands' businesses and activities, and having some knowledge of responsibility of motherhood, including child care and training.

Any one of these subjective feelings or qualities which we desire in an individual whom we might marry could be the basis of a great deal of conflict depending upon how much importance an individual placed upon it. On the other hand, there are perhaps more examples than not of individuals saying, before marriage, that there were certain things which they would always insist upon in the person whom they married, and yet, in nine cases out of ten, they do not find an individual who can do the things they consider important beforehand. The subjective qualities which are important are those which are more basically related to fundamental ideals and needs which we have, rather than those which imply specific knowledge or skills, such as being a good dancer, being a good cook, or other, similar specific things. While many of these attributes might contribute to the pleasure of any two individuals who married, they are certainly not in and of themselves basic to success or failure in marriage.

The most important aspect of subjective goals with reference to success or failure in one's marriage is the extent to which there is agreement and understanding of what each person expects from the marriage and expects the other person to contribute to the marriage. While it is not always possible to state just what it is we want our marriage to be, it is possible to discover, without too great an effort, those goals which we are seeking to satisfy through marriage and which may greatly differ among individuals. It is this discrepancy between the desires which two individuals are attempting to satisfy through marriage that is often the basis for initial and continuous conflict which leads not only to unhappiness but too often to separation and divorce. There are two things which it might be desirable for every young person to know as he contemplates marriage, and those are, first, what motives in his life does he expect marriage to satisfy, and what motives in the life of the person he is to marry is that person expecting marriage to satisfy; and, second, to what extent are these expectancies compatible, and to what extent are they incompatible.

Contrasting Factors Related to Mate Selection

Let us now look at another approach to the matter of mate selection and particularly those factors which seem to be an important basis for successful mating. Of all of the factors which might be considered important, such as age, age difference, religion, education, economic status, nationality, emotional stability, occupation, and so on, none can be considered in and of itself to be the determining one as a basis upon which to make a choice of someone to marry. On the other hand, a single factor may be important enough for one person, but not for another, to be considered the basis for breaking off an engagement and not marrying a particular person.

The really significant thing is, therefore, the value one places upon any single factor. One person may have come to feel that for a college woman to marry a noncollege man would be exceedingly bad, whereas neither of them might object to marrying into a different nationality group from his own.

Let us look, therefore, at some of these factors in more detail and see how much weight they should be given.

Age for Marriage

While we do not have enough studies to indicate conclusively at what age individuals might most successfully

marry, we can draw the general conclusion that maturity is essential for a wise marriage choice.

When couples contemplate marriage at ages considerably younger than the general average found in these studies, particularly if they are in their teens, they should consider the following questions, namely: Are they physically, intellectually, socially, and emotionally mature and grown up enough to understand and assume the responsibility which marriage entails; are they sure that theirs is not just another of those transitory, adolescent "crushes" which occur between fourteen and eighteen years of age; is their attraction largely based upon physical factors, including sex appeal, rather than other important elements; are they economically able and ready to be self-sufficient in raising and supporting a family; to what extent will their choice of a marriage partner under the age of twenty possibly forestall a better choice later; to what extent are they ready to settle down with the companionship of one person?

Marriages consummated too young are likely to interfere with education and vocational preparation. For students in college there are the problems of completing their formal education, possible pregnancy, the question of economic support, of being separated if attending different schools, the girl's ability to help her husband by working and, at the same time, being a wife and companion, which he will expect, and running into parental and college administrative objections. The advantages are, of course, those of being together at all times, the security of marriage, and joint planning and working for future goals. It may mean, in some cases, the loss of the one person one loves most if the engagement is allowed to drag along for years. There is little doubt that couples of eighteen or nineteen years of age are biologically ready to mate, but biological mating and marriage are two quite different things.

Age Difference

The matter of age difference comes in for a great deal of consideration. A young college man of twenty-one asks if he should become engaged to a young woman of twenty-six. Ordinarily, in our society, the man is from two to four years older than the girl he marries. Many couples marry where the ages are equal, and others are happily married where the wife is two or three years older than the husband. The basic consideration is that of determining the reasons for marriage where there is a wide discrepancy from the norm. In terms of what each person supplies the other emotionally and otherwise, this reversal of age may be a satisfactory one. On the other hand, the very needs which this kind of union seems to satisfy may be the cause, later, for unhappiness. Although married women live longer than married men, a man of fifty may be much more attracted to a wife in her middle forties than to one fifty-five or over, whereas the wife of forty may prefer, as she gets older, a husband more mature and older than she did at twenty-five, and especially so if she has had children to mother. The factors of need, which make persons of these ages attractive to each other, are more important to consider than the fact of numerical age itself. Probably age difference acts as a selective factor, that is, only a particular type of woman, either one with maternal interests or a dominating woman, is generally liable to marry a man younger than herself. The younger man, in turn, may have needs which this type of woman's personality may supply. The woman who marries an older man may do so in order to secure a surrogate type of person to her father. There are no grounds, however, for thinking that such marriages would bring happiness to men and women in general.

Length of Acquaintance and Engagement

Over-night and week-end marriages, which are consummated on the spur of the moment, almost invariably end in unhappiness or divorce. It seems only good, common sense, and research bears this out, that where people have known each other for several years and have been engaged from a year to eighteen months, they have a better outlook for a successful marriage. They have had a chance to know each other under a wide variety of circumstances and to have learned each other's personal habits, personality characteristics, ambitions, and philosophies of life. This item is important because it indicates opportunity for acquaintance to be tested and either ripen into engagement or give way to other possibilities.

There seems to be a point at which increasing length of engagement may reduce the probability of good adjustment, but data are not sufficient as yet on this point. We know that, in general, the proportion of couples with poor adjustment declines from 50 per cent, where they have been engaged under three months, to 18 per cent where the engagement has lasted somewhere from nine to twenty-three months. It then tends to increase slightly where the engagement extends beyond a period of twenty-three months.

Education and Mate Selection

Most of the studies on this factor are over-weighted with case histories of college graduates and professional people. There is considerable conflict in opinion among experts as to what effect higher education has upon success in marriage.

Burgess and Cottrell (6) found increased success in marriage with the rising level in education. Terman (7) found no consistent relation between happiness and the amount of schooling. Popenoe (8), as the result of his studies, seems to feel that college education, particularly for women, may have a very definite negative influence upon their ability to make a good adjustment in marriage.

Higher education seems to have a greater effect upon the percentage of women who marry than men. It seems to result, in some instances, in setting up a competitive relationship in the mind of the person between the status value of a career and fulfilling the marital ambition. The highly trained woman often has higher standards as to the type of man she would marry and the social and economic conditions under which she would accept a proposal of marriage, and she thus narrows her field of choice. There is some evidence which seems to indicate a lower rate of family disorganization among educated classes than among uneducated classes. It is difficult, however, to associate these facts with the single item of education alone, because whether one has an education or not, there may be many differences in cultural standards and behavior which are more important in producing family disorganization than the factor of schooling alone.

Marriages among home economics graduates seem to have an exceedingly high degree of compatibility and permanence, if judged by the small percentage of them who are divorced. While knowledge of this science may, and no doubt does, make a significant contribution, it is also a selective factor in that perhaps many young women choose this field because they already have certain well formed attitudes and ideals with reference to marriage and family life.

Actual differences in schooling seem to be less important as a selective factor to men than to women. The college-trained woman tends to marry a man from the same social and economic background as her own. Those who attend coeducational schools seem to marry men whose economic income is lower than do those who attend women's colleges. In the latter case, there seems to be a tendency for them to marry men in business who come from their own higher economic class, although they may not be equal in formal schooling.

The meaning of a college degree may be such that one person or the other is constantly striving to achieve it to be the equal of the partner. It may be born of so strong a feeling of inadequacy as to cause serious conflict in a family. How one feels about a particular item, the value he places upon it, is often more important than the fact itself.

Educational difference is less important than differences in intelligence and general culture, which, in the first instance, is not given one in college and, in the second case, may not necessarily be dependent upon higher education but rather upon family background and the social strata in which one is reared.

A good example of this is the case of a young woman who, a few years ago, came seeking advice as to whether or not she should marry a young man who was not a college graduate. She herself had graduated from a midwestern university and had, for two years, been working in a professional job in a large city. She had met this young man, and her story was that he met in every way the personal, social, and cultural standards of all her friends who were college graduates, and she could see no reason why she should not marry him. He had a business of his own and was doing well financially. The only difficulty in her mind was the fact that her mother objected to the marriage on the grounds that he was not a university graduate. In this young woman's family the mother was a university graduate, whereas the father was not. To the mother it was tremendously important that the daughter marry a man with a college education. The young woman insisted to her that this fact was of little importance. However, in the course of the discussion, she revealed that her emotional feelings about the situation were different than her intellectual statements when she proceeded to point out to the interviewer that she had been able to encourage her fiance to go to night school and finish the last year of high-school work, and that she was sure that after they married she would be able to encourage his night-school work until he had obtained a college degree. This is only one of many instances which might be cited to show the value which she actually placed upon this single factor of having a college education. This illustrates the difficulties of placing an equal amount of weight on any single factor because of the varying degrees of importance which different individuals place upon any particular item.

Economic Status

People usually marry in, or near, their socioeconomic class. The matter of one's financial obligations, economic responsibility for others after marriage, pattern of money handling in one's family background, plans for the distribution of one's income, and stability of one's position and its future possibilities are important considerations.

Debts incurred prior to marriage often hamper immediate marriage, particularly on the part of women. Unless these financial obligations are unusually large they would seem to offer no serious barrier to engagement or immediate marriage but should be understood and recognized in the marriage plans. More often a young man or woman feels that he cannot marry because he thinks a parent is dependent upon him. It means the parent is holding on to a child emotionally, and the child, even though a grown young man or woman, is too emotionally dependent upon the parent to break away, financial responsibility often being a minor problem. Perhaps more important in the marriage are the ideas which each person has about money, how it should be utilized, who should handle it, and the degree of stability of the income. After marriage, it is over these details that most conflict arises. The actual amount of income seems to be of little significance as far as good mating and successful marriage is concerned.

Nationality and Religious Differences

Nationality and race differences are significant because they represent different backgrounds of custom, cultural attitudes, and feelings about so many things of everyday living. In general, within the range of similar cultural ideals, there is no problem involved in selecting a mate of different nationality background. For example, citizens of the English-speaking countries marry freely among themselves even though of different nationality, and, within limits, intermarry with French, German, Scandinavian, and other similar racial and nationality groups. When one contemplates marriage where the nationality or racial differences are more extreme from one's own cultural background, as, for example, Jewish-Gentile marriages, Chinese-English, or Negro-White, then one must be a much more mature, self-sufficient, adaptable person. The wider the range of differences between two individual cultural and religious backgrounds, the better persons it requires to make a success of a marriage. By being a better person is meant one who has greater insight, is more mature, tolerant, and understanding. In general, for most people, these wide differences which involve fundamental, cultural patterns and philosophy of life should be avoided.

Where Catholic, Protestant, Jewish, Christian Science, or other radically different religious sentiments exist, the couple should think through the adjustments to be made if such an engagement is to be allowed to mature into matrimony. In general, it is better for Catholics to marry Catholics, conservative Protestants to marry conservative Protestants, and members of unusual cults to marry within their own cults. The reason for this is that deep-seated religious convictions are not easily altered, and, even though we may rationalize to the point of feeling that they may not be important for us, we can rest assured that, in general, they will show up in many ways after marriage. It is not uncommon for young people to find themselves thrown into a social group where close ties of friendship develop, and, before one realizes it, he is "hopelessly" in love with a person whose religious or racial background is radically different from his own. Then comes the agony of trying to decide what to do. More often than not, there is parental objection to such a marriage, and it does not receive the sanction of either church or racial group. One may defy one's family, leave one's church, and disregard racial differences, but experiences indicate that marriages tend to be happier, on the whole, where they have parental approval, where there is at least some conventional form of religious marriage ceremony.

Let us take as an illustration a young couple of Catholic-Protestant background who contemplate marriage. There can be little objection to such a marriage if one or the other of the couple wishes to become affiliated with the religious faith of the other, provided that this change of religious affiliation is a conviction of the faith, not an act of the hysteria of love. If this is not the case, however, it should be understood that a Catholic, marrying a Protestant, must live up to certain regulations of his church or the marriage cannot be accepted as a valid one by the church. It is necessary that they both agree not to attempt to persuade the marriage partner to leave his particular church; the non-Catholic must agree to allow the children to be raised as Catholics and not to resort to any means whatsoever which would interfere with the normal process of childbearing. These general rules must be accepted by both individuals and lived up to honestly if subsequent conflict over them is not to arise.

What little research evidence we have on this matter of religious background seems to show that husbands and wives who have never attended Sunday school, or who stopped going after the age of ten, show a markedly lower proportion of highly successful marriages. Those who continued their religious affiliation and activity until the age of nineteen to twenty-five, or older, seem to have had a better chance for marital happiness than other groups.

With reference to nationality differences, which may or may not involve religious differences, we need to recognize the fact that, as a result of having grown up in that particular cultural environment, we have many ingrained habits and attitudes which, during the period of courtship and engagement, may not be particularly significant, but which, unless understood and accepted, may lead to difficulty later. These differences will become intensified with the coming of postwar global contacts. These cultural differences do not need to be necessarily as wide apart as a Chinese-American marriage might be in order to cause difficulty. There are often great enough differences in the cultural backgrounds of individuals who are reared in New England and Alabama, or New Jersey and Nebraska, to create many problems of adjustment growing out of these differences in basic attitudes and feelings about how life should be lived to wreck what, otherwise, might be a successful marriage had the couple really analyzed and thought through some of these important factors prior to marriage.

It is desirable, however, that every couple have some basic religious philosophy, the practice of which they can agree upon. The important thing is acceptance of each other's philosophy, and, if possible, the practice of that philosophy in a common way of life.

Physical Vigor

Although we have little actual research evidence on this point, it seems from what data are available that the health of the husband has more to do with good adjustment than the health of the wife. This may be due to the fact that poor health on the part of the husband would be an economic handicap, whereas, if the wife were in poor health, it might enhance the already existing ties of affection. From observation and some clinical experience, however, it would seem that more importance should be given to the matter of physical health and vigor than has been done in the past. We know from observation of families that anything which lowers the resistance of an individual tends to increase the possibility of irritability and conflict and places an added burden upon the marriage partner, that is, an added burden in terms of meeting the additional strain attendant upon the other person's chronic irritability and near illness.

Occupation

The relationship of one's occupation to success or failure indicates that where there is a minimum of mobility and where a minimum of separation of husband and wife for either constant, intermittent periods or continuous periods of time is involved, there is the highest tendency toward happiness. Such occupations as the ministry and teaching are examples of this type. The occupations which seem to have the lowest rating for happiness are those of unskilled labor and traveling salesmen, both of these having a high degree of mobility and the absence of social control over conduct. We know from many sources the tendency to a higher degree to family disorganization among the artistic profession as contrasted with the more stabilized pursuits of engineering, medicine, banking, etc. These differences are perhaps due more to personality factors than to factors of mobility.

Income and Savings

In selecting someone to marry, the sheer amount of financial savings before marriage is not a satisfactory indication of economic security but only of the fact that the husband has saved something. As to the amount of income one should have at the time of marriage, a moderate income gives a higher chance of success than either an unusually low one or an exceptionally high one. The training and ability of the persons who marry, the possible future for advancement in their particular field, would seem to be more important elements than actual income itself.

Gainful Employment After Marriage

The question often arises as to whether or not a wife should continue to work at some form of gainful employment after marriage. The factor that seems to be important here is the wife's attitude rather than the fact that she works or does not. The best adjustments seem to be made where both the husband and wife desire this type of arrangement, or where they both do not desire it. As far as future success or failure in marriage is concerned, one can only say that it takes a more capable person, unless the income is sufficiently large to provide adequate household help, to manage two full time careers as well as a household and the rearing of children. There is little evidence to show that where a couple plan and desire a home and family, as well as the continuance of their professional interests, their family life and rearing of their children may not be equally as satisfactory as that of homes in which the wife devotes her entire time to homemaking responsibilities. It depends largely upon the persons involved rather than upon the cold fact of whether they do or do not work outside the home.

Summary

After considering the many and varied factors which enter into mate selection, we see that it is difficult to arrive at any conclusion as to which ones are the basic and most important, while, as we have said, any one of them may have so much emotional significance for a particular person that it may become the cause of serious conflict after marriage. In general, the following, from all points of view, seem to have the highest degree of significance: having, at the outset and as a result of one's training and experience, basic personality characteristics which we have previously indicated to be socially and emotionally mature; one's living in a home which fostered consistent training; a sense of affectional security; engendered love and respect between ourselves and our parents by allowing for growth and independence and frankness in consideration of all questions, including sex, during our development from infancy through adolescence; having lived in a home which fostered social development, education, religious attitudes, participation in the social activities of the neighborhood, encouraged our normal heterosexual development and had respect for conformity to social conventions; having acquired good physical and mental health and the practice of good health habits; and having acquired a socially constructive philosophy of life.

CHAPTER VI

LOOKING FORWARD TO MARRIAGE

Engagement

Engagement serves two purposes. One, and perhaps the most important, is the opportunity it gives the couple to feel free to discuss the many questions which marriage entails. It is not that these cannot and are not discussed during courtship, but that when a couple reach the stage of becoming engaged, they are emotionally ready to consider the more serious problems and opportunities confronting them, if and when they marry. Second, their relationship has social sanction, and their community accepts their more intimate and constant association. An engagement extending over a period of from a year to three years has a greater chance of future marital happiness than one which exists only a few days or weeks. During this longer period, it is possible for the persons to actually know each other better, to become better acquainted with each other's family, to discuss the ideals each has in mind for his marriage, when to marry and the kind of ceremony they want, how to have what they want on the man's income, the question of the wife's working, the question of children, a discussion of the type of place they wish to live in, what their plans are to be if the husband is in the armed forces, arrangement for premarital physical examination, self-education on matters of housekeeping, finance, sex, etc., on which they may need help. Many other questions, such as those arising from radically different religions, should be carefully and intelligently discussed. If these discussions do not result in a workable agreement, the engagement should be broken. A broken engagement is better than an unhappy or a broken marriage.

Questions of personal confessions or confidential family or personal secrets often arise and are perplexing problems. Each person wants to be honest with the other and yet often fears the other may misunderstand and thus break the engagement if they are told certain things which have occurred in one's past life. In general, it is perhaps wise to consult a marriage counselor and discuss such worries as you may have. The very act of discussing them with an expert may relieve your sense of guilt about them, or he may be able to suggest how you might best proceed. If a counselor is not available, face the reality of the situation and discuss it. If real love exists, it will be accepted, and a sane adjustment made. In general, girls seem to be able to accept past indiscretions on the part of their fiances better than boys are able to accept similar actions on the part of their fiances. Honesty is always the best policy, and if the sense of guilt is very great or the situation is likely to recur, then it should by all means be discussed beforehand, even at the risk of breaking the engagement.

Breaking and accepting a broken engagement is never an easy matter. Couples often let an engagement drag on for years, to the detriment of each party, because neither wants to say the final word that will sever the relationship. Sometimes this is because each says he hates to hurt the other person when, in reality, it is because he cannot stand to hurt himself. In other cases, each would break the engagement if he could maneuver the other person into the position of taking the decisive step, thereby relieving himself of the responsibility. In such cases, the person would then feel that he could project the blame on the other party, thus protecting his own ego from injury.

A good rule to follow is this: when in doubt about marriage, even though you have been engaged for several years, wait or try out someone else. It may be that your relationship is not basically a mature enough one to insure a happy marriage for you. Engagements should be broken if either person is not sure, if he has definitely changed his feelings about the other person, if there is doubt as to the wisdom of carrying out the promise to marry, or if the engagement has been brought about by pressure on the part of relatives or others.

A proposal of marriage is a serious matter. It is a legal contract, and one should not impose his company upon another for an undue length of time unless one has serious intentions of matrimony. It is especially not fair to the girl, who is, by the man's monopoly of her time, taken out of circulation, so to speak, and whose chances of another marriage may thus be impaired.

Wedding Arrangements

One of the first considerations in getting married is to acquaint one's self with the legal requirements for matrimony in the particular state where the marriage is to take place. Since these requirements vary from state to state, one should consult the county clerk's office in the county of residence and find out what the general procedure is. For example, common law marriages are valid in some states and not others. In most states a marriage may be annulled if the relationship is nearer than prescribed by law, if there are certain kinds of physical or mental disabilities, if the parties are not of legal age or are already married to someone else, if fraud is involved, or if the marriage is consummated under duress or in jest. Some young couples are in such great haste to marry that they elope or are secretly wed. Such plans are extremely unwise. There are no good reasons for elopement or secrecy which do not have to be faced and dealt with at some near future date. It would seem better to face the problem and settle it before marriage than to evade it until later. Marriages executed on this basis tend to have less permanence and happiness than those which have parental approval and follow the forms approved by the church and state. The church and state have a stake in your marriage, whether you like it or not. Organized society created the institution of marriage to care more systematically for children, protect them and insure their legitimacy, to regulate sex conduct in the interest of health and morals, the inheritance of property, and to protect innocent parties from exploitation.

Marriages performed by a justice of the peace are legitimate. The majority of brides and grooms usually prefer a home or church wedding. There are advantages to this type of marriage over the more casual forms. A marriage is entered into for a lifetime. The actual occasion of one's marriage should be something upon which one can look back as a happy and joyous event, performed in the presence of one's family and dearest friends. Studies show that, in general, marriages of this type last longer and are happier.

Plans for the actual arrangements are usually assumed by the bride and her family. They arrange for the invitations, the minister, and provide the usual things which go to make the wedding a memorable one. The date of the wedding is usually set by the bride in order to avoid the time of her menstrual period. About the only things the groom must attend to are the license, the ring, and the bride's bouquet. The size and pretentiousness of the wedding will depend upon the taste and wealth of the families involved.

The Premarital Physical Examination

In most states the law requires that a blood test be made to determine the individual's freedom from syphilis. This procedure is often referred to as a premarital examination. A truly valuable and complete premarital examination should include much more than this. Both the young man and young woman should have a complete physical examination given by a physician trained to do premarital examinations. For both men and women, a blood test should be made whether required by state law or not, and vaginal and urethral smears made to check on latent gonorrhea infection. This type of physical examination provides the individual with a good check on his general health and the basis for the correction of minor defects before marriage. It also gives the physician or marriage counselor data concerning the eugenic background of the couple.

The premarital physical examination should be accompanied by an opportunity for consultation with the doctor or counselor on matters of a personal nature.

The Premarital Interview

The majority of young men and women have questions they wish to discuss and often anxieties about previous experiences which they think may affect their marital adjustment. The premarital interview with a physician or other counselor is to determine and help you with your educational needs.

The most frequent questions which others have asked during these interviews include such matters as:

1. A knowledge of the anatomy and physiology of male and female, including the process of reproduction. Most young people of college age know very little of the process of reproduction or the structure of their internal and external reproductive organs.

2. Fears and inhibitions associated with sex due to their early training and lack of education.

3. Remembrance of experiences or shock from early childhood which may still be the cause of anxiety or fear.

4. The effects upon marital adjustment of previous masturbation, prolonged continence, or previous sex experiences.

5. Fears which center around pregnancy and childbearing.

6. Methods of child spacing.

7. An understanding of proper ways of initiating and conducting one's sex life to insure success and enjoyment for each person. This question usually concerns what to do at the outset, what procedure and methods are best, the rightness of various forms of sex practice

involving frankness as to time, posture, contacts and methods, frequency, desirable preliminaries, things to be avoided, how to know when each person is satisfied, and dozens of other similar questions.

8. A clarification of many things which may have been heard or read that are in the realm of folklore and have no legitimate basis in fact.

9. Less frequently, but occasionally, questions arise about "crushes" on one of the same sex, frigidity, ovulation, impotence, sterility, and so on.

Such an interview may require one or several conferences supplemented by assigned material for reading, depending upon the degree of knowledge the couple may already possess. The purpose of the premarital interview is to inform and to allay fears and anxiety. The normalcy of sex in married life and the philosophy and attitudes of the individuals entering marriage concerning their sex relations are just as important, if not more so, than cold facts alone. It is advisable that you return for a check-up interview with your physician or counselor in a month or two after marriage, to clarify any questions or difficulties that may have arisen.

Honeymoons Are Fun

The purpose of a honeymoon is, of course, to get away from one's family and friends, in order to have an initial, uninterrupted time together. It is a transition period between single life and married life. After one returns from this high-peak experience, married life will bring more day-to-day work, cares, and responsibilities, although it does not decrease the joy of living with the person to whom one has chosen to be married.

The length of the honeymoon is important. Long, ocean voyages or train and bus trips often bring fatigue and irritability which mar this initial stage of married life. A shorter trip, with more time to be together and do the things together one wishes to do, seems most desirable. If there are other places you wish to go, save some of them for year-to-year vacations together. Many married women report that their honeymoons are the only vacations they have had alone with their husbands in ten to twenty years of married life. This is too bad. Many a family has had its morale lifted and romance reincarnated by the husband's and wife's taking a short vacation or business trip away from children, family, the job, and the house they live in. It is, perhaps, unnecessary to stress the importance of leaving an itinerary of one's trip behind in case necessity demands a return home on account of some unforeseen calamity.

Do not go to a resort where one has constantly to be involved in the social life of other people, unless by choice. The amount of money one has to spend will limit the type of honeymoon, but in no way does the amount of money spent, be it large or small, affect the quality of the experience. Plans for the honeymoon should be made jointly. Do not take relatives or third parties along. Take a little time each day for privacy. Remember that every person likes privacy, even in the most intimate and enjoyable relationship.

Married life begins upon the return from the honeymoon. Selecting a place to live, furnishing it, getting settled, organizing the household routine, and learning the job of running a home and being a husband or a wife now become the paramount concern for each.

Every couple in love, no doubt, feels certain that their union will be the successful one and that they will live romantically happy ever after. It would be nice if this were literally true. Yet, very soon after marriage, girls especially ask why it is that romance, the same glorious continuation of romantic relationships, does not carry over into marriage. The fact of the matter is, it does, but they do not recognize it. One of the ingredients of happiness is an ample supply of love and romance at the outset. But this alone is not the basis, but the expression, of true love and understanding. One of the important things to take with one into marriage is a knowledge of how to preserve the essence of that same romance which was so much in evidence during the last days of engagement and during the period of the honeymoon. Some of the things which tend to preserve this love ingredient in marriage are the following: the other's attitude and having one's interest and loyalty predominantly and paramountly in the other person's welfare and wellbeing; an attitude of reciprocal appreciation, tolerance, and sympathetic understanding; a recognition of the fact that no couple ever married and lived happily ever after; searching each day for some one thing, however trivial, about that man or woman we married and giving it our approval. There is no medicine so soothing to the human soul as recognition and approval by someone one loves. There is no illness so devastating to a relationship as feeling unimportant, lacking in status, and not having the encouragement and support of the other person. We cannot afford to take the other person for granted. A case in point is that of the bride of a year and a half who began to feel a growing antagonism toward her husband. She wanted to avoid and withdraw from his advances and had increasingly little interest in keeping her home an orderly, congenial place for him to come home to. He was a good husband. He helped with the housework, kept things in repair about the home, and helped with the baby. He did not drink nor go out nights. He liked his home. He loved his wife but was also worried about her increasing indifference. An apparently silly thing was the cause. Upon their return from a one-day honeymoon he went to work, came home, ate his supper, and immediately got on his work clothes, went to the garage, and worked on his car until nearly midnight. This was repeated Tuesday, Wednesday, Thursday, and for ten days. He needed his car to get to work. It was important that he put it in good condition for winter. But the young bride felt neglected and taken for granted. Romance was over, and she was left with only her own hurt feelings and disappointment. After a year and a half, this hurt was showing its depth by her unconscious gradual rejection of her husband, for his hurt to her, which, until he came to an advisor to talk it over, he had never sensed was the reason for causing their union to be unsuccessful.

The Illusion of Disillusionment

We need to have a true picture of what happens after marriage. For the man, it is usually a return to a job in which he is already established. For the girl, it is her first day on the job. She is confronted, for the first time in her life, with the responsibility of organizing and managing a home with all the new experiences and detail that this may involve. There is buying, preparing, and serving the food for the family on time. There is laundry, cleaning, and bedmaking. There is dishwashing, planning for leisure, and entertaining. There is mending, pressing, and furnace care. Any bride can add a dozen or more such items, all, or most all of them, new, with the task of organizing them all into a system which is efficient and leaves time for personal pleasures and a rested wife to receive a tired husband in the evening, and one has a picture of the new bride's job. This requires time. It needs understanding, patience, and sometimes tact on the part of the husband until she has her new job running as smoothly as he has his old one at the office.

A realization on the part of each that the other has his own interests is important. This apparent loss of romance is well portrayed in the following letter from a newly married woman:

"*The one thing I found hard to accept in marriage* (I am finding it increasingly less hard to accept because we are working out a happy adjustment) *was the settling down to everyday living after my rather excessive expectations before marriage*, especially since we were both very busy last year, L. with his last year at law school and I finishing up my master's thesis. Before marriage, whenever we weren't studying together at the library or occasionally going out, we spent every minute of our free time making love. After marriage we found it harder to study up to ten o'clock, for example, and then say, 'Well, that's enough of that now,' and start making love. In the first place, we stopped studying at the library (which was the only quiet place we could find before marriage) and started studying (?) at home, and there was always the temptation to make love instead of studying, so we ended up doing little studying and yet not very much love-making that was free of guilt feelings about the fact that we ought to be studying. And I resented the fact that even though we were married, something we had been looking forward to for years, we didn't seem to have any more time for ourselves than we had before marriage. Fortunately, things are working out much better this year. But I would be very much interested in a discussion, both of the problems of marriage confronting people who marry while going to school and the much broader problems of settling down to marriage in general.

"Money is an ever-present problem of course, much more serious in some cases than in others, but there naturally isn't any one answer — everything has to be worked out to suit the individual couple. From my parents' marriage I gained a real appreciation of how much of a problem money can be (although I suspect that often it's a cover-up for a more basic problem), but money problems have been such a negligible part of our marriage (although we never have any money!) that I'm beginning to forget that financial problems are really important."

Here is what happens to romance after marriage. Before engagement, couples work, sleep, eat, play, worship, study, do miscellaneous things, and spend a little time courting.

BEFORE ENGAGEMENT	DURING ENGAGEMENT	AFTER MARRIAGE
Dating	Dating and Love Making	Love Making
Play		Play
Eating — Leisure	Play — Religion	Eating — Leisure
Religion — Leisure	Eating — Leisure	Religion — Leisure
Work — School	Work — School	Work
Sleep	Sleep	Sleep
Miscellaneous	Miscellaneous	Miscellaneous

As engagement approaches and becomes a fact, the actual time spent together is every minute possible, so this part of the twenty-four-hour day expands, pushing the other areas closer together like the folds of an accordion. Work is not affected much except, perhaps, in efficiency, sleep is reduced play with each other is increased, religion actually may not change, study will be cut, and what was formerly a small amount of courting time is now a large segment. And not only is it a large segment of each twenty-four hours, but this time together is spent in complete adoration of each other with no other interferences. Then the marriage occurs. One needs to catch up on one's sleep, the jobs of the household have to be done, friends invite you out and return entertaining has to be done, Mother visits the new bride for a week, added study is necessary for the man to advance in his profession, and, when the twenty-four hours are over, there is left relatively little time for uninterrupted, complete, and undivided attention to each other. In quantity, the actual, romantic lovemaking time has decreased. But it is still there if one can see it. Everything that is being done is shot through with love for the other person, and the energy put into everything done has added significance because it is for the other person's happiness and the achievement of jointly planned goals. This is what happens when often a girl, particularly, feels disillusioned. Then the engagement romance seems not to linger beyond the first few weeks of married life. This burden of work, planning, decisions to be made and not always without conflict of opinion, goes on with increasing complexity as children arrive, illness enters the home, income is reduced, and other normal life happenings occur. One can see, therefore, how necessary it is for both husband and wife to keep their own relationship, even though it be small in time available for each other apart from the demands of family, job, and community life, filled with mutual encouragement, love, and support of each other. These are the basic things, which, if planned for, enhance the happiness of the initial period of marital life together.

Part III

Evolving a Satisfactory Family Life

To be able, as Confucius indicates, to follow what the heart desires without coming into collision with the stubborn facts of life is the privilege of the utterly innocent and the utterly wise. It is the privilege of the infant because the world ministers to his heart's desire, and of the sage because he has learned what to desire.

— Lippmann, Walter, *A Preface to Morals*, ch. 9, p. 193, lines 1–7. The Macmillan Company, New York, 1929.

CHAPTER VII

THE FIRST YEAR OF MARRIAGE

Adjustments Are Normal — Problems Inevitable

Perhaps one of the most significant characteristics of the first year of marriage is the fact that each couple faces practically every kind of problem they will have to face in the course of their marriage, with the possible exception of pregnancy and the rearing of children. They will have decisions and adjustments to make in relation to finances, their own personal habits and personality characteristics, ambitions and ideals, health, friends, associates, recreation, social life, housekeeping management and routines, relatives and in-laws, sex, religion, education, community participation, their job, and possibly crises.

All that this means is that the first year of marriage is one of the greatest adjustment and perhaps the most crucial of any of the years that follow. It is significant that approximately 40 per cent of all marriages which occur in any one year end in separation or divorce by the end of the first five years. The causes of these broken marriages usually have their basis, first, in bad mating and, second, in the inability of the individuals to establish a satisfactory basis for meeting life's problems during the first year.

We can predict with assurance that many marriages will fail. But at all times in our history an all too high proportion of marriages have failed. People who marry too often labor under the romantic notion that all one has to do to gain happiness, if single, is to marry. There is the case of a young woman who was worrying about whether, if she married, she would be happy. When asked if she was happy now her reply was, "Some days I am and some days I am not." It will not be any different after one is married. Getting married does not change the kinds of persons we are. Our personality, our fundamental emotional and social patterns, our prejudices, sentiments, and ambitions, our reactions to success and failure, and other similar characteristics continue to be the same after we marry as they were before.

Problems are a part of life. The person who has no problems does not exist. What is most important in present day life is not so much the fact that one is confronted with problems and disappointments, as whether that person has learned how to meet problems when they come his way.

The following excerpts from letters, written by young people married during the past two years, are not to emphasize the problem side of marriage, but rather to show how every couple is faced with one kind of situation or another, which it is hard for him to understand and solve.

Mrs. L. G. writes about loss of romance :

"I am a young bride of one month. It may seem to you that one month of marriage is not enough time to voice an opinion on married life, but I feel that I have already acquired a problem that many couples may run into.

"First, before I state my problem, I'd like to stress the fact that I believe the happiness obtained in married life far exceeds the many little misunderstandings that may occur.

"The problem is, why can't married folks continue to be sweethearts after marriage? Why must there be such a change? When you get married, courtship suddenly stops. Your life merely becomes a matter of fact routine. The excitement of something new happening is gone. The sweet nothings suddenly become nothing. You're taken for granted and he's taken for granted. I feel that this attitude should not exist. I believe if young married couples could do away with the above difficulty, there would be less chance for other conflicts."

Mrs. A. writes about her first nine months of married life:

"We were married August 6, 1947, in the Methodist Church of my home town. Our wedding was formal and took place at 8 p.m. It was a rather large wedding — about 100 guests were present.

The entire affair seemed to be perfect. Yes, we had just the kind of wedding we both had always wanted.

"After this wonderful beginning, we started off on our honeymoon. We drove 50 miles that night to a hotel where we had the bridal suite reserved. We didn't get to our room until about midnight, and we were very tired after all the excitement. My husband did have enough strength left to carry me over the threshold, though! I was rather shy that first night about undressing in front of my husband. I made him go into the bathroom to undress while I used the bedroom. We had no sexual relations the first three nights of our honeymoon as I was menstruating. My husband knew about this beforehand, so he did not press the issue.

"I knew one of my greatest adjustments to married life would be the sexual adjustment. I had been raised under a very strict and domineering mother who taught me during my childhood that sex was bad and dirty. Then she tried to tell me right before I was married that sex was perfectly normal and healthy after marriage. However, I could not get rid of all my inhibitions on such a short notice. I was fortunate enough to have had three years of college work, which included Anatomy and Physiology, so I was not entirely ignorant about sex. I believe the broad viewpoint on sex that I gained in college helped me adjust more quickly to married life than any other factor.

"The next day we continued our honeymoon trip. We took a plane and went to Bermuda for four short days. We had a wonderful time. We knew no-one and no-one knew us. We were completely absorbed in each other and our first adjustments seemed to be made quite readily. We took in all the interesting sights and all the interesting night clubs, although we weren't on the move all the time. Almost every afternoon we took time out for a little nap; then later on in the afternoon we would have a 'spot' of tea. I was especially happy during the first few days that we didn't have sexual intercourse as it gave me a chance to get over some of my inhibitions and gave me a better chance for making satisfactory adjustments in other fields. It was such a new feeling to even sleep with my husband that it was nice to only have one thing happen at a time. In thinking back upon my experience, I am wondering if more honeymooners might be happier if the husband weren't so eager to have relations with his wife the first night of married life. I think this is especially true if the wife is a virgin and has been brought up in a strict family environment. I believe it's easier not to have so many adjustments to make all the first day or so.

"The first night that we had sexual relations was not **very** pleasant, especially for me. However, I had been to an obstetrician for a pre-marital examination, so I knew pretty well what to expect. He had informed me that it would take awhile for me to adjust to intercourse as the vagina was quite small. Knowing this, I tried especially hard to overcome all my fears and inhibitions. I also had a very considerate and understanding husband, which is a big help in a period of adjustment.

"Anyway, we had a thoroughly delightful honeymoon, and we returned to my home very happy newlyweds. As the saying goes, 'The honeymoon was short, but sweet.'

"After visiting my home for a few days, we started for Colorado, my husband's home. We rode back in the car with my husband's parents. It took us five days to reach our destination, much of the time being spent in sight-seeing along the way.

"A week later, we returned to our own home, which was quite hot. We stayed in a friend's apartment while looking for a place to live. We both adjusted to our new residence very readily. There are so many young couples living here in the same circumstances as we that we all seem to unite as one big, happy family. It seemed nice to have a home of our own at long last!

"Both my husband and I attend the University now, and we face practically the same marital problems that confront most university couples. Our one large problem is finances. My husband makes $65.00 a month above his G.I. pay, but this amount still isn't sufficient if you try to save a little each month. Neither my husband nor I keep a budget. We've started many times, but never keep it up. To us it seems more trouble than it's worth. We have a pretty good idea where our money goes each month without the budget. We spend on the average of $175.00 a month, which includes the upkeep on our Ford, which usually requires some kind of repairs each month. When we were married we had a bank account of $600.00, and we have reduced it to $100.00 now. This money was used for setting up housekeeping as well as supplementing our income for living expenses. We have had no quarrels over money or who should handle it, but we have had several talks about how and where we can cut expenses. We have a joint bank account, which works out fine for us. I balance both check books with the bank statement every month to make sure neither of us has made a mistake on our entries.

"One problem we have not had to deal with is in-laws. We live about 400 miles from my husband's parents and about 1800 miles from my parents. However, this summer my mother is coming to visit us for a month, and my husband has decided that a month is too long for her to stay. So we compromised on one month!

"I think most of our disagreeing and arguing takes place when we are tired or are worrying about school. I know I'm most disagreeable when I'm studying for examinations. I seem to resent the fact that I have to make dinner, do dishes, and other housework when I should be studying for a test. My husband and I usually share the household chores unless one of us is especially busy, then the one who has the most time takes over. I always have to do the cooking, though, as my husband doesn't know the slightest thing about it. When I'm especially tired, I become very irritable and often find fault with my husband about things that usually don't bother me at all. He reacts the same way, although he seems to have more energy than I and doesn't complain so often. Several times we've quarrelled over such a silly issue as who's going to pack the lunch at night. By the time we both study all evening, we're ready to go to bed and don't want to bother packing a lunch. As a rule, we pack the lunch together or my husband packs it.

"We have not had an occasion to meet the problem of jealousy yet. Before marriage neither of us exhibited any tendencies toward this problem. We both like people and are happy when they like us. When we're on a party, we like to exchange dances with other couples. Then it seems that we enjoy each other's company more than ever when we dance together. Since neither of us has shown any interest in another person, that problem of jealousy has not entered our life.

"As for our sexual relationships, I have fairly well adjusted to the problem by now. Most of my inhibitions have disappeared, although I still don't feel the need of sexual intercourse as often as my husband. After a day at school and an evening of studying, I'm tired and want to go right to sleep without any love making. My husband usually respects my wishes, and we mostly confine our relationships to the week-ends. This seems to work out most satisfactorily for both of us.

"Our largest problem now is our lack of time for recreation. It seems that we're always so busy with studies, housework, or working in the yard that we don't have time to do things like picnicking, playing cards, hiking, or just sitting home enjoying each other's company. We hope this problem will be solved when we're graduated from college.

"In conclusion, I want to say that my first nine months of married life has been one of many adjustments and many enjoyments. I had to adjust to living with my husband; adjust to sharing everything with another person. I think we have made a satisfactory adjustment through a great love for one another and the desire to always satisfy each other before oneself. The various small problems that have arisen during our nine months of marriage have been solved by our being able to sit down and talk our problems over without either of us becoming too emotional. Yes, married life has its ups and downs, but with a deep understanding of each other's needs and wants, an unselfish personality, and a lasting love, marriage can be fun and wonderful!"

Mrs. L. M. tells about meeting a personal problem:

"Harry and I became engaged in December, 1946, and we were married on July 15, 1947, at 3 p.m. in the Presbyterian Church parlor with only relatives and close friends present. A reception followed the ceremony. When the necessities were over, an aunt and uncle slipped us out the back door and we rode with them to the city where we had a reservation at one of the hotels. On the way, we were caught in a terrific rain, and the highway and streets were flooded. We joked at the time that the rain was God's wrath on us for getting married.

"Finally we were deposited at the hotel about 9 o'clock which was too late to indulge in any entertainment. We unpacked our suitcases, explored the room, and sent for some ice cubes, glasses, and '7 Up.' I had the queerest, most wonderful feeling in this nice room, sipping '7 Up' and listening to some good music with my brand-new husband — yet, I had to keep assuring myself that being alone with him in this room was strictly legal, and that if anyone knocked on the door it wouldn't be a fellow church member checking up on us.

"The shower curtain around the bathtub and shower was real protection, and I kept one eye on it to see that Harry didn't peek as I took my shower. I brushed my teeth and dressed while he showered, and I noticed that he was quite modest too. I don't believe I ever fully assured myself that being in the bathroom together was alright.

"We went to bed and followed the usual pattern of behavior. We had no problems, and enjoyed our sexual relations; although I reached no climax. Later Harry went to sleep, and as hard as I tried, I couldn't do more than doze all night. At daybreak I got up and roamed around the room. I sat on the window sill and watched the city awaken. There was an ice tub of melted cubes so I poured the water out the window and watched it disappear before it reached the street below. We were on the 13th floor. Later I want back to bed and by 10 I was ready to sleep, but Harry was ready to get up. We showered, dressed, and went out to eat lunch.

"In the afternoon we went to a studio to have a picture made. Then we visited the Barrell in the hotel, went to the Roof Room, and back to the Barrell. In the evening we had dinner and danced in the Hollywood Room. We took a walk and stopped at the Starlight Room. There wasn't anything we wanted to do so we went back to enjoy our room.

"Tuesday morning we ate lunch at the Grecian Gardens. We saw 'Duel in the Sun,' and then went out to the aunt and uncle's home for dinner. After dinner Harry and I went to see a baseball game.

"Wednesday morning we ate lunch and had fun shopping for gifts and books to take home. I felt as though I was going to step out of Paradise when we left our room so we decided to enjoy it as long as possible, and read until time to start packing to leave. We visited the Roof and then went to the station to get train tickets. We went back uptown for dinner and then it was train time. My folks met us at the train, and there was a terrible let-down feeling to being home.

"Next day we started packing everything we owned, and on the following day we moved into our own apartment. We cleaned the whole thing and spent the next few days unpacking and putting away. Our honeymoon had been wonderful, but short and pretty uneventful. Being in our apartment seemed like a continuation of our honeymoon — as we had told ourselves when we had to leave the hotel.

"Our apartment is a nice, 4-room and bath, basement apartment. There are two other apartments and two nice couples in the basement with us so we feel quite lucky. Harry is the assistant to the caretaker so we have our apartment and utilities at no cost, and receive $25 a month also. There is very little work to do, but we must be here to do what there is to be done.

"During the summer neither of us worked at any job. Harry took care of his work here at the house and helped an old man with some odd jobs, and I kept busy with my housekeeping. We had an old car that we used to go shopping, to drive out in the country to visit relatives and get eggs, go home occasionally, drive to the city, and used around town.

"A short time after we were married Harry's 15-year-old sister was killed. This was quite a shock — especially since his mother died when he was in grade school, but it gave me a better chance to get acquainted with my husband and also his father and other relatives.

"The summer went pretty fast and I can't remember anything of much importance that we did except live each day to the fullest. We enjoyed a friend's beautiful country home with a big swimming pool in the back yard.

"Along toward the end of the summer, Harry began to act as though he didn't care if I stayed around or not. He didn't bother to make conversation or help keep it going, he was very unpleasant, his attention was given to everything but me, it seemed that he seldom talked that he wasn't complaining about something or just being disagreeable. I was terribly hurt and puzzled. I tried to please him, tried to be nice and ignore his catty remarks, got angry and told him off, and gave him the silent treatment; but nothing helped. Just before fall, I went home to do some sewing with Mother. I was sort of glad to get away from a person who didn't appreciate my presence. I was home about 3 days and when I came back, Harry was rather cold until my folks left (they brought me back), then he began beaming with pleasure over my return. He was so sweet and considerate that I decided the best answer to the problem was just to go home and get away awhile.

"After school started, our lives consisted of going to classes, studying, visiting friends, inviting friends in, and keeping house. Harry thinks that even though I go to school, it's still my job to do the housework. Yet he is always willing to dry the dishes, and help out with some job if I ask him to do so.

"For his birthday we invited his father, my parents, and some aunts and uncles up for the weekend. I believe this was one of the bright spots during the winter.

"Before Christmas we painted our apartment — with yours truly doing little more than keeping the painter company. We had fun choosing the paint, planning our time, and getting the job done. Of course the Christmas atmosphere, and our plans for Christmas were big factors in our enjoyment.

"On Christmas we had a big family dinner in our apartment, and had a wonderful time opening our presents. There were lots of joke packages, and gobs of laughs. I had enjoyed our tree so much that I felt like crying when it was robbed of its packages, and began to shatter. Harry wasn't very sympathetic, but he let the tree stand until it added more work than beauty.

"We went to my home for Easter, and enjoyed being away from the apartment for a short vacation. There was illness in the family so we didn't get to do all the things we planned to do, but we saw a lot of old friends. When school is out we plan to spend a few days with Harry's father to equal our visits.

"Every so often my husband gets in an unpleasant mood and I have to try all the techniques I've ever heard of to make him see how much he's missing in life. There was another time during the winter that he became unbearable, and it happened that I needed to go home for some more sewing, — so when I came back in four days he was an old prince charming. He had bought a record album for me, cleaned the house, and unpacked some new silverware.

"As far as children, we haven't made any definite plans. We both want children, but we feel that we should wait until I get out of school, and if possible, wait until he gets out of school. A child would mean that we would have to move from our apartment and the job that goes with it, all of which is pretty convenient with being a student. Although we aren't ready for a baby until we have a chance to get settled in life, we wouldn't resent one. Several times where there was some doubt and I got worried, Harry said that if we were going to have a baby we would just have it and there was nothing to do about it. He seemed so unworried, and teased me calling me 'Mommy.' His attitude made me wonder if maybe he was secretly hoping.

"We seldom talk about the future. I plan to teach school for a few years after I graduate from college. Some day Harry wants a business of his own, but that will have to come after he has gotten some actual experience and a sum set aside for the purpose. We don't see a divorce in our future, although I sometimes wonder if we'll ever have a completely harmonious marriage. We have gained a much better understanding of each other during this first year of marriage, but I feel that it will take much longer before he can tell me what I've done to give him reason for pouting, or before I can tell him what he's done that hurt my feelings.

"All in all we have had a very happy marriage so far. There have been little misunderstandings and hurt feelings that could have been discussed and remedied if we had felt free to discuss them instead of letting them come between us for several days. There were times when we became quite angry with each other, and had big arguments, but the anger never lasted even if we wanted to pretend it did. The night before we were married the minister told us that we wouldn't 'see eye to eye' on everything and that we might as well expect it, so perhaps we are just following the usual pattern. There were no real problems, except some little personal habits on the part of each of us, and maybe this is a good place to learn tolerance."

Marriage — A Social Responsibility

All forms of animal life mate, but mating alone does not constitute a marriage. Mating is a biological term denoting the physical union of any two animals, human or otherwise.

Marriage, however, is known only to human beings in all parts of the world. It is a social and legal plan by which the relationships of the two sexes is controlled by society in the interest of children as well as of wholesome morals, good health, and mental hygiene. It involves public social sanction as well as systematic social control. While two individuals may meet and fall in love, when they marry, their families and the community are involved. We need to realize, therefore, that in our country, as well as in every other country of the known world, society has certain sanctions and restrictions it has set up. As a guide to marriage, it directs who shall marry, from what groups mates may or may not be chosen, by whom one's mate may be chosen, the procedure by which a mate may be secured, where the couple shall live, their rights and responsibilities as husband, wife, and parents, the causes and methods by which the marriage may be terminated, and how and by what means the single, widowed, divorced, orphaned, and childless are to be related to the entire scheme of life in that society.

Most couples, however, consider marriage a private affair. They do not consciously marry to preserve or perpetuate the race, but rather because they love each other and see eternal happiness in living their lives together and heartache at the thought of separation.

Marriage — A Personal Matter

Both a short and a long view of marriage are desirable. From the immediate point of view one is concerned with marrying the other person as soon as possible and getting on with the business of lovemaking, homemaking, and living together.

Given a basis to expect a good mating, this is without question the thing to do. But, however good or bad the match may be, every couple must recognize that their marriage will succeed or fail to the degree, at least, that they have considered the following points:

1. The recognition that every marriage brings together two different personalities, with varying degrees of similarity in their

background of training, attitudes, and understanding of themselves
and the things each thinks he will get out of the marriage.

2. The extent to which each individual is prepared for marriage.

3. The determination, ability, and zest which the couple has for
making their life together a happy one.

4. A recognition of the fact that many situations, apart from
their own personal relationship and beyond their control, will have
to be met and adjusted to.

5. That one must work at the job of staying successfully married
as hard at least as they do at the job of getting engaged and getting
married.

It should be self-evident to anyone that the individuals
who marry are different in many ways and have perhaps
different ideas about marriage, many of which they have
acquired as a result of growing up in the particular kind of
family and environment they did. But herein lies one of the
danger points in many marriages. It is difficult to recognize
one's own inadequacies and to be tolerant of another person's
personal habits and attitudes which may be radically different from one's own. Personal habits and attitudes and differences in what each is striving to get from their marriage
will be discussed in more detail later.

Specifically, there is much knowledge and information on
every aspect of family life available in public libraries, good
magazines, at public lectures, and to be had from classes in
public schools and colleges. Food preparation, consumer
buying, sewing, remodeling garments, child care, budgeting,
household management, family relationships, mental hygiene, health education, religion, and home recreation are
only a few. But whatever preparation one has made along
these lines, there still remains those personality differences
expressed in attitudes, feelings, and early formed habits,
about husbands, wives, homes, sex, money, housekeeping,
social life, finances, children, and one's relatives which will
play an important part in whether you and your newly
acquired husband or wife succeed or fail.

The matter of entering marriage with a zest to perpetuate
its romance and happiness needs little comment. It can be

assumed that practically all couples enter marriage, with some apprehension, to be sure, but with great expectations and determination that theirs will be one that will continue to be happy and succeed. Given, along with this high enthusiasm, good mating to begin with, adequate preparation, and a willingness to work at the job, there is every reason to count on success. Most couples have to work for the happiness, joy, and satisfaction that come from life together, make many adjustments, and meet many hardships not easy to bear.

The last item, working at the job of marriage, is one which many seem to overlook. Suppose a person devoted months of his time to getting ready for a position — clerical, mechanical or professional; he entered the first opening with enthusiasm, and, then, just sat there, expecting salary checks, promotion, and success to come sailing along. How long would it take this career to go on the rocks? Marriage is no different and is, in some ways, more difficult than most occupations, except that there are two persons who should be working equally hard, and each must be a semi-specialist in many fields — a mechanic (be able to fix the lawnmower, etc.), a biologist, a nutritionist (to feed the family properly), a good and economical buyer, a psychologist (to get along with each other, the children, and one's relatives), a business manager (to run the home within one's income), a teacher (to help and guide children in their development), a nurse and physician (to handle adequately the illness of family members), and many others. The home is no place for the incompetent and the inefficient. The best hereditary stock and the best brains in the nation are needed to found and carry on happy and successful marriage and family life.

Characteristics of the First Year of Marriage

The first year of marriage may be likened to building the framework of a new house. While the blueprints may be changed, and the foundation or superstructure modified, it costs less to do one's planning well in advance. With human beings, it also costs less to be well mated and well adapted to each other's needs and interests, than to have to make too many alterations in one's habits, attitudes, and philosophy of life after marriage. The first year is especially important for several reasons.

It is the period of the establishment of the family, the time when a couple is getting settled in their new home and organizing other activities and habits to accommodate them to the joint sharing of life. It is like the beginning of most new ventures; no matter how carefully we have planned everything, there are always little changes and adjustments that have to be made in order that things run smoothly. Take, for example, the following letter from a young bride, who says:

"The first problem that I am confronted with is household routines, such as washing and ironing. We have to go out for our meals and since I only have one room I cannot entertain my friends. I am also attending school which keeps me busy many an evening. If I did go to housekeeping and my husband should move to a job in another city while I finish school, I would have to dispose of my furniture, as my parents could not keep it for me.

"My husband's folks live out of town which causes us inconvenience. Laundering is my big problem and my husband works seven days a week.

"In regards to health, it is perfect.

"I am writing this letter as problems and not complaints as I am very happily married, but I am still troubled."

As can be seen, this statement represents both actual, immediate problems in the establishment of the family as well as other problems which she fears may arise in the future. Today, more than in times before World War II, these adjustments, attendant upon establishing a home, are complicated by many factors. The following letter of another young husband shows some of the problems which arise today in trying to stabilize and establish a common and satisfactory mode of living in one's early married life.

"My wife and I had been going with each other for about five years before we were married. This five-year period, however, included thirty months in which I was in the army. All in all, I would say that we were very well acquainted before we were married. I might add that we waited six months after my return from the army to get married.

"We had a small church wedding. Immediately after the ceremony we left on a honeymoon. We thoroughly enjoyed ourselves during this ten-day period. It was the first vacation my wife had had in over a year and the first vacation I had had in three years. I believe this fact made our honeymoon even more enjoyable.

"Due to the housing shortage we stayed with my parents for a few days after our return from our honeymoon. We did succeed in getting a small apartment after this 'few day' period, fortunately, so we got off to a pretty good start on our marriage. We can't remember too much about the short time we spent in our first home but we do remember that we were very happy. My wife was still working during the day and I was working intermittently.

"We stayed in this location for about a month. We decided that my wife would stay home and I would return to college until I could locate a place to live. She had a very fine position which contributed to our decision for her to stay there. I was going to drive home every week end.

"I returned to school and made the trips back and forth every week end. We soon discovered that this living apart just didn't work. Too, right at the time when school began we found out that my wife was pregnant. This was quite a surprise to us and we just quite didn't know how to receive the news.

"After about two months of school I succeeded in finding a place for us to live. My wife moved and we really started being married. I say this because it seemed before that with her working in the daytime and then being separated for quite a while that we actually didn't have time to enjoy just being with each other.

"My wife didn't work after she moved and I was taking courses that didn't require laboratory work so I had a lot of time to spend at home. It was during this time, I feel, that we began to get an understanding of how happy we both were about our marriage. Too, the fact that we were going to have a baby lost its element of surprise and doubt and we began to look forward to having a child.

"After we had been married ten months the baby arrived. A fine, healthy boy came to rule our home and to add greatly to the happiness we already had. My wife had a normal delivery of the baby but complications arose when she had fed him for a few weeks. She had to return to the hospital for two minor operations which caused us a little bit of trouble but certainly didn't impair our marriage relations.

"The above, briefly, describes what transpired our first year of marriage. With this as a background I can point out some points which might be of interest as far as marriage relations are concerned.

"First of all I want to preface any of the statements I am going to make with the underlying idea that my wife and I get along very well. In fact, after talking to a great number of married men, that I know quite well, I would say that my marriage is almost phenomenal in its success. (Both of us agree on this point.)

"One point of mental controversy arises when we go to our home town for short vacation periods. It is rather a trying experience in that both of our parents live in the same town, both live in apartments without adequate accommodations for guests and my wife's mother works during the day as does my father. In trying to arrange our visiting time with our parents we both try to be very careful. We never have any words about it but sometimes I think we stay too long at her mother's house and sometimes my wife thinks we stay too long at my parents' home. Actually neither of us cares too much about where we do stay but the point of friction occurs in making sure that we don't offend either parent. Even above this difficulty we both enjoy being with our parents and their proudness of their first grandchild even makes the visits more enjoyable.

"A lot of people I have talked to seem to think that a person trying to go to college is handicapped by having a wife and baby. Well, I can say, at least in my situation, that it has worked out quite well. Personally I have had more time for my wife and baby while in school than I ever expect to have later when I am working. I have made a special point to try to learn how to take care of the baby since I have the time and opportunity. I believe that I have learned how to take care of him competently. I might add that a course on Marriage and Family Relationships helped me a great deal in this phase of my married life. It is true that, financially speaking, there is some added burden. Luckily my wife had savings from her working years and I had savings accumulated while serving in the army. Of course we have had to dip into these savings substantially and I have worked part time frequently, yet, all in all, this period while in school has been a happy period and not one of any sort of hardship (except housing).

"Both my wife and I agree that we would be better off if we had a better background in the elements of sex and sex behavior. My father contributed some information to me when I was in my early teens which was helpful yet not extensive. My wife came from a family which left her to pick up a knowledge of sex and she failed to gain any information at all about the subject. Perhaps this will sound ridiculous, but my wife actually did not know how reproduction in humans took place. I have told her as much about it as I know and have acquired books to add to our information about sex. Actually, as I mentioned before, we have minimized the importance of sex in our marriage quite a bit. My wife, so far, has not experienced any enjoyment in our unions. For the past year we have not had any intercourse. The main reason for this is that we did not want another child for a couple of years. This is rather difficult on me at times since there are many times when I desire sexual activity and know that my wife gets no enjoyment from it. I have thought about getting my wife to go to a doctor about this repugnant feeling towards sex but actually I believe that the trouble is mental rather than physical. Somewhere in her background something must have frightened her or disillusioned her about sex. I do know that during her late teens she was walking home from town at night (alone) and was chased by a mentally unbalanced man who was completely nude. This upset her considerably at the time (which is certainly understandable) and later when she told me about the incident it frightened her just to tell me about it. Too, my wife led, relatively speaking, a rather protected existence.

"Although the sex problem is not too important now, I personally feel, that unless something is done, there could be a chance for a rift in our feelings later in life."

It is a time when husband-wife relationships are dominant. The couple are alone and usually have little time or interest for others. Children may come and thus complicate their early relationships, while parents, friends, or others no longer have the right to make their decisions. All choices, decisions, and activities are now jointly those of the husband and wife. Their own happiness, their own future, and their own plans are paramount concerns for them alone. The following excerpts from an account of the first year of married life of one young couple will serve to show their preoccupation with each other. Theirs has been a happy and fortunate year compared with some other couples. The reason, in part, is due to the fact that they were well mated to begin with. Being well mated means that they were old enough to marry, their ages were not too far apart, they had known each other more than twelve months, they were of comparable educational background, similar in their religious beliefs and racial backgrounds, were healthy, came from good hereditary stock, were mentally average or better, came from unbroken homes, knew each other's families before marriage, both wanted children, had sufficient income to be self-supporting and prospects for advancement in job were good, both were born in a similar environment, had no economic responsibility other than themselves, were interested in a number of common social and recreational activities, and each was tolerant of those in which he did not take part, had had good early sex education, were given premarital physical examinations before marriage, held to a monogamous philosophy as to their own relationships, and were married under conventional, home, religious conditions.

Of all the factors which go into the making of a good prospect for a happy marriage, there were only two on which they had to be careful. These were their dependence upon their parents at the time of marriage and the fact that they lived close to each of their families. As you read their story, however, you will see how this affected their happiness, and what the outcome was.

While everyone who marries need not have as many factors in their favor as did this couple, the more common factors they have, the easier it is to succeed, and the less the chance of conflict which leads to continuous unhappiness or even separation or divorce.

"Tom and I have been married just a year. I realize that a mere twelve-months of experience doesn't rate you very high as an authority on matrimony, but at least it's long enough to have given me time to try out some of the advice usually given to newlyweds. And to have discovered all by myself one principle which seems to me more important than all the others put together, and which I have never read in any book or heard mentioned in any discussion. *Trying to learn anything about marriage before you're actually married is a lot like trying to learn to swim from a book.*

"Both our families approved of our getting married. Tom was working under Father — in fact, that was how I happened to meet

him — and Dad thought he had good stuff in him. Dad approved
of early marriages and would do all he could to help us along.
Tom's mother was a widow, and he was her oldest and favorite son.
Of course, she didn't think I was half good enough for him. (I'd
like one look at the girl she'd have thought was!) But Tom was
determined, so I could just feel her deciding to make the best of it.

"Our first night alone in our new home it snowed. We'd had a
two weeks' honeymoon trip, and the few nights we'd been back we'd
been sleeping in Tom's mother's house, till we got the apartment
settled. Now the gold-colored curtains were up, our books were
in the low bookcases and there was a fire in the Franklin stove.
We sat on the antique love seat that had been a wedding present,
Tom's arm around me. Everything was very quiet, the way it is
when it's snowing.

" 'I wonder,' Tom said suddenly, 'whether any other two people
ever sat on this old seat in front of a stove like this — when they
were first married.'

"It was a queer, scary sort of thought, that maybe two people
who once felt the same way we were feeling were old now, or dead.
Or, worse, were still living but didn't feel this way any more. I
held on to Tom's hand a little tighter, and I guess he was thinking
the same thing, because he drew me closer to him.

" 'Bunny,' he said — and his voice sounded solemn — 'whatever comes, we must hang on to this wonderful thing we've got.'

"I didn't say anything, just pressed my cheek harder against
his rough, tweedy shoulder. Almost held my breath. It's the
strangest thing, but for a moment it seemed as though the room
were filled with a different sort of air from the kind we ordinarily
breathe. Bright, light air, almost quivering, mysterious. Maybe
that's what people mean when they talk about love making the
whole world seem 'different.'

"For several minutes, neither of us spoke; we just kept close to
each other, breathing in the magic. After a bit, slowly, the air of
everyday living came back into the room. We both felt strong and
gay and competent, as though we could figure out any problem,
tackle any sort of difficulty. It seemed to me that I could do anything in the world as long as I had Tom, as you might say, on my
side." (9)

Early marriage adjustments are being made and patterns
of managing one's family affairs are in the process of formation. Each individual is trying to put into practice his living
philosophy, and each is modifying and integrating his be-

liefs and behavior into a joint and compatible one, consistent with happiness and success in his new relationship.

Summary

Much happiness is, and should be, a part of the first year of marriage. Much lovemaking, many good times together, a growing sense of satisfaction and pride in each other, and a settling down to a better understanding of the person to whom one is married. This first year is one in which husband and wife belong predominantly to each other, their expenses are usually low, health is usually good, housing needs are simple, each is becoming established in the routine of his job, whether the wife is gainfully employed or not, and the evaluation of their own, unique plan and philosophy is in the making. This is a most important year — the entrance upon the road to success or the road to disappointment, disillusionment, heartache, and failure.

Most of the decisions about life together are in the making — adjusting to each other's personal peculiarities, habits, and ways of life; working out a routine between themselves; handling the family's money; planning social and recreational life with friends, and alone; initiating and adjusting to sex relations; establishing satisfactory relationships with parents and inlaws after marriage; evolving a religious philosophy and practice; and, later on, planning for, and adjusting to, the coming of children into the home.

If there were any formula for success it might include:

1. Being honest — talking things over — being frank, but, at the same time, considerate and understanding of the other person.
2. Making joint decisions as to what you want, how you want things done, and what each person's responsibility is to be.
3. Doing your best to make the other person happy and proud of you.
4. Remembering that each partner has to be successful at three jobs. A woman must be a good wife, a good mother, and a good home manager; a man must be a good husband, a good father, and a good provider, although the wife, many times, may also add to this part of the family task.

CHAPTER VIII

PERSONALITY FACTORS IN RELATIONSHIPS

A decision must be made about most matters of importance. The decision may be easy because one has a well
thought out philosophy of life and has enough maturity
and experience to make the decision with a minimum of
frustration. Another person may become involved with a
problem to the extent that he is in such a state of conflict
and anxiety that he never seems able to come to grips with
the reality of the situation. We need to recognize the reality
of the problems of everyday living and go about trying to
solve them. Evading, projecting, rationalizing, and other
forms of running away from responsibility are bad techniques.

Most Problems Are Personality Problems

A recent study (10) of married college women reveals the
large percentage and wide range of problems confronted by
each, both before, during, and after graduation from college.
All the women apparently had some difficulty in meeting
the normal life situations which had confronted them in the
course of their development, especially personality and human relations difficulties, which tended to remain the source
of problems in later years. In this group there were more
problems after graduation from college than at any time
before. The married women had to meet many new situations and had a wider range of problems than single women.
As new problems were met in life, not all of the old ones had
been resolved, so the cumulative effect on personality was
evident.

Basically most of these conflicts existed because two personalities, a husband and wife, a wife and a mother-in-law, or an employed girl and her employer or associate, were unable to achieve a common basis for making a satisfactory decision.

Type of Problem	Percentage of Married Women	Percentage of Single Women
Personality	98	100
Finances	97	95
Health	96	100
Husband-wife	89	—
Relations with associates	88	100
Recreation	84	86
Housekeeping	82	—
Relations with relatives	80	77
Parent-child	78	—
Crisis	74	73
In-law	60	—
Sex	56	59
Religion	52	50
Vocation	34	91
Education	20	36

Most of the difficulty couples have in making a good adjustment arises from their basic personality and conditioned habits and attitudes. There are, for example, many adequate and satisfying ways for a couple to handle their money, organize their household routines, and plan their social activities, but it is often the value one places on a certain form or idea, which makes it difficult for him to see the other person's point of view or make a modification of his own belief or behavior in the interest of harmony. It hurts one's pride to adjust and most people do not like to be hurt. This is one reason why many individuals like to have the other person make whatever change there is to be made.

One young bride was terribly disturbed because her husband did not "dress" for dinner. She said that her father always did, and that her standards would not let her accept slovenly habits at meals. This illustrates the value placed upon a single bit of behavior by this young woman. She, of course, like all of us, was confronted with a choice between changing her husband's habit and feeling about dressing for dinner, changing her own feeling about it and, thus, accepting his pattern, or leaving the situation by separation or divorce. She did not want a divorce and felt she could not change him. She was forced to decide between enduring the pain of having her standards violated or the worse pain of separation. She actually compromised on a plan whereby he would dress for dinner when there was company and on Saturday and Sunday evenings and be informal the rest of the time. The wife did not quite like this, but it seemed to be a lesser pain to endure than any of the other alternatives. Her problem was, then, one of trying to re-examine the basis for her set of values on dressing for dinner and accept the compromise in relation to all the other desirable aspects of their married life. It was evident that the basic problem they had was a struggle for domination. Neither would admit he might be wrong or compromise on any point. Each had to be right.

The majority of problems in husband-wife relationships are, basically, personality problems, essentially conflict situations between a husband and wife or other family member, and most so-called money, sex, social, or other types of problems are only symptomatic of the underlying problem. Take, for example, a young woman who seeks advice about her husband who drinks. To her, the problem is that he drinks, spends the family income, abuses her and the children, and is wrecking his own life. The drinking, however, is usually only symptomatic of deeper needs which ought to be found and treated before he can really be considered helped. There are thousands of examples in our everyday life where we define the problem as bad sex adjustment, a nagging wife, or an unruly child, when the problem is essentially conflicting personality patterns and characteristics.

Figure 1 suggests the relationship between basic personality factors and other areas in which problems occur.

Let us now consider, in order, the types of adjustment every young married couple must inevitably meet.

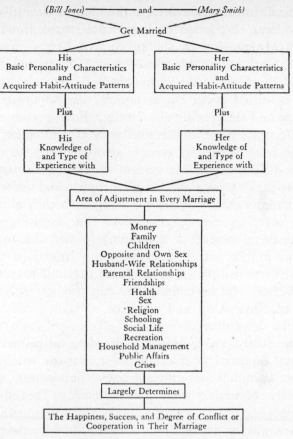

Fig. *1.* *A theory of marital adjustment.*

Husband and Wife

There is no rule of thumb by which individuals may be taught to find for themselves, in advance of marriage, the key to the solution of the problem situations which will confront them after the step has been taken. There is much in education which may contribute to one's knowledge of the biological, sociological, economic, psychological, and other data useful to any person in the management of their lives in our society. Here, however, there is only need to consider the importance of there being a close correlation between the theoretical information which one learns from books or lectures and the kinds of experience through which the learners are passing in the process of being "educated." There is perhaps no experience which places upon the individual so great a need for insight and adaptability as that which is called forth by assuming the responsibilities of marriage and the rearing of a family. Each person, the man and wife, regardless of the similarity of the cultural backgrounds from which he comes, always brings to marriage enough differences in his system of habits, attitudes, and beliefs to make it necessary to compromise and make adaptations at many points in getting along with each other. Success in marriage not only involves the acquiring of facts, but the development of a philosophy and the techniques involved in the art of understanding human nature and human relationships. It is both an art and a technology.

That there will be conflict one can predict with assuredness, but the nature and outcome of that conflict cannot always be determined.

In one study, struggle for domination, adjustment to sex relations, financial conflict, and adjustment to differences in personal habits and cultural backgrounds were the most frequently occurring causes of difficulty in the marital relationships.

In struggle for domination, one can see demonstrated the way in which husband and wife each work out their individual personality characteristics in terms of the other's. The previously acquired patterns of projection, withdrawal, evasion, or acceptance, of which neither is aware, or the facing of each situation as it arises, as a mature and well adjusted person, is presented in this human drama.

The way in which the personality functions often determines what conflicts regarding money, sex, in-laws, and other matters arise. A woman may have struggled with parents, siblings, teachers, and vocational associates all her life up to the time of her marriage to maintain the integrity of her own individuality. She must have some way of achieving a sense of importance in this relationship, as in others. The degree to which her husband recognizes her need and gives her status and a sense of significance may do much to enhance the entire marriage relation. Individual variation in the ability to make adjustments is also a factor. Some men and some women, to avoid conflict, make all the major adjustments, while, in other cases, there is continuous conflict between husband and wife, and a lack of adjustment made by either.

In one case the wife says, "If he wants to handle the money, let him. He can do a better job of it than I can, so why should he not be responsible?" In another case his wife is constantly complaining that her husband handles the money, that she has no voice as to what they spend and no knowledge of their financial situation. These examples show the way in which the wife's personality pattern functions in relation to her husband in money matters. In the second case, competition is shown between husband and wife for domination in family decisions.

The husband-wife problem is predominantly a personality adjustment-conflict pattern. This pattern, in turn, colors, though it does not entirely determine, the adequacy of husband and wife in handling money, sex, child, in-law, and other phases of their personal, social, and professional life. The reader should not fail to see the significance of this fact. So often money, sex, in-law, and other problems are given more weight than they deserve as causal factors in family disorganization because they are considered in isolation and not as a whole, or partial, reflection of the personality of the individual.

There are, of course, situations, such as maids' quitting, losing one's job, or the failure of health, which are problems in themselves. However, the stride with which we meet these unpleasant phases of daily routine is largely a personality habit.

The following excerpts from one wife's case (11) are cited to show the way in which family conflicts involve not only specific husband-wife adjustments but numerous other factors as well. They emphasize particularly the interrelationships of problems, their dependence upon the personality factor, and their relevance to early conditioning.

HUSBAND-WIFE RELATIONS:
  Many arguments over religion.
  Disagreement over husband's resistance to having a wider group of friends.
  Conflict over sending child to Sunday school.
  Arguments over calling on people.
  Lack of orderliness about house, producing conflict with husband.
  Many hurt feelings on part of both husband and wife in first year of marriage.
  Sex adjustment difficulties because husband too inhibited and modest.
  Conflict over rush and strain.
  Irregularity of husband's hours, causing differences and irritation.

RELATIONS WITH ASSOCIATES:
  Wife and husband shy; "did not talk about things much" before marriage.
  Bashful with associates.
  More critical of friends than formerly.
  Difficulty in keeping up relations with old friends because they bore her husband.
  Answering the child's questions frankly, about the origin of babies, causes conflict with neighbor.

ATTITUDE TOWARD SELF:
  Worries about not doing more "outside things."
  Was very uncertain and shy about getting married.
  Considers herself lax in budgeting her time.
  Is not very orderly.
  Glad that she does not have to suffer the hurt feelings she experienced when they lived in town with their families.
  Thinks she has too little ambition.
  Feels herself to be losing her pep.
  Feels bashful and shy with associates.
  Is becoming more critical of her friends.
  Fears death.
  Likes to avoid issues.
  Is an easygoing person.
  Was very inhibited and shy when going with husband.

Was ignorant of what married life meant.

Was sensitive and cried over the slightest things.

Was never satisfied with her accomplishments while working.

Felt exhausted at the end of each day.

Was homesick for her college friends when she first began to work.

RECREATION :

Visits of friends overtaxing following illness.

Conflict with husband over visiting and having people in the home.

Social life bored her when she lived near her own family.

Missed college life after she began working.

Social contacts with friends were difficult because of her husband's attitude.

RELATIONS WITH RELATIVES :

Too many family demands upon them when living in the same town with their families.

Conflict with mother over child's not attending church.

Could not have carried out her own child-training plan while living near her mother.

IN-LAW RELATIONS :

Too many demands; hurt feelings when living near her in-laws.

Conflict with mother-in-law over not belonging to church.

Conflict with mother-in-law over trying to "iron out" differences between her and the children.

Wife could not have carried out her own child-training plan while living near her in-laws.

CLIENT'S EVALUATION OF HER HUSBAND :

Hard to interest in social activities; quickly bored with people; his attitude toward religion a reaction against his strict upbringing; argues too much with his mother; is a shy, retiring person; contributes little in conversation; is not anxious for them to have another child; was not able to help wife with early sex adjustment; always gives vent to his feelings, regardless of consequences; has irregular work hours and does not call to notify his wife when he is to be late.

HOMEMAKING SKILLS AND ACTIVITIES :

Getting housework done in orderly fashion and on time difficult.

Hates dirty work of housekeeping.

Lacked household skills and had a hard time adjusting herself to homemaking.

Had great difficulty in organizing her time.

Personal Habits

Another important problem in husband-wife relations is that of personal habits, which include such seemingly trivial matters as punctuality at meals, picking up clothes, cleanliness of person, food idiosyncrasies, observing social conventions, formality and informality in the home, remembering anniversaries, arrangement of housekeeping activities, and being together or isolated during evenings at home. Conflict over such matters becomes closely tied up with the struggle for domination, and any one of these items might become the point around which serious and lasting conflicts arise. Each is apparently unable to tolerate differences in the other when the matter in question touches upon some emotionally inviolable area. Ash trays, for example, must be in certain places, not because the matter is important in itself, but because the entire situation has become a symbol of the total personality of the individual and has important meaning to him.

Status

One element of compatibility often lies in the degree to which the husband can make his wife feel that she is an important person — has status and comes first in his planning and consideration. The following comments from several cases show evidence of how often wives feel this lack:

MRS. B.
Felt husband was indifferent during month preceding marriage.

Husband's tendency to consider the needs of his business prior to those of his wife annoying.

Feels husband is too engrossed in his own work and resents her asking him questions.

MRS. F.
Husband is very upsetting and disrupting to home situation.

Husband has no confidence in her.

Husband does not sit and chat with her much.

Husband seems to have no confidence in her taking responsibility.

Generally forgets to bring his wife something from his trips.

MRS. A. T.
Husband has never given her feeling of being essential to him.

MRS. B. Q.
Felt husband was not attracted by her appearance.
Feels husband should spend more time with his family, instead of devoting all his time to reading.
Feels husband is bored by accounts of her daily activities.

MRS. B. W.
Husband disliked client's interests.
Husband immediately changed in attitude toward client after marriage.
Husband made fun of wife's activities.
Husband completely disregarded her when out with friends.

These excerpts indicate many questions of status, of the husband's accepting the wife as competent within the field of her responsibility as far as being a wife, a mother, and a housekeeper is concerned. A lack of status is probably one of the most important factors leading to frustration with which these women are confronted. These excerpts may also indicate a lack of maturity, self-sufficiency, and breadth of interests on the part of the wife.

Take, for example, such an item as, "The husband tends to consider the needs of his business prior to those of his wife." This shift in attention and interest often occurs immediately after marriage when a man resumes his interest in his work, and his wife at certain times becomes somewhat secondary in importance to him. It is a very difficult transition period, and, in the development of their marriage, it is difficult for many women to accept the fact that anything else in life is as important to their husbands as they were before marriage and as they feel they should continue to be following marriage. There is perhaps no actual loss of interest but merely a shift in relative emphasis, which must, of necessity, take precedence when a wider range of responsibility is again resumed by each.

Other more specific problems involving the feeling of being accepted by one's husband are these: "Husband belittles whatever she knows or attempts to do." "Husband is continually complaining because she is a poor housekeeper." "Husband does not consider her interests and activities of great importance." "Feels that husband is bored by accounts of her daily activities." "Husband never notices what she wears or how she is dressed."

Summary

Success in marriage, therefore, involves not only a knowledge of the relevant facts but also an understanding of human nature and a philosophy of human relations. Regardless of how alike or different the husband and wife may be, there will always be adjustments and adaptations to be made, and the responsibility for making them falls upon the man and woman individually. That there will be conflict between them can be predicted with certainty. The nature and outcome of the conflict cannot always be determined.

There is no better explanation of the basis for many of these husband-wife conflicts than the following quotation from an article by Lawrence K. Frank (12), which appeared in the *Parent Teacher Magazine* for December, 1938:

"We need only remember that underneath the outer mask of adult size and dignity, behind the official position, rank, or prestige of the grown-up man or woman, there is always a little boy or little girl, still living over the hurts, the injustices, the unhappiness of a forgotten childhood. It is these little boys and little girls who run our social life and create the social problems and difficulties we suffer from — not because they are deliberately wicked, sinful, selfish, or antisocial, but because they are dominated by these childish feelings which govern their lives and direct their conduct. Usually they are unaware of the long forgotten occasions for the resentments and anxieties that so potently influence their present lives; but as we gain insight into personality development and trace back the individual's adult career to these early emotional experiences, we can see how the need to 'get even' with parents and teachers, to build up defenses against early anxieties, to atone for guilt over childish misbehavior, are all operating as effectively as if the individual were indeed a little boy or little girl."

CHAPTER IX

SEX AS A FACTOR IN FAMILY LIFE

Sex is important. If it were not for the fact of reproduction, life would cease to exist, and the human race would perish. Not only would it perish if humans did not marry, copulate, and produce children, but, without it, the farmer no longer could reproduce plants and animals and their products for human consumption. The farmer's job is that of wholesale reproduction.

Good sex adjustment in marriage depends as much upon your attitudes as upon your knowledge of facts. These attitudes are formed early in life. If, as a young child, you were told that questions about sex were vulgar and nasty, if you were punished for asking questions or observed your mother's or father's embarrassment or avoidance when questions of origin of babies or sex came up, you probably turned to books and friends for your sex education. In such case the chances are that much that you learned gave you an abnormal attitude and wrong information on the whole subject of sex.

In order to do a good job as a sex partner in marriage, one must, therefore, have sane, balanced attitudes about sex as a part of life and some sound and correct information about sex.

Personal and Social Aspects of Sex

The individual couple is interested in sex to the extent that they may achieve a satisfactory adjustment — so that the act is enjoyable to both and comes to be accepted as a true expression of existing love between them. They are interested in knowing about the anatomy and physiology of both man and woman, and how each functions in his or her reproductive capacity. Each is interested in sex because it leads to the creation of offspring, and because they, as parents, will in turn have to give their young children sound information and good guidance in sex as they grow to maturity. How to achieve a sound knowledge, proper attitudes, and successful sex relationships is the main purpose of this discussion.

From a social point of view, sex is important because, properly handled, it is the source of great happiness to married people and the means whereby the quantity and quality of the human population is increased. On the other hand, the improper use of sex may lead to great individual conflict, social problems of many kinds, and the breakdown of many fine marriages.

Let us first recognize sex and human reproduction as physical functions belonging to the field of biology. As such, they have no ethical or social importance. They have no more moral quality than eating, breathing, or sleeping. But, wherever there exists any group of human beings, certain sanctions and restrictions are set up which act as a means of social control of this set of human relationships. The relationships of the sexes, male and female, are controlled by this set of rules called the mores. It then becomes right or wrong to do certain things in certain ways. Sexual behavior and all the relationships of courting, engagement, marriage, and the birth of children are largely social and more far reaching than the purely biological. They involve psychological, social, and ethical values. Human reproduction is not an individual matter in this sense. The lives of two persons, two families and two generations, parents and progeny are involved. Yet, the problems of sex and reproduction are, at the same time, highly individualized for every couple. Success depends upon the intelligent handling of this relationship.

Men and Women Are Different

Everything that is bisexual reproduces its kind through the association of two different cell types, i.e., male and female cells known, in human beings, as the sperm cell of the male and the ova or egg cell of the female. While in flowers the male pollen is scattered by the wind or carried by insects to the female cell of the female plant, in human beings direct physical contact between the man and woman is necessary for reproduction or conception to occur. This process of physical contact is called sexual intercourse, copulation, and sometimes by other scientific or common names.

While male and female are different in cell structure, in metabolic rate, in glandular secretions, and, possibly, in certain intellectual and emotional functions, we are concerned here with their physical structural differences for the purpose of sex function and reproduction.

The sex cells, male and female, are different. One, the male, is motile, active, the aggressor, and instinctively seeks its complement in the more inactive female cell.

What Men Should Know About Women

Women are different from men in many ways. They have a different combination of chromosomes; their metabolism is lower, blood temperature warmer, and heart rate faster; their internal, glandular secretions tend to make the differences between secretions of the ovaries and testicles; and they are physically different. Women have breasts for providing food for the young, and their specific organs of reproduction are constructed for a different function than that of the male. Women are functionally different. They are built so that they can copulate, menstruate, and carry a child through pregnancy to childbirth. All these physiological differences may make for certain emotional and intellectual differences, about which much less is known than about their physical functioning. Women are expected to be different, live differently, and act differently because of many traditional beliefs and attitudes we have in our society. As a result, women and girls have been more protected, allowed less freedom, kept ignorant of sex matters. These social taboos have resulted, for many women, in ignorance and lack of appreciation of their most important attribute, and often in unwholesome attitudes as well.

What Women Should Know About Men

Men, as a rule, are less inhibited on matters of sex than women. This is partly accounted for by differences in the upbringing of boys and girls. Men are more aggressive in their desire for sex contact.

On the other hand, many men are just as ignorant about good sex practice, although less inhibited than women. Their need for information and education is ofttimes covered up by a false show of self-sufficiency. They do not want their bride or anyone else to suspect their inadequacies. As a consequence, they many times continue their bungling methods. They seem to be more sensitive to criticism or to being wrong than women. Man is the "big shot" in our society; he is often pampered and spoiled by his mother and sisters and finds it difficult to face any sense of inadequacy. But once this protective shield is broken, he may become the best of students of the subject and a thoroughly considerate and understanding sex partner.

Beginning One's Sex Life After Marriage

There are three things necessary to insure satisfactory sex adjustment — knowledge, proper attitude, and experience. The condition of married life offers the best opportunity for practice. Previous and continuing attitudes toward and about sex are a most important factor. They condition every act, no matter what one's knowledge or experience may have been.

What kind of information helps one make and carry on a satisfactory sex life?

1. Simple facts about the anatomy and physiology of one's own reproductive system and that of one's mate.

2. The consummation of marriage.

3. What to expect in the way of results.

4. One's own attitude about sex and the attitude of one's partner.

When you start your married life, it is not always easy to accustom yourself to intimacies with a person of the opposite sex. If you have been a heavy "petter" and engaged in premarital sex relations, then what is to follow may be of little value to you. But the great majority of women and many men who marry have not had sex relations prior to marriage. Neither have they been free to discuss sex questions at home, and only a few have discussed the matter in detail during engagement. So, the initiation of the sex act in marriage involves the breaking down of much shyness and embarrassment through a slow process of becoming accustomed to dressing and undressing, bathing, sleeping, and living with a person of the opposite sex whom we love. To accomplish this demands a certain amount of self-control on the part of the man and no small courage on the part of the wife. Little things which later are not very important may seem very significant in this early, beginning stage of adjustment. A good rule for a man to follow is that of trying to help make this adjustment easy for his new bride, not be in too big a hurry, and to keep his mind on satisfying and making his bride happy, rather than sexually satisfying himself. An ounce of patience and self-control at the outset will lead to more than a pound of reward later on.

One may assume that any man or woman who marries has some knowledge of his own reproductive system, but often this is not true. If you do not know, find out, and, as you live together, you will gradually come to know, not just facts in general, but the particular facts about each other. Any book can give general information but cannot take into account the peculiar, individual characteristics of a Bill Jones and Mary Smith who may marry.

In general, then, the following are the simple facts which any young couple should know.

Male and Female Sex Anatomy

Both male and female have external and internal organs which are essential and important in the process of reproduction. The man has certain external organs which are best described in Chapter 24 of Kimber and Gray, *A Textbook of Anatomy and Physiology*, 11th ed. The organ used in actual copulation is called by various common names, but is best known as the penis. The organ is usually soft and, because of the rush of blood to that part of the body when thinking about sex preparatory to intercourse, easily becomes stiff and rigid. The size of the penis is not very important. Usually it is never too large nor too small to function satisfactorily.

Just below, and attached to the lower part of the penis, is a loose skin sack like an appendage, called the scrotum. Within this are two soft, tender, almond-shaped, fleshy organs called testicles. In these are manufactured the male germ cells (spermatozoa). As they escape from the testicles they pass through a series of organs or canals called the epididymis and the vas deferens to a glandular sac named the seminal vesicle. Here the male cell is joined by other secretions and held in readiness for mixing with a fluid from the prostate gland, forming the semen or seminal fluid.

The urethra, another tube which leads from the bladder through the penis and serves ordinarily to pass the urine secreted by the kidneys, also acts as the canal through which the seminal fluid is ejaculated into the vagina of the female during intercourse.

The woman's reproductive system is more complicated than that of the man. The external organs are situated between the thighs and to the front of the anus. This elongated slit, running from the upper front to the lower part of this portion of the body, opens back to each side easily. Beneath these lips, or labia, you will discover, toward the upper part of the groove, a small fleshy organ about the size of a large pea, covered with a fold of skin.

This is a very highly sensitive organ called the clitoris. During intercourse this organ becomes gorged with blood and is highly sensitive. Stimulation of this organ in normal intercourse leads to what is called an orgasm for the woman. The orgasm is the climax and termination of the peak of sexual excitement.

Below the clitoris is a small opening from the bladder. Below this is another opening, the entrance to the vagina, partially covered by a thick skin, the hymen, which is stretched or broken at time of first intercourse. The vagina is the sheath which the male organ enters during intercourse and into which it ejaculates the fluid containing male spermatozoa.

The internal organs are as follows: At the back or posterior end of the vaginal canal, is the mouth of the womb or uterus. This has a small opening through which the male sperms may pass and, from this organ, then enter a tube running from the uterus to the female ovary. It is here that conception or pregnancy begins, if the male and female egg should meet.

The ovaries produce small cells called ova which, during the month between menstrual periods, pass from the ovary to the uterus by means of the Fallopian tube. If no male sperm is there to meet it, it passes on down and deteriorates and is sloughed off with the rest of the cell lining of the uterus at the menstrual period.

The cell lining of the uterus prepares each month to receive a fertilized egg which, if conception takes place, attaches itself to the uterine wall and grows for nine months into a human infant. In case no fertilized egg arrives, this cell lining breaks down, deteriorates, and is discharged each month as the menstrual flow.

The breasts of the woman are closely related to her sexual feelings and reproductive function. They supply milk for the newborn infant and, by gentle stimulation, particularly of the nipples, act as sensitive zones during the normal love foreplay prior to actual intercourse. Briefly, this is the reproductive process and the nature of you and your spouse. The process of pregnancy and prenatal development of the infant and his early care will be discussed in a later chapter.

Sex Practice During Marriage

Sex attitudes, as previously emphasized, are determined by our early sex education at home, school, our associations with other young people, and, to a degree, our religious background. Those attitudes we bring to marriage with us. Emotions of shame, disgust, fear, and guilt all tend to hinder the normal sex adjustment.

Fears and inhibitions are common to both sexes. When men marry they usually have had more experience with masturbation than girls have had. (Masturbation is the process of getting sexual stimulation by means of manual manipulation of the penis or gently stroking the female clitoris region.) Because they have been told of the harmful mental effects of masturbation, they have some anxieties about its effect upon their marriage.

Masturbation is a habit. Most men and many women have practiced masturbation either as children or young adults. It does not ordinarily, if practiced only a short time as a young person or child, offset one's ability to marry and carry on normal sexual relations. Prolonged and chronic masturbation may build up mental attitudes which affect one's ability to withhold ejaculation long enough to satisfy one's partner or may lead to irritation of certain parts of the male reproductive mechanism.

The question of undesirable experiences is another source of concern. It may have been a childhood sex episode of intercourse one may have had prior to marriage. These experiences, if they persist to bother one in memory, should be talked over with a good counselor. They need not greatly affect one's marital adjustment, but they may do so, if the shock attending them was great enough. At the time of first intercourse or for a short time after marriage, some men are embarrassed either by ejaculation that comes too soon or by getting an erection and losing it before making an entry. Both man and woman should know that this often happens. It takes weeks and sometimes months of experience and practice, under the tense excitement of sexual conduct, to be able to control the time of ejaculation. Some authorities advise a longer time of preliminary lovemaking, so that the female reaches an orgasm more quickly after entrance of the penis into the vagina is made. This may work for many. The prolonged foreplay sometimes makes it even more difficult for some men to enter and proceed normally. Do not worry, but practice mental self-control until you get the desired result and make the kind of adjustment that suits you both. The loss of erection may also be due to over-excitation, and the thing to do is not to feel badly, but to relax a little while and try again or wait until morning or the next evening.

There is one point for all couples to remember. Every time you have sex relations, it will be a new experience, no matter how many times you have had them before. So many factors affect this relationship that it can be said to be almost a barometer of the harmony or disharmony in the other areas of your married life. Conditions are different every time. You may be more tired, there may be more people nearby, thus making noise an inhibiting factor, you may have had a spat over a mother-in-law or the monthly bills or one of a hundred other things may affect the results. Having adequate time, so as not to be hurried, and conditions free from interruption or the anticipation of interruption are both good insurance against unsatisfactory sex relations.

Another set of fears many newly married girls have has to do with the proper response and attitude they have toward their sex relations. Husbands often want sex relations more frequently, at first, than most brides do.

The rightness of mutual contact as to time, place, methods, and physical caresses and contacts cannot be overly stressed. To become accustomed to these normal, physical contacts is a part of the early sex adjustment in marriage

A girl may think her husband is over-sexed at first, but usually, as she gains experience and her own sense of guilt and shame about sex expression are overcome, her desire and satisfaction will tend to equal that of her husband's, because this is one of their most intimate ways of expressing their love for each other. We do not love a person because we have sexual relations with them; we have sex relations because we love them and as an unselfish expression of that love.

Frequency of intercourse is an individual matter. At first couples usually want to be together more often, and it is not uncommon for them to engage in intercourse daily or oftener. As a rule, however, as they become more accustomed to living together, intercourse is practiced from one to two times a week. The frequency may vary so that some weeks they may have intercourse three or four times and other weeks none at all.

Some couples have intercourse during menstruation, but this is an aesthetic and hygienic, rather than a physical, problem. There seems to be no reason why they should not if they care to. The same holds true of intercourse during pregnancy. It may not be advised the first two or three months, but between the end of the third to the sixth month it can be practiced with reasonable safety. However, consult the obstetrician caring for you during pregnancy in each particular case.

Planning for Children

Many couples wish to use some form of contraception to space their children. There are many kinds — condoms, douche, jellies, pessaries, and so on — none of which are 100 per cent safe. The best advice can be had by the couple's going to a reputable physician, preferably a gynecologist. If you are a Catholic, you should seek advice along this line from a physician or have a priest refer you to the proper person for advice on how to practice the rhythm for your particular menstrual cycle.

Abortion is dangerous. While there are thousands performed every year, they are done under secretive and illegal conditions which make the risk to life greater. If pregnant, and for some health reason you feel you cannot give birth to a child, consult a good physician. It is always good practice to go to an obstetrician when you think you are pregnant and stay under his care throughout pregnancy until the baby arrives. You get better care in the long run, and it usually costs no more.

When Problems Arise

When problems of sex adjustment arise in marriage they usually are due to (1) unfavorable attitude toward sex which involves unresolved fears, anxieties, and insecurities about the sex relations between husband and wife and about the sex education and behavior of their children; (2) a gross ignorance about sex, inadequate and incomplete sex education; (3) conflict over courtship and engagement practices; (4) specific marital sex difficulties, including such items as fear of pregnancy, lack of responsiveness, differences in response of husband and wife, frequency of coitus, husband's idea of sex technique and practice, and the kind and use of contraceptives; or, most important of all, (5) conflicts in other matters which are reflected in sex responsiveness.

If you feel that your sex adjustment is not what it should be, do not let it get worse. Find a good counselor at once, let him aid you in finding out where the trouble lies and help you to do something about it. If you do not know a person from whom to seek advice, consult a physician, your religious counselor, your family welfare department, or write to your state department of public health. One of these sources should be able to find the right counselor for you.

CHAPTER X

PARENTS AND IN-LAW RELATIONSHIPS

"How can we divide our holidays between our two families in a satisfactory manner? What if the mother of an only son cries if 75 per cent of the time is not spent with her?"

"What can be done about my wife's mother, who persists in taking over the responsibility of raising the children?"

Our parents, or those who become in-law parents, can make or break a marriage. They exert a powerful influence on our lives from infancy until death. The wise parents help us to "grow up," to mature and become self-sufficient, so that we are not handicapped by fear and guilt when we make our own decisions.

Over-domination by our parents seems to be one of the most usual problems of relationships in the family. This may be due to many things. Fathers often feel that we should obey instantly any whim or wish. They often believe that physical punishment is the best method of control. As a result, we have in many homes a system whereby the mother goes as far as she can in child management, and then the father is called in when more brute strength is needed. In this respect he is sort of a policeman who administers the rod, when mother is at the end of her rope.

On the other hand, many mothers find in their children a love object, which takes the place of a diminishing, affectional relationship between her and her husband. She lives her life for and through her children with the result that they become crippled in their growth toward maturity. They find it unusually hard to leave home, or else they may resent

family "love" and domination and break from the family
at an early age with an undue amount of hostility toward
their family.

In other cases, a father may undertake to make his son
into the kind of person he himself always wanted to be but
did not become. Often this is evidenced in pushing the boy
into a type of vocational pursuit for which he has no interest
nor aptitude.

Parents also often interfere too much with the choices
which children make in their friends and especially with the
girl or boy whom they choose to marry. After marriage
fathers, as well as mothers, attempt to "hold on" to their
children by money contributions, gifts, nagging, depreciating
the child's mate, and by trying to dominate every detail of
their home and family life. Of course, this may be done by
brothers or sisters, aunts or uncles and grandparents, as well
as by one's parents. What is important here is the fact that
the "in-law" problem is an outgrowth of the kind of parent-
child relationships that each person in a marriage has been
exposed to.

After marriage we all still feel a certain love for, and
obligation to, our parents and often find it difficult to maintain the dual role of dependence upon our old home and independence in the new one. Both revolt and guilt are likely to
be experienced in trying to reconcile the two.

Too often we never fully realize when the offending parent
is our own mother or father. This is clearly shown in the
following excerpt from the first year of marriage of one young
couple, whose only basic conflict arose over parental attachment on the part of each. (13)

"About the third danger point, the in-law situation, we didn't
have so much to say. Which might, I suppose, have been a warn-
ing.

"I did say a little dubiously that I supposed it would have been
easier if we hadn't been going to live quite so close to Tom's
mother. Tom seemed really surprised at that, assured me that his
mother thought I was swell and that, anyway, she'd never be the
interfering kind of mother-in-law. Then he surprised me just as

much as I had him by saying that he wished he weren't working for my father. I couldn't understand that. I could have, of course, if Dad had been like some men. But I knew Dad approved of Tom, both in a business way and as a husband for me. And, besides, I knew how very sympathetic a person Dad is. He seemed the last person in the world who would ever make trouble for any son-in-law. Moreover, Tom and I both felt that in-law trouble was sort of funny-paper stuff and that well-bred people could avoid it just by being kind and tactful.

"Tom commenced stopping in to see his mother a few minutes every afternoon on his way home from the office. I felt that I oughtn't mind it, but I did. . . . Then I soon realized that Bess — well, it wasn't exactly that she was criticizing me to Tom, but she was always giving him little suggestions that 'would be better for both of us.' And I knew, too, that she must have suggested to him that it would be more tactful if they seemed to come to me as his own ideas. That's the sort of subtle method that would never have occurred to Tom in a million years.

"It might have worked all right if I'd been a dumb bunny, but I'd have had to be a pretty dumb one not to have seen through it. Tom would look at some new curtains I'd just made and that I'd seen Bess glancing at that morning, and would say sort of casually: 'Wouldn't it have been a good idea to have had that material shrunk before you made it up?'

"Naturally it didn't take any Sherlock Holmes to recognize Bess' fine Italian hand back of that question. Tom doesn't know any more about curtain-making than he does about milking reindeer. And when the first time I washed the curtains they did shrink so that I couldn't use them any more, I felt some way mad at both Tom and his mother about it.

"Bess would glance up from planting sweet peas in her yard of a spring morning and see me on our porch, putting Tom's heavy suit away in a moth bag. That evening Tom would say, 'Oh, hon, I don't believe those moth bags you bought are the safest kind. There's another brand that seals much tighter.'

'And so on — all such petty trifles that I was ashamed of the way they bothered me. But there were dozens and dozens and dozens of them. It was like mosquitoes. When I'd complain of any one to Tom, he would say oh, that wasn't worth worrying about — as indeed, just by itself, it seldom was.

"I don't know how things might have worked out if it hadn't been for a totally unexpected break of luck. Tom came home with the news that he'd been offered a job in the firm's Denver branch office, a thousand miles away.

"It suddenly seemed to me that I might even make Tom understand how I felt about his mother. Tom must have been having the same sort of feeling, because suddenly, before I had time to speak, he did.

"'Listen, Bunny,' he said, holding me very tightly, 'please don't get sore at what I'm going to say. Because — I don't know just how to say it, but — I mean it right; honestly, I do. You won't get sore, will you?'

"I promised that I wouldn't. And then Tom told me something that almost knocked me off the love seat with sheer amazement. The reason he was gladdest about the new job was that it would take us such a long way from my family.

"'It's such dinky little things,' he explained, 'that I hate to tell 'em to you. Things like —, oh, like when I got that raise in July. You kept saying how grand it was of your father, how he'd written to the home office praising my work, how he was going to push me right ahead just as fast as I could possibly go. It was all true — but — well, you see, I'd worked like a dog for that raise and I felt I'd earned it entirely on my own. And — it sounds fluky to say it, but — I couldn't help feeling that if I'd been working for a stranger, you'd have been thinking how good I was instead of how kind the boss had been.'

"'Oh, Tom!' I fairly gasped. Of course, that's just what I should have felt if Tom's boss had been anybody but my father. 'That's absolutely true. I was dead wrong about it, wrong and mean to you! But I honestly never thought of your feeling that way. Why didn't you tell me?'

"Only half of me was really Tom's wife; the other half was still trying to stay the little girl in her own family. Still feeling that having her parents understand and approve of her was the most important thing in the world; that the way they did everything, from believing in God to having pancakes for Sunday-morning breakfast was, for some mysterious reason that mustn't even be questioned, the only way to do.

"Our going to Denver is going to make things easier for us. Not only by removing the daily irritations that come to Tom through working for Dad, but to me through living so close to Bess. Much more valuable than that, we'll be forced to turn just to each other because there won't be anybody else within a thousand miles to turn to. That may be hard at the minute, but it'll be all to the good in the long run. And I'm going to remember that lots of young people don't get such breaks as we had, that plenty of them have to work out their difficulties right under their parents' roof. I'll remember, too, that a good many of these do work it out."

In this case we see not only the unconscious and well meaning acts of each parent, as he tried to be helpful to this young couple, but also the degree to which each child was still dependent and leaning on his parents after his marriage was underway. At the risk of tedious repetition, it may be well to point out again the importance of acquiring a balance in living which was discussed earlier. When mothers and

fathers devote some of their love and energy to each other, some to the care and training of their children, and some to a wide variety of interests and outlets, both related and unrelated to their primary responsibility to their home life, their own need to absorb an undue amount of the maturing child's affection and obedience is minimized. The satisfaction of the parent's own need for love, security, new experience, and other creative experiences, does not have to be directed entirely toward his children, nor do the children feel crippled and hemmed about by undue possessiveness on the part of the parent.

Handling Parental Relationships

The first essential in handling one's relationship with either parental family is for the young couple to sit down and talk over what they want in the way of family routines, recreation, child education and training, and other matters. They must come to some common understanding as to what kind of family life they want for themselves. After deciding upon each issue as it arises, then it is the responsibility of the husband to talk over with his parent or parents the decisions they have made, and of the wife to talk over with her mother or father these same decisions, if it is her folks who are interfering with their family happiness. We often evade the matter, of actually taking the responsibility for making it clear to our own parents that they must accede to the way of life which we as a couple have decided upon, and the plans we may make from time to time. Let me illustrate this. A young couple were very happily married, but for the fact that the husband's mother insisted that they spend every holiday with her. Both husband and wife wanted to have their own home celebrations occasionally and also go to the home of the wife's parents. This seems a simple matter, but the husband was not able to go to his mother and tell her what he and his wife had decided to do. Instead he would evade the issue and leave his wife to try and work out the embarrassing situation with her mother-in-law. The job was his, not his wife's. If the offending party had been the wife's mother then it would have been her responsibility. Mary is no longer Mrs. Smith's little girl, nor is John any longer Mrs. Jones' little boy. You are now Mr. and Mrs. John Jones. You are establishing a home for your own happiness and in order to achieve for yourselves certain long-term objectives of, possibly, home ownership, children, success in a job, accepted social status, insurance for old age and others.

Each issue should be decided in this manner and in terms of your future.

Often there is economic necessity to explain the presence of in-laws in the home. The parents of husband and wife have not been able to become economically independent, they must live somewhere, the child or children cannot afford to maintain a separate home for them, and the only answer is for them to live in the same household. There is obvious need for more sympathetic understanding of this problem and the development of means by which parents, living in their children's homes, may find interesting outlets for themselves, and achieve a greater understanding of their role in their children's homes. Older people in the family need to feel important and should develop interests, outlets, and activities which will enhance the spirit and purpose of family life.

If one is economically self-supporting, it is always advantageous to start married life living apart from either parental home. Distance helps a couple to work out their own problems rather than depend upon mother or father to make decisions for them.

A second aspect of the in-law problem is the competition between the wife and the husband's mother. Until her son's marriage, the mother feels she is first in his life and assumes great responsibility for his welfare. Then, suddenly, another woman is first with him and assumes, in most respects, what was formerly the mother's role. The mother then feels that she is no longer needed, while the wife feels that her mother-in-law is a threat to her. This competitive situation seems to be met if the husband makes the wife feel that she is first because she has the unique relation of wifehood to him. At the same time, he should persuade his mother to recognize the fact. The whole situation reflects the extent to which the mother has helped her son to mature and to become independent of family protection, while she, at the same time, has found other interests for herself.

Summary

As we grow from infancy (the period when we are more or less cherished objects), through childhood (when we are real competitors in the family, competing for the love and affection of mother and father and our brothers and sisters for the material things of life), to late adolescence (when we should have learned to be participants in family affairs), the habit of talking things over with our parents should be developed. Parents do not have to be "Hitlers," except in making certain decisions in our early lives. If this mutual love and mutual confidence is developed, we will go to our parents for advice and respect it. If our parents are continually clubbing us, either verbally or actually, we will go elsewhere for counsel.

Our parents love us, are proud of our successes and sorry when we fail. We should, when possible, seek their advice when we need it and try to raise our own children in such a way that they will be the right kind of in-laws when they marry.

CHAPTER XI

RELATIONSHIPS INVOLVING MONEY

Sufficiency of Income

There is a common saying that no matter how much money a person makes he never has enough. This is almost literally true when one studies the results of research. Families in the economic income class of from $5,000 to $10,000 per year have as many financial difficulties as those in the $1,800 to $2,500 income class. The basic problem of economic stability is usually not the amount of income one receives, but the amount of excess spending one does over and above that income.

There is, of course, the problem, which faces many families, of actual low income in relation to cost of living. In periods of financial depression, thousands of individuals are out of work and have to look to public relief for the means of livelihood. In normal times, the majority of those gainfully employed are earning under $2,000 per year. The problem of low income and that of irregular income, due to unemployment, are economic questions which do not concern us here. We are more concerned with the individual family problem of financial management.

Division of Labor between Husband and Wife

The most important factors in money management are honesty as to income and expenditure, agreement as to what things the money is to be used for, and a suitable division of responsibility between husband and wife in the handling of the family's money.

156

When two individuals quarrel over the fact that the husband got a bonus of $50 and did not tell his wife about it, and she got a gift of $25 from her mother which she did not tell her husband about, there is no basis for sound, financial management. The entire basis of their personal relationship needs to be examined. This is no money problem. It is a human relations problem. There are, of course, many different patterns used in families for handling finances. There is the joint planning method, the dole method, the allowance method, and many others. The system which brings about the highest degree of satisfaction for any couple is the plan to use. If a man enjoys keeping his income a secret and giving his wife money only when she asks for it, and the wife enjoys this plan, there seems no good reason to change. There are other families where the wife has a certain planned allowance each week or month, and she pays certain parts of the family's expenses from that, whereas the husband pays the remaining bills. The following excerpts from the cases of the Beattie and Cavanaugh families show how some wives work out their problems by adjusting to their husband's ideas and wishes.

THE BEATTIES

"After her marriage Mrs. Beattie was very worried about being kept in ignorance of family finances, since in her own home these things had been discussed quite frankly, and, during the period that she was teaching, the distribution of her salary was entirely her own. 'Mr. Beattie has the idea that money worries belong entirely to the man in the family and that it is up to him to worry about these things and not me. I have reached the point that I feel that it is best to comply with my husband's wishes in this matter and not to make an issue of it. At present I know that we have nothing and so buy only the absolute essentials.' " (14)

THE CAVANAUGHS

" 'Mr. Cavanaugh handles all the money and I am to see that we don't spend it.' She laughed and said that this was probably a funny way — that he wanted to handle it and yet she was probably more conscious of careful spending than he. They charge most of their groceries. Most of their bills are paid by check and her husband writes the checks. She does not have any money for her own and when she needs it 'I have to inveigle money out of him for spending. This bothers me a little because, whenever I do ask for money and then need some again very soon, he will say: "What on earth did you do with the money I gave you? I don't see how you could use it all."' The client says when getting money from her husband she has to be pretty sure of his attitude and the right time. 'I generally have to get him at the first of the month and when he feels in a good humor. This bothers me a little bit but not to any great extent. I try to be careful in spending but would like to have an allowance of my own.'" (15)

The following examples of money management in the Johnson and Holt families illustrate the plan of joint control and show some of the effects this plan had in the case of the Holts.

THE JOHNSON FAMILY FINANCIAL PLAN

The case of the Johnson family shows what can be done when an entire family cooperates in the planning of its activities together:
"'Often when our children were small they were disappointed because their father had to go to work when they wanted him to stay and play. In order to justify his leaving, I would say, "Dad has to work to earn our bread and butter." Later one time when our young son was overloading his cereal with sugar, I said, "That's too much sugar, child. When it's all gone, Dad will have to buy more." He thought a bit. "Mother," he said, "I know Dad has to earn the bread and butter, but does he have to earn the sugar too?"

"'Since the beginning of our family life we have kept accurate accounts and budgets. We now have set up a family council that we call Johnson and Johnson. We have a formal meeting once a month. We have officers and keep a record book. The aim of this organization is to discuss all kinds of family problems. We are trying to get away from adult domination by considering the viewpoints of the children as important as those of the adults. We listed our income on a month's basis. Children cannot grasp an income on a yearly basis so well. Then we listed our "musts." By subtracting the "Bread and Butter" from our income, we had the "Sugar." It was a revelation to the children to see how large a percentage of our income went for "Bread and Butter."

"'We had a frank discussion of personal allowances, individual contributions in time and energy for the privilege of belonging to the corporation, ways of earning money in the family, kinds of jobs and basis of payment, and many other things that have contributed greatly in developing a happy family unit.

"'Clothes were not listed in our "musts." We realize that clothes can be a big or smaller item. We make a clothes plan for each individual at the beginning of the year. We then try to buy out of season because we can get better materials and better color satisfactions for less. We also make some things because we can have more for our money than with buying moderate-priced ready-mades. So far the children do their clothes account on a credit basis. I act only as purchasing agent.

"'May I show how this council plan works? We decided to take an Easter trip. The question was: Given an amount of money and four days, what shall we do? Shall we go deluxe, hotels, tea-rooms, etc., or shall we go farther, see more, and stay at tourist homes, and eat at cafeterias and lunch counters? We decided on the latter. We had a grand trip. We came home with four dollars, part of which we spent for Snow White music.

"'Another question: Shall we buy summer rugs and curtains for the living room or shall we screen the front porch? There were many pros and cons based on estimates for the various items. We bought the summer rugs and curtains and are happy over our decision.

"'We feel that in frankly talking over the amount of money that is available for "Bread and Butter" as well as "Sugar," we are getting immediate interest, understanding, and satisfaction. We are also hoping that we may be helping these young Americans to develop a philosophy of life that will be a satisfaction to them and to other lives they may contact.'" (16)

A CHANGE IN FINANCIAL ARRANGEMENTS

"Mr. Holt had for several years gone on the basis that the responsibility for all expenditures in the family was his. The effect of a change to a more democratic procedure is shown by the following statement made by the husband in a recent interview. He says:

"'You have suggested for me a willingness to agree to extra spending where Mrs. Holt desired it. In decorating and painting our house, my wife was keenly interested in extra money for more expensive paper and to do a more artistic job. So we followed her plans and I find the result most attractive and she is very happy about it. Then again, I proposed that we should make a change in the manner in which all extra expenses are met; that we should do away with the idea of myself as the sole guardian of our savings against raids and instead substitute the notion of full rights to each of us, and if at any time she wished to buy something as an extra, I should not have to be consulted. She said she had waited for years for this to come from me voluntarily; that the lack of it was probably a reason for her notions of "trying to get things out of me;" that she might do some silly things at first but that it would all work out very well.'" (17)

Conditions differ in families. In some, the husband is away a great deal, in others the income may be a fluctuating one or uncertain, as in the professional family, and in still others there may be a steady salary to be planned for. In every case, the division of responsibility should be allocated in accordance with the time and ability of the persons. A wife may be the best person to manage the family income if she has had previous professional experience, or if she is, by temperament, best qualified. The barrier most often to joint planning and management is the cultural pattern in the background from which each has been reared. The man's ego may be so sensitive that he must dominate the entire money situation, or the wife may have become so accustomed to a pattern of nagging and quarreling over money in her own home that she will do anything to keep peace in the family.

The Budget

Money management is often given as the most difficult problem in homemaking, and the one that causes most worry. Some of the reasons why this might be true, according to experienced homemakers, are:

Income not large enough.
Income irregular or uncertain.
Money not available when needed.
Lack of planning ahead.
Lack of good buymanship.
No margin for emergencies.
Underestimation of expenditures.
Overestimation of income.
Too many fixed expenses.

Lack of cooperation between members of family.
Difficulty over who shall control the money.
Differences in attitudes about money.
Differences in judgment of values in things purchased.
Period in the family cycle — what demands are made and what preparation has been made for them.

Budgeting or planning is one way to eliminate some of these worries, and to see the financial picture more clearly. The budget can never tell one what to want nor what to spend one's money for. It can, however, be a helpful tool in aiding one to do with his money what he wants to do with it. A study of the budgets of any family over a period of years is a fair index of the basic values which that family holds to be important. Often a couple will want help on how to draw up a budget. This would no doubt be helpful to them, but it is not the answer to their problem. Take, for example, a young woman who grew up in a home where she had practically no experience in buying or in housekeeping activities, and where the income was $20,000 a year. She was to marry a young graduate student who had a job in a small college at a starting salary of $1,800 a year. This young woman wanted a budget. She did not know what the clothes she wore cost, had never cooked a meal in her life, and never shopped for food or anything else, and she thought a budget would solve her problem. What she will have to learn is how to live on $1,800 a year when she has been accustomed to a $20,000 standard of living at home, how to buy, how to economize and do without, how to plan, manage, and learn to love it, along with her husband. These are personal adjustments no budget can solve.

Take another couple who wanted help on a budget. The wife was earning $150 a month and the husband $250 a month. They wished to live on his income and save all of hers but seemed unable to do so. While there were points of economy which a budget was helpful in bringing to their attention, the basic problem was conflict over the values for which their money was to be spent. For example, the husband complained that the wife ought to be able to get along without a telephone, since they both worked, whereas the wife thought that, since they had a full time maid for the cleaning, meals, and laundry, the husband ought to let her do his shirts instead of insisting that they be sent out. The telephone cost $30 a year and so did the extra laundering of his shirts. They rented a summer cottage, which the husband liked, and they spent $150 for a vacation trip, which the wife wanted. Each wanted the other to give up the thing that the other liked, in order to balance the budget. This, as you again can see, is no money problem, nor is it a budget problem. It is a struggle for domination — a personality conflict between husband and wife.

It would naturally seem that the couples who have small or irregular incomes would have a harder problem to get money to work as they wish, but it depends so much on the individuals' ability to plan ahead, to limit wants, to get their money's worth, whether or not the income is "enough." Some couples never have enough and are always behind, while others have a wonderful time on much less. Just as planning is important to housekeeping and meal provision, so planning is a key to success in solving money problems. Ready-made plans or schemes for accounting and budgeting seldom fit individual cases, so need not be considered here. All one really needs is a dozen sheets of paper and a pencil. Use a sheet for each month. On this sheet write down everything you can think of that will have to be bought or paid for in that month. Estimate amounts that you cannot state definitely. Be sure to allow for medical and dental care, and emergencies. For example:

JULY — 1949

Food	$ 50.00
Rent	60.00
Gas	1.50
Light	2.00
Savings	37.50
Church	4.00
Insurance	18.00
Shoes (Jane)	6.50
Clothing (Jane and John) . .	15.00
Emergency	10.00
	$204.50

Be sure each month's outgo has enough income, either from that month or from the previous month's savings. In this way one can see clearly what will be due, and whether one can meet all demands and so make provision for them. An easy way to keep accounts is to write the actual figure for the items beside the planned figure. Accounts alone are of little value except to estimate future expenses. Every home-maker should have a special place to keep financial papers, such as plans, receipts, bills, etc., so that these can easily be found when needed.

Regardless of the amount of the income, each person should have some part, even though small, which is his own to spend as he will, without accounting. This practice gives a sense of freedom to even the most restricted scale of living.

Extra Economic Responsibilities

There may come times when one needs to assume an un-expected responsibility for a relative, face a period of pro-longed illness or unemployment or the debts of the husband or wife. All of these can be partially offset through various forms of savings, investment, and insurance, but many times the reverse is so great, that one must go deeply in debt or begin from scratch again after ten years of hard work. There is no way to avoid risk. One can, however, reduce risk by intelligent and cooperative planning and handling of his financial affairs, including his wants.

Laying By for the Future

Planning one's financial future is a difficult task at any time. Twenty-five years ago everyone was trying to get rich quick in the stock market. In 1929, nearly everyone who got rich quick, along with many others, went broke in the crash and years of depression which followed. From 1932 to 1936, there was widespread unemployment, and people were looking for ways of providing economic security for themselves. Social legislation was passed by Congress allowing for unemployment compensation and old age social security benefits. A new step had been taken by govern-ment in the interest of economic security for the masses.

There has been a marked increase in wages for most classes of the population, but an even more rapid rise in the cost of living. If we allow unrestricted inflation, which will benefit those who have large investments in property and common stocks, the great majority of the population will suffer. If prices, wages, and costs are controlled, we stand a better chance of living comfortably and investing some of our earnings for the future. What future conditions will be, no one seems to know. It will be necessary for every couple to acquaint themselves with changing conditions and to gauge their economic planning accordingly.

The rules for sound, financial planning vary with the direction the price level is tending, but over a long period of time one can feel relatively safe in investing a certain amount of surplus over actual necessary living costs in government bonds. Next in line for protection of one's family is a reasonable amount of life insurance, selected to meet your needs. These needs will change as you grow older and your children mature, so your life insurance plan should be reviewed occasionally to see if it needs changing. A third investment is property, especially a home for oneself if engaged in the type of occupation or living in a type of community where owning a home is practical and desirable. Beyond these three items, one's planning for future economic security will be determined by one's ideals, the amount of additional money one has to invest, and other factors. As to methods of spending, it is generally wise to pay up any outstanding debts and limit drastically the taking on of any additional, long-time obligations. Cash buying is usually cheaper than buying on long-term credit. Charge accounts for some individuals lead them to excess spending.

Summary

The important aspect of the money problem is its significance as a point of agreement or conflict between husband and wife. The differing experiences with money and differing patterns and standards of economic life of the husband and wife enter into conflicts in this area, as does the struggle for personal dominance. In the beginning of marriage, there are two sets of values and two competing sets of desires for the things which money commands, those of the husband and the wife, as well as differences between them in ideas about handling money. The conflict between husband and wife over money is one of divergent personality strivings, values, and roles. It is not always money, in itself, that constitutes the problem, but rather the question of how money is to be spent, and who is to make the decision about its use.

CHAPTER XII

MANAGING THE HOME AND HOME RELATIONSHIPS

A family's resources are their collective time, energy, money, and personal qualities. If they know how to put these to work, a family group can do much toward getting what they want out of life. To be sure, each family and its home is unique. There is no other just like it in the world. Two unique individuals, each with his own particular background, ideals, and goals, have founded the home and in their way are striving toward their goals for themselves and setting up goals for their children.

Even though each home is unique, all families have much in common. In the early years of marriage, all couples go through a period of learning to live together, experimenting with ways of handling money and of dividing and sharing responsibility. All families with children go through years of concern over behavior and health and times of struggle to set the child on his own feet as an adult. All fathers and mothers experience the sometimes difficult period of replanning their lives after the children are reared.

Making a home, then, is a job which changes as the years pass. It is a job that calls for constant alertness. It can never grow stale or boring if the husband and wife keep the purpose of the home in mind. *A home may be made anywhere — in a mansion, a cottage, a flat, or a trailer.* It *is not a place, but a relationship, an atmosphere.*

Each bride and her husband come to the new job of homemaking with a desire to make the same kind of a home in which each grew up, if those childhood homes were happy; but if they were not happy, then there is a desire to create something different. What the wife wants and what the husband wants may also vary, but reconciling the two and creating a new structure is part of the adjustment during courtship and early marriage. Every young man and woman should realize that homes do not just grow, like Topsy, but that real homes are fashioned after a plan, constantly nurtured and occasionally checked up on to see how they are developing, how they are fulfilling their purpose. And what is the purpose of a home? Briefly, to make the people in it happy individuals. Happiness comes only from purposeful living. So what we do in our homes should stand the test of, "How does this contribute to the happiness and wholesome growth of the members of this family?"

Every young man and woman should realize that, in the job of homemaking, *many skills are necessary, certain attitudes are indispensable, and other personal characteristics are desirable.* Even in the most modest home and at the very beginning of family life, somebody has to know how to prepare food, keep the house orderly, see to the laundry, wash the dishes, do the shopping, take care of the furnishings, and do the mending. In addition to these minimum essentials, a wife, sooner or later, has to know how to handle the sick, the weary, or the discouraged mate. She must at all times be ready to be his companion, ready to make adjustments in her own work to take care of emergencies. She must be a manager, a worker, a companion, an adviser, and a sweetheart, all in one. In return for this, she deserves appreciation from her husband. It behooves him to make her feel that being a homemaker is a grand job, and that he is proud of her. He must realize that, while he gets satisfaction and approval from his fellow workers and superiors, she works alone and has only him to look to for approval. A wise husband, for example, never fails to comment on an especially good dinner. The wife's status comes largely from her husband.

Since every bride has chosen to be a homemaker, she should do her best. She should see in homemaking a great work which cannot be delegated to someone else, and an intangible atmosphere that grows out of many little acts.

> "The common tasks are beautiful if we
> Have eyes to see their shining ministry . . .
> A woman with her eyes and cheeks aglow,
> Watching a kettle, tending a scarlet flame,
> Guarding a little child — there is no name
> For this great ministry. But eyes are dull
> That do not see that it is beautiful;
> That do not see within the common tasks
> The simple answer to the thing God asks
> Of any child, a pride within His breast:
> That at our given work we do our best."
> — Grace Noll Crowell (18)

Homemaking can be fun, adventure, and joy when each family member does his part. Homemaking is essentially a woman's job, and she must expect to carry the greater share of the job. Husbands should realize, however, that they will miss much pleasure if they cannot or do not share in home activities, be it ever so little. It is also well for a man to be able to do a few things about the house, in case of emergencies. If the husband is also a father, his participation and attitudes affect the children greatly and make it more or less easy to train them to take part in the activities of the home. *Every family has to decide* what *to do*, when *to do it*, how *to do it, and* who *shall do it*. If all concerned have a voice in the planning, it is usually easier to carry out the plan.

Even with planning and sharing there are bound to be some hard spots in every homemaker's day. There are things she dislikes to do, jobs that tire her, things that worry her, situations that irritate her. Some experienced homemakers say, "Oh, if we could just do away with fatigue, worry, and irritation, home would be a happy place." Before these things can be done away with, we must search for their causes. What causes tiredness, irritation, worry?

Tiredness may spring from physical and mental causes or a combination of them. It may be due to poor health, which may come from lack of nutritious food, lack of rest or recreation or attention to some minor ailment. Tiredness may be due to poor attitudes. If one is not happy as a home-maker, the job may grow monotonous and boring. If there is strain and tension in the family, it shows up in fatigue and irritability. Unless one is fairly skillful in doing the work of the house, there may be a great waste of time and energy, so that one becomes unnecessarily tired. Sometimes, home-makers get into poor posture habits. They lean over sinks, tables, and ironing boards that are too low. They sit on stools that give no support to the back. They rest in chairs that are entirely unsuited to healthful sitting. They allow their shoulders to droop forward, their abdomens to protrude, and their chins to drop. All this muscular sagging and drooping contributes to tiredness. Poor grooming may be a factor in fatigue. Who does not feel better after a bath, a fresh dress, and a bit of powder? Housecoats and bedroom slippers are not good costume for housework, from either a health or safety angle. It may be there is too much noise in the home. Blaring radios and street noises affect some people greatly. Or, perhaps, the lighting is poor. There may be too glaring light, or the whole place may be too dark, or perhaps there are several small lamps about, so that the eye must constantly be adjusting from light to dark. Little children usually play on the floor, and it is not uncommon to see Mother or Father reading under a bright light, while Johnny plays in a dark corner or strains his eyes reading in some poorly lighted spot. Let there be light! — in the right places.

One of the common causes of weariness is hurry. Sleeping too late in the morning, a homemaker gets a late start; she plans more than she can do; she is behind all day; she stays up late at night. Hurry, hurry, hurry. Maybe there is too much to do sometimes. If so, do away with some of it.

If a homemaker is really interested in not being tired, she

can find many little ways of saving energy. One of the simplest of these is by body position or posture. Whether standing or sitting one should try to keep the body straight. Every bit of added bending, stooping, or drooping uses extra energy. Since standing requires more energy than sitting, a homemaker should work sitting down when possible. The chair or stool should be of such height in relation to the working surface that stooping is eliminated. Energy may also be saved by lying down for rest rather than sitting.

Other ways of saving energy may be:

1. *Teach each person to care for personal possessions.* Have easy places for them to keep things. Temporary places may have to be devised. Husbands can hang up their own pajamas and put their laundry in the proper place, etc.

2. *Dovetail jobs.* Prepare food for more than one meal at a time. Many small jobs can be done while waiting.

3. *Arrange your equipment and cupboards more conveniently.* Try out different arrangements until you find one that saves the most steps and motions.

4. *Standardize your work.* Do it the best way for you. After you find a good way to do a job, do it that way. It saves strain. There is no one best way for everyone to do a job.

5. *Use simpler standards.* Use simpler meal service, fewer dishes, clothing that requires less care, fewer objects about that need dusting and cleaning.

6. *Plan work better.* Alternate light and heavy jobs. Schedule the heavy jobs over fewer hours. Do not try to clean the house and do the laundry the same day. Leave long enough time for big jobs to make good use of the warming up period, the period of greatest efficiency and lag of effort. Take, for example, ironing. It usually takes quite a long time. Plan on a long time. Begin with easy articles. After you get warmed up to the task, attack the shirts and harder

things. Then, as you begin to get tired, iron some more of the easy things. The tendency is usually to leave the hardest for the last, and then they seem still harder.

7. *Avoid hurry.* Do not plan so much for the day that interruptions upset you.

8. *Have definite rest periods.*

9. *Plan definite routines* for the day, week or longer.

10. *Do be flexible.* Every homemaker must be able to change her plan of work to meet emergencies. Sometimes she cannot do the job as well as she would like. Remember the three ways to dust. Some days you get into every nook and cranny. Other days you must be content with dusting the most important spots, such as table tops, etc. And then, sometimes, there come days when you just pull the shades down a bit farther.

Of all these ways of saving energy, the use of routines is one of the most important. Every family should plan some routines that suit their particular needs. It does not matter what the Smiths do, or when the Johnsons hang out their washing, or when Mrs. Brown does her shopping. It's an individual problem. The family group should experiment with different ways and times for doing things until they find an arrangement that meets their need, and that, for the time, enables them to manage their lives smoothly, with the least expenditure of time and energy and the fewest situations that cause strain and irritation.

An example of replanning one's household routines is shown by the following case. This young woman had married and was the mother of one child. Her training and experience had given her little idea of how to organize her household activities, and, as a result, she was busy from early morning until late at night doing jobs that had to be done. She was expecting a second child and could not face what she would do when this additional responsibility arrived. She was asked to keep an accurate diary of every activity of each day for an entire week. This diary was studied, and a daily work plan was formulated. While she was not able to put this plan into effect, at first, as effectively as a more experienced person might have done, she gradually got her household affairs reorganized on a satisfactory basis for herself and her family. The suggestions which accompanied the schedule were:

1. To save time and energy in washing dishes, use a dish drainer after rinsing dishes in hot water. Cover the drying dishes with a towel and leave until the next meal. This will save many steps and motions, as well as minutes.

2. Fix some place in kitchen, either a low part of a cupboard or drawer, where baby can keep things and such objects as clothespins, pans, covers, etc. She can play with these while mother works in kitchen and will not be so tempted by icebox.

3. Keep as many things in icebox in jars with screw tops as possible, so baby cannot spill them.

4. Cook cereal for breakfast while cooking dinner.

5. Before going to bed put living room in order. Empty ash trays, fold papers, plump up cushions, etc.

6. On washday, plan easy meals, use canned fruits and vegetables, left-overs, etc.

7. On cleaning days, give one room a thorough cleaning, the next week give another room an extra good cleaning, etc., in rotation. In this way, each room comes in for good cleaning about once in six weeks, and this, together with the regular weekly cleaning, keeps the house in good order. I mean such jobs as cleaning windows, woodwork, closets, polishing furniture, etc.

8. Putting baby to bed before parents have dinner makes it more calm for them, as well as relieves baby.

9. These hours are only suggestive and not necessarily to be rigidly followed. But the order of routine might be followed. I believe I have allowed plenty of time for duties which will allow time for taking baby to toilet when necessary. The mother can play with baby as she works, also.

10. In the afternoon schedules, I have not scheduled some of the time between three and five, but at this time, baby may be taken out for a walk, or mother may mend, sew, etc.

11. Extra washing for baby may have to be done. This could be done right after morning dishes or after lunch dishes.

12. Pressing clothes may have to be done. Try to do this after regular ironing, or work it in some afternoon.

13. If a small quantity of staples can be purchased and kept on hand, it will be possible to limit shopping to twice a week; also relieves strain.

14. Taking time some evening to plan the meals for three or four days ahead will be a great help.

15. If water has to be heated for dishes, put it on just before sitting down to eat.

Recommended also are keeping the housework up and clearing up after each meal, so that there is no piling up of jobs. This is what makes it a burden. Unless there is prospect for having help, it would be better for the mother to acquire the habit of getting her work out of the way even in the evening, so that she can start the next day fresh. There will have to be some change in the schedule when the new baby comes, but it is better to handle the job this way now. By that time the first child's routine can be changed enough to work in the new baby's care easily and still provide rest for the mother.

Daily routines help to get the housework out of the way with the least effort. Routines for the week also help one to spread the work so that the amount of energy expended is about equal each day. Then one does not get worn out on one day and have to spend the next recovering, but is ready and able to take each day as it comes. Washing, ironing, cleaning, special cooking, weekly shopping — all these take time and much energy and should be especially planned for. To some people, regularity and routine may seem deadly, but once on the job, they soon will realize that haphazard working leads only to disorder, irritability, fatigue, and dissatisfaction.

Once a satisfactory routine has been established, let no one be so innocent as to believe such bliss can go on forever. Let a baby enter the picture, and an entirely new plan has to be devised. Let the wife but get a job, and the whole setup has to be reorganized. Making a home as a full time job is one thing. But being a homemaker and carrying a full time job outside is quite another. To a man, a job is his life; but even if a woman does have a job, she is still expected to maintain the home at a fairly good level. So the work of the home has to be unusually well planned as to what, when, how and who. Short cuts, simplification, routine, and rest become "musts." Cooperation between husband and wife must be unusually good, and is unusually important, if there is to be real homemaking. Then only can a woman carry two jobs, both of which demand her best.

Feeding the Family

One homemaking job that takes a lot of time, but which most women enjoy, is meal preparation. To save time, energy, and money, and get better nutrition and greater satisfaction, more attention should be given to meal planning. Everyone should know what makes up a nutritious diet and be willing to eat the foods that provide what the body needs for good health. Experts tell us that an adult should consume the following foods every day:

Milk — a pint, or its equivalent in cheese or other milk products.
Vegetables — two or more, besides potatoes. One of these should be green or yellow and one raw, preferably.
Fruit — one citrus or tomato. One other fruit.
Meat, cheese, fish, or dried legumes — one or more servings.
Whole-grain or enriched bread and cereals.
Butter or other fat fortified with Vitamin A — about four tablespoons.

With this standard in mind, meals can be planned to meet the needs of the family. If possible, plan ahead a few days in order to save shopping time, energy, and money. If the planned food is not in the market, one should choose a good alternative. Shopping well ahead of cooking time avoids hurry. Keeping a few extra supplies on hand for emergencies avoids worry.

If vegetables and fruits are purchased ahead of time, they should be kept cool and covered. A withered vegetable has lost much of its food value. Food should be prepared as near meal time as possible to avoid loss of vitamins. Cook vegetables in a small amount of water in a covered vessel to avoid vitamin loss. Use any leftover cooking water in some way. It is rich in minerals and vitamins. If there are leftovers, store them in covered dishes and use as soon as possible.

Cooking for more than one meal at a time saves time, energy and fuel. Extra potatoes, stewed fruit, baked goods, etc., may be prepared ahead. Use the same dish for cooking and serving when possible. It saves dish washing. Arrange cupboards as conveniently as possible. It saves steps. Plan a definite time for food preparation. It relieves bustle and hurry.

If there is a lunch carrier in the family, he should be taken seriously. Carried lunches are notoriously poor. A few suggestions may help:

1. Use a clean container — paper, wood, metal. See that it is free from odors.
2. Wrap each food separately.
3. Use a thermos for hot or cold foods.
4. Provide foods which can be eaten easily.
5. Include something crisp and chewy, juicy and refreshing, as well as substantial.

A good lunch should provide the equivalent of a glass of milk; a large serving of fruit or vegetable; protein-rich food, like meat, cheese, egg or peanut butter sandwiches. The amount of such foods depends upon the person's needs. Lunch should provide about one-third of the day's food.

Just as routine helps to get housework done easily, so the planning of meals insures better food for the family. Nutritious food is necessary to health and good dispositions.

Buying Economically

Getting one's money's worth depends upon knowing one's need and being able to select the thing which most nearly meets that need at the price one can afford to pay. Most young couples, and most families rearing children must give thought to what is really needed. When looking at merchandise, don't buy it unless you need it. If you really need it, then try to get the quality that best fits the need.

1. If one needs service hose, do not buy fine sheers.
2. If one needs work shoes, play shoes won't do.

3. If one needs a durable, washable dress, sleazy, poorly-dyed material will not do.

4. If one needs protein for building body tissues, almost any lean meat will do, as well as other protein-rich foods, like eggs, cheese, etc.

5. If one needs underwear, a hard-working man may need one type, while a sedentary worker can use another.

6. If a woman has limited time for laundry work, she must choose the type of underwear that demands little ironing and care.

Since women do most of the family buying, they have a responsibility for getting the best value for money spent that is possible. They must learn to be good buyers. They must plan ahead. Articles that cost much should be planned for long enough ahead so that funds can be accumulated. One should shop around and compare values, instead of buying the first article seen. Every woman should learn to judge quality, whether it is in sheets, gloves, spinach or beefsteak. Some things are being standardized. There are quality standards for sheets, some canned goods, some hose, and grades of meat. Everyone can read labels and ask for information about goods. He should know what the article is made of, what service to expect, and what care to give it.

Even the smallest margins can be put to good use, if one is a good buyer. Fifty cents a month set aside for the purpose can keep the linen supply in good shape, or furnish new kitchen utensils, or shoe repair, etc. Little leaks and little investments make a difference. Money is only a tool — use it to work toward goals.

Utilizing Conditions as They Are

A house should not be thought of as something for one's friends to admire or envy, or something that is a burden to be kept clean, but rather as an arrangement that provides opportunities for growth and personal development. Besides providing for eating, sleeping and cleanliness, a house or living space should provide opportunities for personal and group recreation and relaxation, for entertaining friends, for privacy for every member of the group, conveniences for work, study, reading, etc., equipment for caring for one's belongings, and equipment necessary for caring for children. Even the smallest apartment can provide all of these if the husband and wife have no false pride and have some imagination. A group of young brides were bewailing the fact that they could not entertain their friends. There was not enough space, not enough chairs, not enough dishes, and so on. Eventually they worked out plans for some group meals to which each couple contributed its share of food, and the meal was served picnic fashion on the floor. Pooling food, dishes, and work, and being very informal solved the problem and provided a great deal of fun.

Another young homemaker bemoaned the fact that they owed the "boss" and his wife a dinner, but just could not think of inviting them to their modest flat — and, anyway, the baby interfered with her time so that she would not be able to prepare the elaborate kind of meal they had been served at the home of the "boss," and anyway they could not afford it. After planning, she and her husband invited the "boss" and his wife to dinner — a simple, well cooked meal, served on a small table, with a minimum of dishes and silver. No show, no apologies, but lots of fun because the "boss" and his wife had been young once, too, and had begun very simply.

Enjoying friends is the main reason for having a party. Adapting what one does to what one has to do with, and avoiding the unnatural, makes for success. One young hostess, whose husband refused to serve food when there were guests, became famous for her attractive buffet suppers. Another, whose time and supplies were unusually limited, enjoyed her friends over waffles and baked apples. There is always a way, if you keep yourself from becoming a slave to things and the fear of other peoples' opinions of you.

Entertaining friends does not have to mean a party. A real friend should be welcome at any time. The house should be kept so that people may drop in without embarrassing the homemaker — or her husband.

Sometimes the house seems so poorly arranged, or so small, that certain necessary pieces of equipment can find no space. In one household, the young husband found it necessary to do a good deal of drawing at home in the evening. There was no place for his drawing table except in the living room. The wife refused to have it there. What would the neighbors say? The husband then found that he would have to do his work elsewhere, while the wife sat alone in her orderly living room. Finally she decided that the drawing table could stand in the living room, and that, regardless of what people would think, she preferred to have her husband working there.

Very often, in small living quarters, there is little room for washing or drying clothes. No one enjoys seeing chairs, towel rods, and radiators strewn with drying laundry. A few clothes lines placed well toward the ceiling, either in bathroom or kitchen, may help. Or lines that can be taken down between washings may be put up in other places. It is usually easier to handle the laundry in such crowded quarters if it is done as it is soiled, rather than leaving it until a big pile accumulates. Ironing may be reduced by hanging wet clothing evenly and smoothly.

The shared closet may become a source of irritation in some homes. Most closets were not meant for anything in particular, but they may easily be made over with simple materials, so that clothing can hang freely, shoes be kept off the floor, and dust removed easily. Rods for hangers, bags or racks for shoes can be provided cheaply. No one can afford to be careless with clothing in these days, and it certainly saves tempers if one can find the garment he wants when he wants it.

Bureau drawers can be divided by using paper boxes. It is much easier to keep small compartments orderly than one large drawer, which becomes a jumble every time it is opened or closed.

If a baby is anticipated, certain equipment must be added, but it need not be costly or elaborate. A homemade bath tray, fashioned from wood or a kitchen pan, can be made very attractive. Add a vessel for bathing and a simple comfortable bed, together with a well thought out layette, and baby has about all he needs. Anything in excess satisfies the parents' pride, but adds little to baby's comfort or well-being.

Once in a while you see a house in which it is impossible to relax. To lie down on the davenport would be a sacrilege. The bedspread is too dainty, the blankets too fine. Chairs were chosen for looks rather than comfort. One of the things a house must provide is an opportunity for its occupants to relax — a studio couch, an army cot, a bed, or some chairs chosen to fit the peculiar anatomy of the people who are going to sit in them the most.

A few well chosen things can be made to meet all the requirements for good furnishing. Young homemakers should not be unhappy if they cannot have everything they want or the things their parents have. Just as Mother and Dad had many adjustments to make in their early marriage and finally achieved something rather grand, so they probably started housekeeping rather simply, building up comforts and furnishings over the years. Children take all this for granted and do not realize that it takes time to make a home the way you want it.

A young couple rented a one-room apartment in a large city. They had very little money for furnishings. They purchased a folding table, a couch-bed, a reading lamp, two straight chairs, and two comfortable chairs. Aside from kitchen equipment and a couple of small rugs, this was all they had. A few pictures and some gay, cheap curtains were added. An older woman came to call and later remarked to a friend, "You know, there is hardly anything in that place, but it's so homey." The house, its arrangement, use and care does affect the congeniality of the family. One needs to think of possible ways her own house could provide a better home.

Managing a home, then, is a job for intelligent people. They realize that fatigue, worry, and irritability are the enemies of happiness and will do all they can to avoid them. They know that skills, attitudes, and successes are closely related.

When a husband and wife see how they may work toward their desired goals, using their own particular set of resources and getting some results — that is good management.

Family Living Should Be Democratic Living

What has been said in the preceding pages is more than rules for managing a home. Its implications go to the very core of democracy itself. We do not learn how to be valuable members of a democratic society by taking high-school or college courses in civics, history, or social studies. We only learn facts and theories about democracy. The greatest contribution of the family to society should be in its practice of those virtues and ways of living which give its members experience in sharing, working cooperatively toward the achievement of common goals, foregoing individual desires in the interest of the welfare of another, and abiding by the decisions of the family group on matters of common concern. These are the essence of what it takes to live as a participating member of a democratic society.

CHAPTER XIII

SOME OTHER FACTORS IN FAMILY RELATIONSHIPS

Social Relationships

Our basic friendliness patterns not only affect our dating, courting, and marital relationships, but also our relationships with teachers, vocational associates, and superiors, and our social and recreational activities. When a couple marry, they usually have either many friends in common, or each has his own set of friends whom the other person has not met. This is particularly true when the bride moves to the place of business of her husband, or when both move into a new community. The problems which sometimes grow out of these situations are numerous.

Under war conditions, the latter of these situations is a most common one. Couples move into an army camp situation, into an industrial city or other locality, neither of them having contacts of a personal sort. The man usually meets other men on the job and more or less quickly has contacts of both a business and social nature. The wife, however, may live for months and have made few, if any, friends. If she is aggressive enough, and they are able to find part time care for the children she may engage in numerous volunteer activities, or, perhaps, contacts can be made through sorority or alumnae groups, sports, attending public lectures, the library and church. Show yourself friendly and interested in other people.

The problems arising from each having his own set of friends are of a different nature. Mainly, they affect the social participation of the family. The husband may find much of his after-office time devoted to lodge, bowling, or cards with his business associates. When this is done to excess, it reduces his contribution to his wife and children and is often the cause of considerable conflict. It may work the other way when the wife is so active in her bridge club, volunteer work, and other social diversions as not to have either the time or patience to meet her responsibilities as wife, mother, and homemaker. A maid can provide the home with household services and the children with safe care and attention, but she cannot provide a husband with the love and encouragement, nor the children with the affectional security which only the parents can supply for them and for each other.

Frequently neither husband nor wife likes the other's social friends. Perhaps the best solution to this kind of situation is for each to arrange a certain amount of time for social and recreational activities with their own friends and reserve a large portion of their time for their own joint recreation at home or away from the home.

We must not overlook the fact that the kind of friendship pattern we establish in our family life not only affects our children's attitude toward friendly association with others, but their future tendency toward repeating the same kind of pattern in their own lives. It is not that we cannot over-come many of these early conditioned feelings and patterns, but that we add to enjoyment and facilitate good marital relations in providing a desirable sociability pattern for our children.

Closely associated with one's relationship with friends and associates is one's social and recreational activities. When couples marry, they usually have had good times enjoying active or passive entertainment. The nature of their activities may be affected by the type of employment, hours of work, and time at home, of the husband as well as the wife, whether or not she is also gainfully employed.

There may be a basic conflict in the setup for fun in many

families in that, when a husband comes home, he may be tired and wish to stay in, read, garden, listen to the radio, or tinker around the house or with his hobby, whereas the wife, in the house most of the day, prefers a change and is desirous of getting out and away for a little while. Many people complain of this situation, rather than each sacrificing part of his leisure time to satisfy the other. It would add to the felicity of family life if, occasionally, husbands made the effort to do something, however simple, in going out with their wives, and if the wives, in turn, would help their husbands enjoy the rest and quiet of their homes on other evenings. When each is concerned only with satisfying his own selfish desires, trouble usually lies ahead.

The problem of social and recreational activities usually arises after children arrive, although, before this time, there may be such wide differences between interests of husband and wife as to allow for little common social bond. There are many cases where the husband likes, and is active in, sports, including golf, riding, etc., and the wife has had little or no experience, hence, no skill in them, and she appreciates and is more interested in music, art, drama, reading, etc. Problems arise when each tries to force his own form of recreation on the other and is scornful of that of the other. Here, again, is our basic problem of husbands' and wives' keeping their emphasis upon the happiness of the other. A wife may well encourage her husband in the things he likes, and she can well afford to acquire enough skill in some of them to participate with him. A husband could, likewise, afford to have the same basic attitude and willingness with reference to the wishes of his wife. In marriage we must sacrifice a certain amount of our individualism, and only those persons who can accept this fact and make adjustments accordingly will make congenial husbands or wives. Marriage, without this cooperative attitude, becomes a master-servant relationship or a continuum of conflicts and estrangements.

Vacations are another matter for joint consideration. Men often have different interests as well as needs from their wives. The amount that can be spent and time available is usually the determining factor. Where it is possible, there is an advantage in the husband's having some vacation time of his own, completely away from job and family responsibility. It may be a hunting trip, a boat trip, a week at the beach, or some other type of recreation. The wife also needs to have time when she can be relieved of the care and responsibility of home and children. A father can contribute a great deal to the children, as well as learn much about them and the daily problems of the mother, by looking after them a few days himself while the wife is away. Then there is an advantage in the entire family's vacationing for a few days where everyone can have fun together, as well as the desirability of the husband's and wife's having some time away from the rest of the family each year. I know dozens of wives who have been married from ten to twenty years and who have not been on a vacation trip alone with their husbands since their honeymoon.

Physical and Mental Health and Hygiene

The most prevalent kinds of physical and mental illnesses which affect the everyday life of most families are those symptomatic and undiagnosed conditions, such as headaches, chronic fatigue, malnourishment, backache, insomnia, colds, sinuses, eye strain, and nervous tension. Not much is known about these conditions but there is some evidence that many are related to diet, rest, exercise, and emotional maturity. While every kind of physical or mental illness has its effect upon the normal routine and relationships in family life, it is these constant and intermittent little half-physical, half-emotional conditions which form the basis for much conflict, bickering, and unhappiness in the home. It is easier for one to be irritable when one is fatigued, headache-y, and has had little sleep.

In war time, we saw many people who worked long hours, seven days a week; mothers were also employed who were trying to keep expenses down, taxes paid, bonds purchased, the children sent to school, insurance and other payments made, and, in addition, were perhaps under the added emotional strain of having a son or daughter in the armed forces and of undergoing the day-to-day bombardment of radio commentators and newspaper headlines. No wonder thousands of families deserted their homes, seeking release from the turmoil of life by desertion of responsibility, neglect of children, and the refuge of divorce. Everyone might well afford arbitrarily to set aside a small amount of time for uninterrupted fun — a good mental hygiene insurance against family conflict, breaks in health, or even complete family disorganization.

These conditions are of such proportion today that it becomes a nation-wide, social, as well as an individual, family problem. It raises the question of the desirability of letting anyone work seven days a week, or of letting both members of the family work outside the home where there are children under ten years of age. A population whose physical and mental health is at this breaking point may easily become unduly hysterical in times of national crisis. The home, presided over by a rested, intelligent, and socially active mother, can do much to enhance the physical and emotional strength of its members and, thus, perhaps make a vital contribution to national welfare.

Continuing Education

The home is the most important seat of learning for the young child. As we grow older, we are exposed to many other influences which add to both our fund of knowledge and our attitude toward learning. When a couple marries, they may have both completed only eight grades of formal schooling, or they may both have doctor's degrees in economics, psychology, medicine, or one of many other fields of knowledge. There seems to be little correlation between years of formal schooling and our knowledge and insight into human personality and our ability to manage human relationships successfully. What elements of human capacity are the essential ones, to insure successful marriages and successful family relationships, we do not definitely know. In spite of this, it is important that every couple use their intelligence to the end that they are continually learning and educating themselves in matters pertaining to the management of their family affairs. In many matters of home management there is little excuse for failure due to ignorance, although the acquiring of skill is a matter of practice. One need not necessarily take a course in school to be up to date with the amount of good material available in current magazines, newspapers, and books. The increasing and continuous desire to apply the contributions of science and the arts to our personal problems and development is the all-important factor in the ongoing of successful living.

Religion

Religion is important to everyone because we all feel ourselves a part of the universe and are affected by and influence the world in which we live.

"No man is an Iland, intire of it selfe; every man is a peace of the continent; a part of the maine; if a Clod bee washed away by the Sea, Europe is the lesse, as well as if a Promontorie were, as well as if a Mannor of thy friends or of thine owne were; any man's death diminishes me, because I am involved in Mankinde; And therefore never send to know for whom the bell tolls; It tolls for thee." (19)

Many of us find ourselves, however, in conflict with our family over religious practices. Religion may become for some a symbol of restricted social and recreational life. We all ponder at one time or another the question of our origin and our destiny as well as our individual relation to the universe. We need religious education at home and at the church of our choice to help educate and give us a sense of security with regard to these important matters. Here, as well as in food habit training, it is necessary for parents to do more than say to us, "Do as I say, but not as I do."

As we get older, we pass through a stage of conflict between the religious beliefs we have been taught and our family's beliefs, as well as the beliefs of others, and the ideas of science and philosophy with which we come to grips, particularly in college. It appears that many traditional religious beliefs are uprooted by the study of science in college, and the individual is unable afterward to reintegrate his thinking in terms of newly acquired points of view, or to achieve for himself a new philosophy of life in terms of modern science and a newer conception of the universe.

The impact of the more critical and objective view fostered by institutions of higher learning seems to cause many to question for the first time the traditional teachings of the church.

At maturity, certain ones of us avoid making any very definite decision about our religious philosophy. Some of us accept our earlier pattern of religious belief and practice, although with qualms. Others reject this early pattern with obvious feelings of guilt. Of these last, some fail to arrive at any satisfactory substitute for this early pattern, while a few work out a new philosophy of life.

When one marries, this issue has to be met squarely, for, as one's children begin to grow up and questions of the religious practices they wish to observe arise, they serve to renew one's confusion over religious beliefs and to bring the problem into focus again, if these matters have not been settled.

The child's revolt is often not so much against the idea or belief itself as against the method used in pressing it upon him. He needs the insight gained through experience as much as the intellectual knowledge gained through being told. In religious matters the family, as well as the child, labors under the difficulty of living in a rapidly changing world where the values held important by society are less well defined and less generally accepted than formerly and where even the church is finding it necessary to redefine and restate some of its interpretations of the meaning and function of religion in the light of modern conditions.

Modern research seems to indicate that some forms of religious philosophy tend to act as a stabilizing influence in the life of the individual and family. The rejection of basic religious principles (not controversial theological and doctrinal issues) is more often due to the lack of a capacity on the part of the individual to grasp its significance in historical perspective in relation to the ongoing of our culture, its conplementary relationship to the discoveries of science, its basically constructive philosophy of the worth and importance of human personality, and its emphasis upon democratic social relationships, than to any fundamental quarrel with those principles themselves.

CHAPTER XIV

THE COMING OF CHILDREN

Becoming pregnant is a condition which every young bride looks forward to, with both joy and anticipation as well as with a certain amount of fear and anxiety. It is a completely new experience for both husband and wife. And, like all new experiences, we wonder how we will get along. Will the pregnancy be a successful one? Will the baby be normal? Will it be a boy or girl? What will it cost? These are just a few of the questions which the bride, pregnant for the first time, asks herself.

But before these questions are answered, there are two others which newly married couples are pondering today. First, should they have a child now or wait until they are economically better off or more settled in their plans? Second, if they decide to have a baby, how will the wife know when she is pregnant, what should she do if she is, and how should she arrange her affairs if she has an outside job?

Should We Have Babies?

In normal times, most young couples do not debate this question. They usually want babies. They may not want them the first year of marriage nor want ten or twelve, but they want some. And, in normal times, the question of when to have them and how many to have is not a debatable question if you are a good Catholic. But for non-Catholics many couples prefer to devote the first year or two to becoming well adjusted to each other and established in their new mode of life, before undertaking pregnancy and child rearing. The non-Catholic may also choose to space his children, rather than leave pregnancy entirely to chance. In so doing, he may consult a reputable physician for sound contraceptive advice, whereas the Catholic couple will consult a good Catholic physician concerning the use of the rhythm method which is approved by the church.

Young women seem to want a child, preferring to face childbirth while young. This may or may not be a good motive for having children, but the motive is certainly as valid as the one often used for not having children, that is, until the couple are economically well established.

Young men seem to feel there is time and that to wait until they are better established professionally is preferable. They say they can have them then, and that in this way the young woman is relieved of the economic risks involved.

Certainly where pregnancy is decided upon, the child should be wanted by both father and mother, and there should be some consideration given to the health of the parents, the conditions under which the couple or wife will live if the husband is away, and the financial means of support. While there are day care centers for children of mothers working in defense plants, the day care plan is not an adequate substitute for the home and the mother. Children should not be parked and reclaimed every day like a satchel. To have a child may be a great satisfaction to a wife or husband, but the responsibility for his welfare does not end, but begins, there. It is not society's job to look after your children for you. It is your job. Therefore, the decision to have children, and the responsibility for them if they arrive, are personal problems. These matters should be taken into account before marriage and before chances which lead to pregnancy are taken. But support, proper care, and mother contact are important.

Pregnancy is a family affair. The husband is just as definitely affected as the wife. Even though fathers do not contribute as much constant care to the children's development, they should begin early to assume a father's part.

During pregnancy, the routine of the marriage is somewhat changed. The prospective mother may not feel like being as active in certain athletic and social ways as previously. Sex relations will be interrupted for a couple of months and greatly reduced when carried on during the middle months of pregnancy. The woman may be more concerned with herself and preparation for the arrival of the new baby than the father. If the father is away, there will be times of great loneliness for each other, particularly as the time of delivery approaches.

Considerations Before Pregnancy

* Before having children every couple should, *first*, be in the best possible health. An examination by a physician should check one's present condition and readiness for undertaking the strain of childbearing, as well as any hereditary conditions which might affect the pregnancy. Even though most couples wish to have children, there are often undisclosed fears and anxieties about pregnancy that should be discussed and cleared up in so far as possible.

The *second* thing which will affect the child is the attitude of husband, wife, relatives, and friends toward pregnancy. These attitudes may center around the fear of the added responsibility of children on the part of the husband, that other children will entail too much additional expense, as well as strain, on the mother, or that a child will interrupt and interfere with the career of the wife. Or the wife, particularly, may have certain feelings of embarrassment about the condition of pregnancy, its effect upon her social life and marital relations with her husband, or she may feel insecure because she is lacking knowledge of what pregnancy is like and what to expect from it.

Third, there are social and environmental factors also to be taken into consideration. There are certain changes in marital life during pregnancy. One's normal recreation and leisure time pursuits need not be greatly interrupted. The advice of one's obstetrician should be followed, because every individual must be prescribed for in terms of her own situation.

Fourth, problems may arise in actual home management. If it is the first child, it may be necessary to alter living arrangements, particularly sleeping arrangements, for a time, and help will be needed by the new mother from other members of the family. There will be interruptions in adult routines to meet the demands of the new member of the family. Occasional household help will be desirable for cleaning, laundry, and heavy work for a period of months.

Fifth, the added cost of having and caring for a baby is greatly overestimated by many couples, who complain that they cannot afford to have children. Ordinarily, the actual cost of doctor's care and confinement in a good hospital for a week can be found to meet the income of practically all economic classes. During World War II the difficult problem was to get hospital and obstetrical care at any price. An estimate of costs involved in pregnancy and hospital or home care will vary according to your income and depending upon services received. The cost of maintenance after the child is born varies, depending upon whether the child is breast fed, as it ordinarily should be, given expensive artificial foods and taken to the most expensive or a less expensive pediatrician. The place of residence as well as the general cost of living will be factors in both of these last items.

What to Learn about Reproduction and Childbearing

The average couple could well afford to know more than they do about what is involved in the entire reproductive process, especially if they have not had a premarital examination and consultation which included this. A good time to acquire this knowledge is when pregnancy is contemplated. In Chapter IX the discussion of sex was primarily concerned with the matter of adjustment on sex matters between husband and wife. Here we shall discuss briefly only those additional matters pertinent to pregnancy.

Menstruation and Pregnancy

Each month a female egg ripens in the ovaries and is expelled. It passes down the ovi-duct or Fallopian tube. This occurs, as far as is known, sometime between the end of one and beginning of the next menstrual period. Throughout this span of time, which may vary from twenty to forty days, but is usually from twenty-five to thirty days in most women, if the ova reaches the uterus without having been fertilized, the cell lining of the uterus, which has been built up to receive a fertilized ova, begins to deteriorate and, at the beginning of the time for the next menstrual period, is passed off, constituting, with the unfertilized egg, the menstrual flow. If the egg has become fertile, it begins to grow and is about the size of the end of a pin when it reaches the uterus. Here it becomes attached or implanted in the lining of the uterine wall and begins to grow. This new life cell develops its own protective layers of surrounding covering, called the amniotic sac, the chorion and decidua. Where the new life cell is attached to the wall lining of the uterus there develops a mass of rootlets or branching placenta blood vessels, which are attached to the child by the umbilical cord. Through this connection the child receives his nutriment during the period of pregnancy. There is no direct connection between the fetal and maternal blood vessels. The exchange of nutritive and waste materials is carried on by the process of osmosis between these two sets of capillaries.

This entire mass of material which provides attachment, protection, and nutrition for the growing fetus is called the placenta.

The baby grows for approximately 280 days in its uterine home and is then born through the cervical opening of the uterus and the vaginal or birth canal. After birth occurs, the entire placenta or after-birth, as it is called, is expelled.

Questions about Pregnancy

One of the first things one wishes to know is the signs of pregnancy. While many people may miss an occasional menstrual period, if a woman of childbearing age has had sexual intercourse and stops menstruating, pregnancy must be suspected. This is the most characteristic early sign that conception has taken place. Shortly following the first omitted menstrual period there may occur slight nausea on arising in the morning. Other later signs are tenderness around the nipples and enlargement of the breasts, a darkening of aureola around the nipple, and a desire to urinate more frequently. If you have any one or a combination of these signs, the best practice is to consult a good obstetrician, a doctor whose specialty is caring for women during pregnancy and delivery of the child. He will make a certain test which will be a fairly accurate answer to your question, if an early diagnosis of pregnancy is desired. This test can be made with a high degree of reliability about two weeks after missing your first menstrual period. For the average, healthy woman, pregnancy is not a great hardship, but many times her general health may be improved. The best way to insure a normal delivery is to go to a doctor when you think you are pregnant and remain under his care throughout the nine months' period. He will examine you each month, advise you as to diet, rest, exercises, etc., and if you follow his advice, you will have little to fear.

There is no way of telling whether your child will be a boy or a girl. Be glad whichever it is and expect your child to be as normal as most children are at birth. There are many complex growth processes which take place from the time of conception until a baby is born, and the result cannot be predicted. Most children are born normal, healthy youngsters. When they are not, it is not usually a reflection upon the parent but just one of those deviations in biological development which cannot be predicted or helped.

The actual sign that the time for delivery is near is the settling down of the child in the pelvis. The lower part of the abdomen becomes larger, the woman breathes more easily, may have a return of constipation and frequent urination, and she may, usually from one to four weeks before actual labor, begin to feel slight labor pains. Then from twenty-four to forty-eight hours before actual birth, true labor begins, and the birth is completed. The actual dilation of the uterus and other pelvic parts may take from twelve to twenty-four hours, at the end of which the soft amniotic sac or bag of water breaks. The second stage of expulsion may last from a few minutes to an hour or longer. After a brief rest, the uterus contracts vigorously and expels the placenta. With the exception of pains due to the contraction of the uterus, this concludes the birth process. Sometimes the whole birth process takes a much shorter time.

The Baby's First Year

The art of child rearing and training is something to be learned. Love alone will not teach the mother the principles of good physical care and proper feeding of her child. Love will not tell the mother how to instill proper habits and attitudes in the child. These can only be done when one studies how best to do them and works diligently at the task. Some of the simple rules to follow are:

1. Register the child's birth and get a copy of the birth certificate.
2. Have a doctor examine him at frequent intervals and advise you as to proper diet and feeding.
3. Nurse your baby, if possible, and give him plenty of cuddling and affection.
4. See that his surroundings are healthful and free from possible sources of infection.
5. Keep him clean and give him plenty of fresh air, sunshine, and exercise.
6. Have a schedule for him based upon a rhythm of his own which you can learn after a little careful observation.
7. Remember, babies are human beings, not playthings. Each one is different from the other in many ways.
8. Raising children requires both father and mother for best results. Both should know what their children are

like, what they need, and how to guide their development. This knowledge by both parents eliminates
much conflict between parents over training methods
and is better for the child.

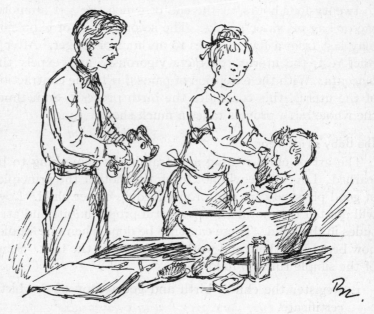

One of the first principles of good child management is to
know your child and to know what to expect of him at different stages of growth. Since children are different at birth,
one should study each child separately and try to work out
a plan for his development in terms of the kind of baby he
is. Remember, learning begins the first hour after birth
and continues throughout his life. His education is now up
to the parents. The first bit of knowledge to acquire is what
to expect of him in physical growth the first year — how
fast and how much he grows.

He will weigh anywhere from 5 to 10 pounds at birth and
will have reached approximately 20 pounds by one year.
His weight will depend upon the size of his parents, the
type of body build he has inherited, and his sex, since boy
babies are a little heavier than girls. He will not be able to

see very much soon after birth. His ability to see and attend to things in his environment increases until, by one year, he is able to see most minute objects. Unlike sight, his hearing is fully developed at birth. While both abilities to taste and smell are pretty well developed at birth, these senses become very acute after a few months. His sense of feeling is well developed at birth, but it is not until he becomes older that he can differentiate between discomforts that are due to various causes. At birth, when lying face down, he can raise his head momentarily but cannot hold it up, whereas, when lying on his back, he cannot raise it at all. He begins to show some interest in sitting up and rolling over at four or five months of age and at seven or eight months may be able to sit alone. He cannot usually walk before a year, although this varies greatly. The child should not be urged to walk. He will walk just as soon as he is ready and able.

He will grasp a finger or rod at birth but will not be able to pick up an object with his thumb and forefinger until toward the end of his first year.

He only cries at first, then in a few weeks coos. It is not until the end of the first year or during the second year that he begins to imitate sounds he hears and adds a few real words to his "Ah-ing" vocabulary.

The infant's learning results, like other people's, through his successes and failures and the experiences which bring satisfaction or dissatisfaction. By the time he is three or four months old, he has learned to focus and coordinate his eyes, pull or push his feet or hands with force and coordination, and by six or eight months is able to move about on the floor by hitching himself along on his stomach. His social development commences the first few months. He begins to learn about people from his contacts with his own family, relatives, and admiring friends. Too much attention may be a bad thing for him, and one should, by the time he is a year old, not talk about him in his presence. Becoming the center of attention constantly is not good for him. It gives him the unfortunate feeling that the entire world revolves around him, and this may lead to difficult problems at four, eight, or sixteen years of age.

The Child and His Family

It has been said that husbands and wives are primary and children are secondary in family life. This seems to be true, as far as training and development are concerned. The parents come first — they decide to have a child — and what he is at birth and how he is cared for and trained is the result of what parents do to, for, and with him. He learns what we teach him, for good or ill, through our conscious and often subtle and unconscious relationship with him. It may safely be said that the family is responsible for everything of importance that is done to the child. But the coming of a first, second, or third child into a family also effects important changes in the relationships in that family.

For a year or more husband and wife have engaged in unrestricted pleasures of their own. They may have, if the first child does not arrive for several years, established for themselves patterns of personal and social relationships which have become both satisfying and fixed. The coming of a baby upsets this balance, and each is forced either to reject the child or, as is true in the great majority of cases, readjust their living pattern to a new scheme of things. The mother has her time, energy, and attention divided between a husband, her house, and her new, helpless infant. As a result, both housekeeping and husband may suffer some neglect, as compared to former days. This rearrangement of human relationships into a new balance requires insight on the part of each into what is happening and an effort to work out a new arrangement which allows the husband, the new baby, the wife, and the home their share of attention and satisfaction. If this were the end of shifting relationships it would be a relatively simple adjustment. But in many families a second child is born a year or two later. Again the focus of attention is drawn away from husband-wife relationships, the house, and baby number one, and is centered on baby number two. The same new rearranging of relationships has to be worked out again. This time the wife has more physical burdens to look after which sap her strength and emotions. Baby number one may notice that he no longer is the center of attention and begin doing many things he never did before, to get attention. There arises for the parents the new problem of how to manage two children so as to reduce the amount of jealousy between them for both the love and attention of mother and father and the material things of life, along with the usual questions of care, training and management, household duties, social and recreational activities, and so on.

Arising out of these new, shifting realignments of human relationships in the family, associated with the coming of children, are the myriad of problems of child care and training which will last, changing for each child according to his own characteristics and sex, as he grows to maturity. This child rearing period in the average family with only two children is approximately a twenty to twenty-five year job.

Looking at the coming of a child into the family a little more specifically, we may conclude that, *first*, he may become the center and source of great joy and happiness. He will add to the happiness and enhance the love of a couple who are in love. He will not be the cure for any couple's conflicts and grievances toward each other. A family about to go on the rocks should work out their adjustment first and not think that having a baby will solve their problems.

Second, he will upset the household routine of the family, and it will be necessary for father and mother to rearrange their accustomed way of life somewhat to allow for three persons instead of two.

Third, he may become the sole object of the parents' attention to the extent that they neglect their own relationship with each other, or he may become the sole object of the mother's time and energy to such a degree that she forgets she has a husband and fails in her role as a wife. This has been the basic cause of the beginning of many estrangements between husband and wife.

Fourth, he may interfere with the amount of social life a couple has become accustomed to if they cannot afford a maid, occasional help, or have a nearby relative stay with the youngster while they go out.

Fifth, he may cause much irritation and conflict between husband and wife because they each have different ideas of how he should be raised. Fathers are usually less well informed on good modern methods of child care and training than modern mothers.

Sixth, he may be the apple of his grandmother's or grandfather's eye and thus cause conflict between mother and her own or her husband's mother over how he should be cared for.

Seventh, he may, because he is learning by experience with things and people, be the source of annoyance to parents who are overly meticulous about their home and the things in it. It is better to move expensive vases and the like out of the way and let a chair or rug be worn out, than to put the baby in a cage.

Eighth, he will no doubt cause the mother more work and thus add to her physical and emotional fatigue. It is well for the mother to have a plan and learn to organize her household so that she can have time for rest and relaxation. She needs some of her emotional energy for her husband, friends, and outside interests.

Ninth, he will cost something. This may necessitate some sacrifices on the part of the parents.

Tenth, when the second or third child arrives, as has been previously pointed out, all of the above mentioned items will still be important and, in addition, a rebalancing of the household will have to be planned. There will arise the new problem of giving attention, affection, and a sense of security and acceptance to each child as well as a proportionate share of the material things which the family can afford. Parents have to be very careful in how they show differences in their feelings toward and about each child. It is so easy to make a child feel rejected, unwanted, or inferior.

On the other hand, the coming of children into the family may bring, *one*, a hope for realization through the child of the desires and ambitions which the parents were not able to enjoy or achieve in their own lives. This can be a great source of satisfaction if the fulfillment comes as a result of what the child can accomplish in terms of his own abilities, interests, and opportunities, but it may be crippling to the child if he is forced into activities and training unsuited to his abilities and interests in order to satisfy a father who was disappointed in not being able to be an engineer or a mother who could not follow a musical career; *two*, a sense of fulfillment into the lives of the couple; *three*, a sense of achievement and an added incentive; *four*, an element of solidarity; *five*, a challenge and opportunity to produce for themselves and society an individual who will be a credit to himself, his parents, and in what he contributes to the world; and, *six*, a lot of fun in watching and guiding his growth from infancy, through early childhood, into adolescence, and on to maturity and marriage.

Part IV

The Family and Democratic Society

Without respect for personality and the human rights of others, without understanding of children, their basic needs and guidance, without cooperatively planned family life which produces patterns of friendliness instead of hostility, there can be no democracy anywhere.

Robert G. Foster

CHAPTER XV

SUCCESS OR FAILURE IN FAMILY DEVELOPMENT

For years, now, we have been accumulating data on the physical, mental, and social growth and development of children. We know from the studies of Gesell and others pretty accurately what to expect in the normal growth and development of children of both sexes from birth through the preschool years. These norms of development are an invaluable basis for understanding child behavior. Prior to the advent of child research centers, our knowledge about children was theoretical, came from cross-sectional studies or from delinquents. While it is possible to learn something about the functioning of human beings by studying failures, one cannot deduce the principles of success from the study of failure alone. One of the most practical bits of advice ever given to students is recorded in the preface to George L. Warren's book on *Farm Management*. He says that if one wants to improve agriculture, one must go out and discover how successful farmers are managing their farms and then teach the unsuccessful ones their methods. His emphasis is on the study of the factors which contribute to success.

In considering success or failure in marriage from a personal point of view, there are three factors to be considered. First, the family, like individuals, passes through similar stages of development from infancy to old age. Second, like the individual, the family must have a chance to fulfill its function at each stage of development, discard its outlived function, and proceed to its new responsibility in the next succeeding stage better prepared to meet it successfully.

For example, the first stage of establishment of the family should lead to the development of those sentiments of affection and solidarity which prepare for the mutual acceptance of the child bearing and rearing stage and not produce adult relationships which resist the transition from this first to the second stage in family progression. Third, success or failure must be evaluated in terms of the expected role and function of each member of the family.

Phases of Family Development

One, the period of the establishment of the family is that time from the day of the marriage until the arrival of the first child. It is the period when the adult husband-wife relationships are dominant, and the couple are working out their plan and philosophy of family procedure. Characteristics of this period vary, but in normal times, in general, the income is often low, current expenses need not be great, health is usually good, and housing needs are simple. There is opportunity in most cases for some savings in the form of insurance, to make the first payment on a home, and other contemplated future necessities. If both the husband and wife are working, this is doubly possible if their wants for luxury goods are not excessive. If not, the man is usually getting established in his job, learning what it means to be a husband, and the wife is learning both the meaning of being a wife and how to manage a household.

The personal relationships and the evolving of a philosophy of family life are paramount. The marriage has the potential possibility of becoming a male dominant one, a female dominant one, a parentally dominated one, or one of a real partnership. The couple, like the new born infant, have first to become acquainted with their new status and relationship, how to see, hear, think, talk, and feel the things which confront them as man and wife. Theirs is no longer a single, but a paired, relationship, although each party to a marriage must give the other freedom for the development of his own individuality.

Two, the next stage in the course of family development consists of the child rearing periods. This actually should be considered in several sub-periods, the first of which is (a) the preschool period. The couple can no longer, as is the case of the infant, be solely concerned with its own pleasures per se. They must begin growing up, becoming more self-sufficient and able to meet the increasing complexities of life.

The first important factor to consider is the way in which the first pregnancy and arrival of the first child changes the concerns, problems, and planning of husband and wife. Their daily routine has to be altered, their activities changed in some respects, there are new things to be learned and new expectant joys ahead. Whereas there are extra costs attendant upon childbearing, both medical and household, there are also possibilities of increased income for the husband as he becomes better established in his vocation.

(b) As the first child reaches school age and another has been added to the family, the balance in the family relationships is again complicated. The second and third arrivals increase the work and responsibility of the mother and demand that both parents give serious thought, if they have not already done so, to their interrelation to the children and the children's growing needs and relationships to each other. There is increasing need for managerial ability on the part of the homemaker and for adapting the housing arrangements to the needs of a larger family. There is continuing increase in current expenses, along with possible increases in income as the man grows more experienced and useful in his job. Laundry, cleaning, and repair costs will be heavy.

(c) By the time the first child reaches the age of budding adolescence, parent-child relationships are of primary importance, and presumably husband-wife relationships have been adjusted to meet their needs as adults and those of their children. This is the beginning of a long stretch of heavy expense. The social life of the older children takes on added significance, and there may be an accentuation of conflict of the generations. The job of parenthood is at its peak throughout this period. There may be in the home children ranging in age from preschool to adolescence, some boys, some girls, each a different personality and with different developmental characteristics, interests, and needs.

(d) The next and last stage in this long child rearing period is one of the most critical for both parent and child. It brings to the fore the test of the skill with which the parents have done their job well. It is the time of freeing the child from dependence on his family and the parent from dominance over the child. Again, the adults may need to readjust their personal relationships both to more mutual enjoyments together and independent, personal participation in community affairs. It will be the time of middle age, with its own health problems peculiar to the late forties and early fifties. For the wife, menopause will be in the offing and, for the man, a gradual readjustment of his strenuous activities. The ability to utilize one's leisure time is increasingly important, especially for women, since no longer is the responsibility for children there to occupy her time. This period of middle life brings with it both retrospect and prospect. There lies ahead a goodly span of years in which the husband and wife may be free to develop many of the most interesting and satisfying activities of their married lives.

Three, the period of recovery begins as the first child goes out into the world on his own and continues to take on significance as each succeeding child goes out into the world market for which he has been preparing these many years. The price he will bring depends upon the heritage we have given him and the skill with which he has been helped to grow and develop into a self-sufficient, mature individual. After the long period of high expense, this period of recovery, when the furniture is worn out, the house is too big and savings are used up, allows for some time to recuperate before active retirement is reached.

Four, approaching old age is only intolerable to the young who have a life to build. One's wants are much fewer, expenses are at a minimum, and there is time to follow as many other interests as one is able and cares to. Due to possible illness, help is often needed, and one must always face the problem of living one's old age alone or with one's children. Realistically, in view of the fact that married women outlive their husbands, there is the desirability of insurance or other protection, so that the wife, now a grandmother, can live her life economically independent of her children. This cannot always be done, and it falls to the children to assume the responsibility for her care or that of the father if he outlives the mother. One of the most unfair of family relationships is the shrinking from responsibility for aging parents by several children, leaving one child to bear the burden and make all the sacrifice. Social security and old age pensions will add materially to the retirement of many older people, but family plans should take into account one's responsibility for caring for one's parents.

The problem of economic support is by no means the only one which confronts us as we reach old age. There are, first, the anxieties about becoming old and facing death. Some satisfactory life philosophy and the maintenance of cultural interests and social contacts is the best solution to the problem. Then there is the psychological problem of lonesomeness and a sense of worthlessness. The older person is often ignored and shunted about by the family and made to feel his insignificance and uselessness. In large measure, we should begin preparing for retirement and old age in our youth. This may be done by equipping ourselves with a wide variety of interests and hobbies and taking active part in church, school, and other community affairs.

Criteria of Success

In light of the foregoing discussion, let us consider certain criteria for evaluating successful family development and relationships.

The test of time has long been one criterion of whether a marriage was a success or failure. That is, how long did

the marriage last. This alone is not all. In addition to sur-
viving, it must be charged with a high quality of domestic
relationships between family members. This is less objective
than the criterion of time, but possible of some degree of
objectivity. There can be degrees, ranging from low to high,
of the quality of domestic relations.

It would seem that quality in human relationships is a
more important criterion of success than quantity or the
amount of time a couple lived together. If we look at any
family in terms of its development, it appears that the quality
of husband-wife relationships tends to remain high the first
few months or years and then tends to decline, whereas
their qualitative relationships toward their children tend to
increase as somewhat of a substitute for their own. On the
other hand, one partner may function very adequately as a
husband, or father, or provider but only at a high level of
effectiveness in one of these. Since family relationships are
personal relationships, the following criteria for success or
failure, applicable to any single stage of development or to
the entire course of the family's existence, might serve as a
practical device for judging the extent to which a family was
operating at a high or low level of effectiveness.

These criteria have to be amplified to delineate those
attributes that are usually associated with each responsibility. The qualities of a good mother may not always be
combined with those of a good wife, and the vocational success of the husband may often interfere with his contribution
as a husband or father. Take each of these items and work
out, to your own satisfaction or for class discussion, the
attributes of a good wife, father, homemaker, child management program. Pick out a family of your acquaintance and
see if you can first describe and then rate it in terms of the
above criteria. It will become clear that a person who is a
good wife for one man may not be for another, and that much
of the formulae for criteria must be considered in a relative
sense, and standards of adequacy of performance set up with
a wide degree of latitude.

CRITERIA FOR JUDGING FAMILY SUCCESS

1. To what extent does the woman function at a high degree of effectiveness:

    a. As a wife.
    b. As a mother.
    c. As a homemaker.
    d. As a person.

2. To what extent does the man function at a high degree of effectiveness:

    a. As a husband.
    b. As a father.
    c. As a homemaker.
    d. As a provider.
    e. As a person.

3. To what extent do the children function at a high degree of effectiveness as they pass through each stage of their development:

    a. In their physical growth.
    b. In their educational advancement.
    c. In their social development.
    d. In their emotional maturity.
    e. In their philosophy of life.
    f. In their economic self-sufficiency.
    g. In their intellectual growth.
    h. In their relationship with the family.
    i. In their relationship with their own and the opposite sex.
    j. In their relationship to the community.
    k. In their ability to utilize their leisure.

4. To what extent does the family maintain for itself and give status to the children:

    a. Through its own position in the community.
    b. Through its relationship to the social, educational, religious, and civic life of the community.

Masculine and Feminine Roles

From the time we are children, we hear such terms as "sissy" applied to boys or "tom-boy" applied to girls who are acting differently from their expected cultural pattern. A boy in our culture is supposed, or expected to be, boisterous, wild, rough, and independent, and he plays baseball, football, cops and robbers and other rough games. He has more freedom to forage about the neighborhood than his sister of the same age, is less protected and has, in a sense, more status in the family than girls. A girl, on the other hand, is expected to be more refined, less boisterous, plays house and with dolls, and never engages in rough and tumble sports. She is more carefully supervised and less free to explore the community on her own. These are supposed to be feminine characteristics. Thus, when a boy shows an interest in domestic things or a girl in boys' rough sports, each is atypical and is called a "sissy" or a "tom-boy."

These traditional roles or expected ways of behaving carry over into our adult life and, along with other traditional ways, constitute the difference in attitude and behavior of each sex toward the other. Not only do we acquire these general patterns of behavior, but we observe relationships outside our respective homes which give us convictions as to how a husband or wife should behave toward each other, how mothers and fathers differ in their relationship to children, and how the affairs of the family are managed. These conceptions we bring to marriage with us, and we tend to expect our partner to operate according to our preconceived notion when he may have acquired an entirely different set of ideas about his role in the family.

Assuming, as we have said, that what is suitable to one person may not be for another, what in general is the man's relationship to his family?

The Man in the Family

As a husband, a man's predominant interest and paramount loyalty is to his wife. He supplies personal and social companionship for her, is considerate of her feelings and needs, tries to understand and assist her with her problems, and tries to satisfy her needs for sex expression as a good lover and faithful husband.

As a father, a man is jointly responsible for the guidance and rearing of the children. While the mother may assume the major responsibility in this regard, the father will plan jointly with her on matters of training, support the mother's acts, and take a share in the actual social development of the children at different periods in their development. Boys and girls both need fathers, especially so at certain times in their development. The father will try to understand his children's needs and attempt to supply them as best he can.

As a homemaker, the man's role is usually a minor one as far as actual housekeeping is concerned. The division of labor between husband and wife as to household responsibilities is an individual matter and varies greatly. There is, however, a cooperating responsibility which it is important that he assume, as well as contributing to the social, recreational, and spiritual quality of the relationship.

As a provider, society expects him to be effective and successful. It is his major role and responsibility, regardless of whether his wife is gainfully employed or not. While most men prefer that their wives do not undertake an outside gainful job, except in cases of necessity, there is today a much higher percentage of married women working than ever before. Jobs are plentiful, wages are good, and opportunities for women are greater than in previous years.

As a person, we all must try to function at a high level of maturity. Whatever our responsibilities as husband, wife, father, mother, or other, we still are unique personalities in our own right and need a certain amount of independent, free opportunity for personal expression. This maintenance of our personality apart from any other must be carried out, however, in terms of mutual confidence and support of each other. Our possessiveness and jealousy can only form the basis of conflict in any human relationship.

The Woman in the Family

As a wife, the woman's role in the family is similar to that of the husband. She is a companion, one who enjoys her physical relationship with her husband, creates a relationship of social friendliness and mutual trust and confidence in all of their relationships. Just as it is the husband's role to give his wife a sense of importance of status in connection with her family responsibilities, so it is the wife's role to give her husband support, encouragement, and sympathy as his mood may demand.

As a mother, the woman has a more demanding task than the man. She carries the child during pregnancy and is tied down to the routine of feeding and care of the infant. Her role demands that she study children, know how to feed, care for, and handle them. This is less expected of fathers but desirable if they assume part of this responsibility. When a woman becomes a mother she needs to remember that she has a husband and has certain obligations as a wife as well as a mother. The husband needs to understand what the burden of motherhood adds to his wife's work and responsibility and adjust his demands accordingly, while at the same time trying to cooperate in reducing the inevitable additional work of parenthood.

As a homemaker, the woman is expected by her husband and by society to be able to manage the affairs of the household efficiently, whether she does the work herself or hires servants to do it. Her role in this regard involves a knowledge of foods and nutrition, economical buying, the execution of household routines, and the creation of a condition and an atmosphere of comfort, ease, and friendliness. Home management is her business, as is gainful employment her husband's. The acquiring of new knowledge and skills to create a wholesome and happy home atmosphere is her main task, just as it is her husband's task to increase his efficiency and successfulness in his vocation. For some, this comes more easily than for others. Many young women have acquired favorable attitudes, knowledge, and skill in homemaking activities throughout the course of development, whereas others start at scratch, so to speak, and have many new things to learn and skills to acquire.

As a person in her own right, every woman who marries

needs to maintain interests which are peculiarly her own and which may not in any way be family interests or joint interests with other members of the family. The job of being a wife, mother, and homemaker are first in terms of responsibility, but those women who have other outside interests seem to bring much to their family life from those contacts and seem to find them useful places to which to turn in times of crisis.

Children in the Family

A family is successful when it fulfills its functions to the satisfactions of husband and wife and the expectancy of the culture in which it exists. The bearing and rearing of children is both a personal satisfaction to married couples and a social contribution to society. Measures of our success lie in the degree to which we produce and rear healthy children, give them a good education, direct their lives in such a way that they achieve a reasonable degree of social, emotional, and intellectual maturity, help them acquire a philosophy of life as a guide in meeting life's problems successfully, enable them to be economically self-sufficient, enable them to establish good relationships with the opposite sex and leave their own family at the time of marriage, help them acquire social habits which insure good mental health, and enable them to live within the conventions of the community.

The Family and Society

The family should strive to attain a respectable place in the community, thus giving children a feeling of status and of being proud of their own family in particular and of the worthwhileness of family life in general.

In addition, that family is more successful which relates itself with, and thereby also introduces its children to, the important institutions of the community, such as those which foster wholesome social and recreational activities and entertainment, good educational advantages, normal religious development, and efficient civic services.

When One Has Problems

It is proper for individuals to be self-sufficient and solve their own problems, but with family problems, just as with medical ones, the individual cannot always diagnose his own case and prescribe the necessary treatment.

There is need for professional counsel. Clinical psychologists, ministers, physicians, teachers, social workers, public health nurses, youth leaders, and marriage counselors are available in most large centers and some smaller ones. Increasingly, each profession is supplementing its training, so that the younger men and women graduating are more competent to advise on family matters than they may have been a generation ago. The first advice, when problems arise that you seem unable to solve, is to seek out the best person you can find in your locality. There are some things, however, that everyone should know about these counselors, which may make it easier to seek their advice.

What Good Counselors Do Not Do

They do not order you to do or forbid you doing what you want to do. They do not ask you to sign any pledges or make any promises to them. They do not pat you on the back and tell you there is nothing the matter and to forget your symptoms. They will not give you specific advice as to what they think you should or should not do. They will not condemn, but will try to understand and help you.

What a Good Counselor Will Try To Do

He will be sympathetic and will try to understand your situation. He will try to help you see your problem in clear perspective. He will try to help you decide what you wish to do about the problem. He will try to help you make decisions when alternative choices are involved. He will try to help you in such a way that you can not only solve your present problem but be able to meet future problems more adequately. He will probably want to see you several times, depending upon the nature of your problems. He will be a person in whom you can confide and have no fear that he will discuss your problem with others. He will keep your ideals and goals in mind at all times. He will try to help you understand the difference between what are symptomatic problems and those which are basic. He will try to help you recognize that you are the one who, throughout and as a result of the counseling process, will work out your own problem in terms of your ideals, goals, and according to your own set of values. He will allow you to take as much time as is needed to arrive at a sound answer for you and will not continue the appointments beyond necessary limits. He will help you, where possible, or find for you a place where you can get help, if he is not the person to deal with your problem.

There are no problems, however trivial they may seem to us, that should not be faced and worked on as soon as possible. Many individuals are afraid to try to solve their problem, because they fear possible fault on their part and that, beyond their own sense of guilt, the counselor or partner, if married, will condemn them. The straightforward, honest couple talk about their differences and arrive at a solution of them. They learn to compromise and reach a decision, whereas many other couples avoid discussing little problems, letting them smoulder until they become crises. It is never a mistake to admit that one is sorry or has been wrong in what he has done. The person who can admit to himself that he needs help and seeks it, from his spouse or a counselor, is ready to be helped and in all likelihood will get results.

CHAPTER XVI

CRISES AND HUMAN RELATIONSHIPS

The Universality of Crises

Life brings change. Change brings with it the inevitable necessity for making adjustments. Many of them, however, begin with little situations which in and of themselves may not be major calamities, but which become crises both because of their persistence and because of the nature of the emotional stability of the individuals who have to meet the problem. Thus, while any trivial situation might become a crisis in the life of an individual, the degree to which it is critical depends largely upon the extent to which he has acquired a personality capable of facing and resolving difficulties.

Kinds of Crises

There are two major kinds of crises which confront families. The one type is that experienced by everyone and includes loss of economic support, death, severe and prolonged illness, and the like. The other type involves social stigmas of various kinds, celibacy, and the major social calamities such as war and economic inflation and depression.

Usual and Expected Crises

Loss of economic support is faced by the majority of couples in the course of their married life. The occasion may be due to conditions beyond an individual's control, such as the severe and prolonged depression which occurred from 1933 to 1936, or it may be related to an accident or prolonged illness. Such conditions are met by different families in different ways. Some go on governmental or social relief or devote their every effort to finding some way of supplementing the family income after their unemployment compensation ends; others become morose, irritable, and frustrated to the point where they are the cause of added strain and conflict between themselves and other family members; and others seek a divorce, desert their families, and, in some cases, commit suicide. Under conditions of prolonged strain such as this it is usually the strong personalities who meet the situation successfully and the weaker ones who have the most difficulty.

I recall two families who, during the depression of 1933, met the crisis in very different ways. One family, consisting of a mother, father, and three children, were reduced from an income of $250 a month to $80 a month. In their case, they hunted for cheaper living quarters in a poorer neighborhood, reduced their living to the barest minimum, and sought aid from experts on buying and budgeting their expenses. The wife wore her old clothes a little longer without complaining, and the family sought ways of enjoying themselves that did not cost money. When times improved, they resumed their former economic status, perhaps the better for having met these reverses the way they did.

The other case, where the parents were also college graduates, concerned a young man, his wife, and young baby. He was out of work and refused to let his wife get a part time job, and he remain home and help with the care of the baby. The wife refused to move to a less pretentious neighborhood, and their differences and unwillingness to meet the situation realistically led to divorce.

Loss of economic support is more serious for women who live on farms, where their husbands may be ill or be taken by death, than for those who live in a large city, where opportunities for gainful employment are greater.

When money ceases to flow through the family as usual, the questions of the wife's working or of what things to give up, such as the family car or an insurance policy, arise. In addition, the children have to be curtailed in their incidental expenditures for candy, movies, contributions to charity drives at school, and so on. All of these adjustments may create continuous grumbling and unhappiness or, when met by more mature adjustment, can draw the family closer together in their common planning, playing, sharing, and living.

Severe and prolonged illness is a crisis in many, if not most, homes at some time or another. The threatened loss of a member brings added anxiety and strain to the family. This, in turn, can bring members closer together, or it may result in more irritability on the part of a tired and overworked mother and frustration to an anxious father.

Every illness disrupts the usual supper at six and other household routines and demands that each well member take some added responsibility and readjust to the new arrangements. When health is regained, routines may again be installed, and the family is more at ease, more normal, and happier in spirit.

When the mother is ill the family routines suffer the most. Many fathers have not become accustomed to sterilizing baby bottles, preparing food, dressing three-year-old Johnny and getting six-year-old Mary off to school. If the family income is low and help scarce or inadequate, he may have to do these things before he goes to work in the morning, and in the evening he may have to get supper and look after household things and the children's bedtime routine. Of course, it is much easier if a practical nurse or a maid can be afforded or obtained at all.

Crises arising from family conflict situations are many and varied. Among the most universal ones are those which are associated with emancipation from the overprotection or dependence upon our families, feeling of being unwanted and rejected by a parent, and conflicts with relatives and between brothers and sisters. These may seem trivial, but the experiences of college age young people and older married couples prove their seriousness.

Mary Lou is an example. She was very fond of her father and thought he was fond of her. He was, but one day when she was in high school she overheard him tell her mother that he liked her younger sister much better than he did her. This nearly broke her heart. She went to her room and cried for what seemed to her hours. From that day until long after she married, her feelings and attitudes toward her father were different. She felt rejected, unwanted, and terribly hurt. It also increased her feeling of resentment toward her younger sister, which continues to persist.

Another similar incident is that of a mother who, because her daughter forgot to send her an invitation to her eighth grade graduation exercises, refused to go, and who, because this daughter was not as "nice" as her younger sister, gave her a candy box with rocks in it for Christmas with a note saying, "If you had learned to be as nice a girl as your sister, you would have gotten candy in your box as she did." This crisis in the life of this child will affect her relationship to her family indefinitely.

A different kind of crisis situation arises between husband and wife when they expect a child which neither wants. They are confronted with the problem of facing an illegal abortion or almost inevitably rejecting the child after birth, thus crippling his development beyond remedy.

Perhaps the greatest threat to a happy marriage is when some other man or woman enters the affections of husband or wife. More often it is the husband who becomes involved, both because of greater opportunity and lesser risk of discovery. The underlying conditions which give rise to such affairs may be the same for each. A nagging, irritable, complaining husband or wife may force the other person to try to find peace and comfort somewhere else. At first it may be at a bridge club or extra work at the office, and later it may become an infatuation with a member of the opposite sex. It may be that a wife, after the arrival of children, devotes all of her time and attention to them, or a husband becomes so absorbed in, or driven by, his job that he forgets to function as a husband. The thing that many young people do when this situation becomes known is to bring the crisis to a head by asking for a divorce. The guilty person will often be defensive or very humble, promising never to err again, and the innocent party may feel overly sorry for himself or punish the offender in many psychological ways, such as being overly suspicious and jealous of his subsequent acts, withholding normal sex relations, and many other personal techniques of punishment. While it takes time to re-establish the same confidence and trust that existed previous to the event, the innocent must try to do just this, and the guilty so conduct himself that there is no need for suspicion.

There are some self-styled liberals who advocate freedom of relations between married people and others outside marriage. Some mature individuals seem to engage in such relationships with those of whom they may be fond and have longstanding friendships, but in general it is not a practice that even the most liberal in theory seem able to adjust to and accept in practice.

Bereavement

Becoming a widow or widower involves a break in the family. It entails both the personal adjustment to bereavement as well as readjustment to a single life again. Both are difficult ones to make. It is, however, an almost certain situation for many married women, since they usually outlive their husbands.

When a husband dies, the first problem which confronts the widow, especially if she has children or if she has never worked or not worked for many years, is a financial one. If she has children, it is often hard to provide for their care during working hours.

The widower faces a different set of problems. He must, if he has children, try to provide for them. He may get a housekeeper, but good ones are hard to find. Often it is necessary to parcel out children temporarily with relatives or place them in foster homes until he can make more permanent arrangements for them. Being a man he often looks around and remarries. This is a solution to some of his problems of personal adjustment but often creates problems of adjustment between the children and the new step-mother. She is often sensitive in her new role, and the husband frequently becomes defensive or over-protective about the children or leans over backward in his desire to back up his wife, causing hostility and antagonism on the part of the children.

The response of a person to the crisis of bereavement may take many forms. A certain amount of emotional hurt and readjustment is expected and necessary. Beyond a certain point, one becomes "chronically bereaved" and is in need of medical attention. The ways of escape or outlets one chooses when meeting a crisis situation will be determined largely by what he has learned to do in similar but less acute situations. If his habit has been to utilize the forms of outlet which, if persisted in, lead to personal disorganization and social maladjustment, he will no doubt turn to these. If he has acquired the socially approved and personally constructive avenues of release, his recovery will be quicker and more assured.

Personal adjustment to bereavement is a matter of mental hygiene and the pattern of response which the individual has acquired for meeting disappointment and sorrow. One person may become so engrossed in self-pity, aided by the unwise counsel of friends, that he will never be able to face life resolutely again. Another may take himself in hand and utilize every channel of work and other creative outlets as an aid to softening the emotional shock. Having met the economic problem and that of the care of one's children, where there are any, one then must reorganize his mode of living on the basis of an interesting job, contacts with friends, participation in social and club activities, and the building of a life for one's self alone or with one's children, until, and if, one remarries. There will be many hours of lonesomeness which cannot be entirely avoided. The loss of constant and happy companionship, the joint building of a home with a person one loves, and the loss of normal, satisfying sex expression can only be partially substituted for. The person who has had these may find it even more difficult to make a satisfactory adjustment than the single person who has not had them in the same sense or the divorced couple who, in many instances, continue to see each other at intervals until they remarry.

Owning one's home, having insurance and other savings may lessen the economic burden. The emotional and personal hurt are lightened only by the degree of maturity of the individuals who remain and the kind of philosophy of life they have evolved for themselves.

Divorce as a Crisis

Divorce has been the cause of much unhappiness, and much of the reason for divorce has been bad mating at the outset. Divorce creates as many problems as it solves, especially where children are involved. The causes of divorce are complex. Basically, they are personality problems due to mismating and conflicting ambitions, values, and needs of the couple. The situation is accentuated by the anonymity of life in large cities, weakening of social control over marriage by the church and state, interference of relatives, and the immaturity of those who marry.

The legal grounds for divorce usually include such things as adultery, bigamy, extreme cruelty, desertion, conviction of crime, habitual drunkenness, and nonsupport. The divergence of opinion as to the factors which cause divorce is shown by the following statements of a psychiatrist, three judges and two ministers:

"Dr. W. J. Hickson, psychiatrist of the Chicago Court of Domestic Relations, believed the principal causes of divorce to be: (1) feeble-mindedness plus dementia praecox; (2) dementia praecox; (3) feeble-mindedness.

"Judge Bradley Hull, once Director of the Bureau of Domestic Relations in Cleveland, rejected the psychopathic theories and listed the main causes as: (1) economic pinch primarily; (2) nerves; (3) faulty education.

"Judge William L. Morgan of Chicago said: (1) poverty; (2) neglect of woman by husband; (3) low mentality; (4) drink; (5) nagging; (6) improper sex mating.

"Judge C. W. Hoffman of the Cincinnati Court of Domestic Relations believed nine out of ten divorces to be due to the sexual degeneracy of the husband.

"Rev. John G. Benson, head of a Methodist Church clinic in New York, listed: (1) adultery; (2) relatives; (3) physical incompatibility; (4) female independence.

"Rev. Ralph H. Ferris, Director of the Bureau of Domestic Relations in Detroit, listed: (1) hasty marriage on physical attraction followed by quarrels when economic pinch occurs; (2) lack of religion; (3) drink; (4) uncontrolled temper." (20)

These, however, represent basic causes for marital conflict which usually begin soon after marriage in the little bickerings and conflicts discussed more in detail in previous chapters on adjustments in marriage.

There are no doubt many mismated couples, in no way suited to each other, who would be better off divorced and married to someone else. Part of the remedy for these divorces lies in less hasty courtship and marriage. On the other hand, successful marriage is a learning process. However well individuals know each other beforehand, they still have to learn how to live together, share, give up, compromise, make adjustments and common plans together. To live, one must experience; and all experience is to some degree new experience. Even the second or tenth game of chess, building one's fourth house, having a third baby, and marrying a second time are new experiences, though the elements common in such repetitions may facilitate the process, reduce anxiety, and enhance the value of the result.

Another important characteristic of experience is the kind of attitudes and feelings accompanying it. The quality of initial experience is unusually potent in determining the effective tone of the individual toward it and toward repetitions of the experience. Thus, a second marriage may be no more successful than a first, if one does not find a person who is a better complement to his needs and in greater harmony with his behavior, standards, ideas, and ambitions. Similarities noted between the experiences of the divorced and the bereaved are often far reaching:

"1. In both there is the loss of a former love-object which changes the whole life situation.

"2. Internal and (usually) external adjustments are slow, and largely unplanned, uncontrolled, automatic. The main outlines of these adjustments are essentially similar. The slower the adjustments, the more apt they are to be thorough, permanent, and satisfactory.

"3. There are similar yearnings, frustrations, and sense of emptiness.

"4. There are many similar insistent habits and impulses to be reconditioned, broken, or transferred piecemeal, and some of these may prove persistent beyond control.

"5. The reintegration of new habits into some new system of living is often similar.

"6. In both experiences there is dream-work and fantasy formation as a phase of unadjustment or reorientation of attitudes.

"7. In each there is a gradual piecemeal canceling of memory by actuality; each memory is checked off with a twinge as no longer true.

"8. The divorced and the bereaved may both reactivate roles played before marriage — though this is probably more frequent for the divorced than for the bereaved.

"9. For both the bereaved and the divorced there is apt to be an increase of self-centeredness; one would be driven in on self even in the absence of self-conscious uncertainties and defenses.

"10. Either group may find recovery through work, or routine, or ceremonials, which are the first activities to regain meaningfulness after the period of 'emptiness.'

"11. Either may indulge in 'confessional' confidences, or in forced pleasures in hope of escaping from or relieving tensions.

"12. In both, the habit of conceiving one's role as unhappy may outlast the tensions which constitute the unhappiness. When spontaneous pain is gone, mourning, if continued, may then become merely ritual or patterned autosuggestion.

"13. In both there is often the gradual discovery of new love-objects; for the divorced oftener than for the widowed they may constitute a series of substitutes.

"14. For both there are similar patterns of personal disorganization or reorganization of life habits, with some new philosophy of life emerging therefrom." (21)

Children and Divorce

Apart from the problem of adult readjustment to divorce, there is a serious problem of its effect upon children. Legally the tendency is to award children of younger age to the mother and older children to the father. This varies in different legal jurisdictions. But more important than who gets their legal custody is the effect upon the normal development and attachments of the children to mother and father and their need for a stable family pattern as a guide for their own values and conduct. There is all too often a pulling and hauling at the child from both sides. His social status in his play group is affected, and his whole attitude toward marriage may become cynical and warped. Juvenile delinquency, youthful sex offenders, and adolescent crime are a few of the results that are, to a large degree, traceable to irregular and disorganized family life.

Childlessness as a Crisis

Occasionally a couple will have to face the problem of sterility, of a miscarriage, or of a stillborn child. These are not the usual experiences of married people but constitute real crises when encountered. True sterility cannot be cured. The best solution, when it is definitely known that one cannot have children of their own, is to adopt one or more babies over a period of years. Taken a few days or weeks after birth, they become as much a part of one's family as if they were one's own. They should be told that they are adopted and given reassurance of one's love for them. Many sad situations arise when children learn of their being adopted only after they are grown or are ready to marry.

Crises Which Involve Social Stigma

Occasionally a family is faced with those kinds of crises which carry with them a certain amount of social stigma. One's husband may become a chronic drinker and create many kinds of family problems. Abuse of the wife and children, spending income for drink when it is needed for the family, neglect of one's job, and physical and mental deterioration are some of the consequences of alcoholism. Expert psychiatric help is the best approach to a solution.

Children may become delinquent and have to go before the juvenile court. Criminal acts may have been committed by an adult or a child. A girl of high-school or college age may unfortunately become pregnant. She and her family are faced with a decision between having the baby and adopting it out immediately after birth or trying to cover up by having a criminal abortion. These are not situations which have to be met by most individuals and families, but when they occur they are not always intelligently met.

Having a baby that is, or becomes, mentally deficient or abnormal is another difficult situation some parents have to face. Usually no social stigma should be attached to such an event. There are too many possibilities of malformation in prenatal development and of birth injuries to feel that there is any stigma associated with it. The shock and adjustment to it are not easy, but in most cases the parent should not indulge in self-blame.

The Crisis of War

War is one form of major calamity which is the result of man's ignorance of how to organize his common life. It grows out of conflicting philosophies of economics, politics, and social and religious welfare. As long as there are both autocratic and democratic forms of government, wars will last. It is only where freedom exists that there is the opportunity for a peaceful solution to conflict, progressive change, and ultimate individual and group advancement. The problem is, how can conflict be so localized and dispersed as to provide socially constructive ways for individuals to give vent to their repressed hostilities? What manner of freedom, of self-expression, of democracy will keep the channels open so that a free people can remain free, and monopolistic and dishonest groups cannot distort the philosophy or techniques of free living. As long as the democratic process has the incentive and the method of organization to function freely, the forces of education and religion can gradually raise the ideals and capacity of mankind to the point where it can endure the sacrifices and enjoy the benefits which peace might bring. Very apropos is the retort of a great preacher who, when asked "Why, if God was so all powerful, he did not stop this horrible war?" replied that God was not concerned with stopping wars but with making a warproof man. The solution to war lies in the kind of philosophy of human personality and human relationships in which the majority of individuals believe. We cannot teach the golden rule in family life and expect our children to become more than cannon fodder if we do not do something to change the selfish cutthroat, dog-eat-dog competition of our economic system, the intolerance which exists in our religious philosophy, and the graft and corruption in political circles. If man wants these things, he has them. He evidently wants them, or he would be less lackadaisical in the performance of his public duties. We must have a vital, dynamic, aggressively democratic education and family experience for everyone if we are to solve the problem of democratic social living.

As Professor Lindeman has so well said:

"Family experience may become a training course for the building of habits on the part of family members which lead either to power over or power with; if it is the former, the family will become a hindrance to democracy, and if the latter, family experience may become a potent source of habit-building for democratic conduct.

"Because of its very intimacy family life becomes at one and the same time the most fruitful and the most fateful of all human relationships since it is due to this intimacy that so many of the ensuing tensions and conflicts are suppressed. The freedom which democracy grants is the antithesis of suppression. Likewise, the authority which is integral to the democratic process is the opposite of that variety of order which accompanies dictatorships and absolute or totalitarian states. Modern absolutists seem to want order for the sake of order. Those who believe in democracy desire order for the sake of true freedom.

"In the intimate processes of family life may be built up attitudes and habits which are basic to the system of values which holds democratic society together." (23)

Marriage in Wartime

Marriage creates for most people as many problems as it solves, war or no war. Even in peacetime a third to a sixth of all marriages end in the divorce court. It is difficult, therefore, to say what effect war, as an isolated fact, has upon success or failure, happiness or unhappiness, stability or instability in marriage. It would seem a fair assumption that individuals who are emotionally mature, intelligent, and earnest are likely to succeed at any time, whereas the weak, ineffectual neurotic person would eventually fail at marriage in any period.

Let us first distinguish between "war marriage" and "marriage in wartime." War marriages, for the most part, are thought of as those over-night or week-end love at first sight affairs, which are entered into with little background of acquaintance or preparation. They satisfy chiefly an immediate lonesomeness on the part of one or both parties, an uncontrolled sex urge, and the social pressure of the time, heightened by the emotion of wartime psychology. Marriages of this kind have always existed, however, and constitute a large clientele of peacetime divorce courts. Most authorities, as well as sensible young men and women, disapprove of these as doomed to failure for the majority at the outset.

But many marriages in wartime are somewhat different. The couple know each other. They have lived in similar surroundings, know something of each other's families, have had at least a year's acquaintance, are as reasonably well matched as a couple in peacetime would be, and their marriage is consummated ahead of schedule only because of the war. These marriages can succeed as well as marriages consummated at any time.

Neither war nor any other catastrophe will bring a stop to the basic needs of human beings, particularly to those needs which are best satisfied through marriage and family life.

In spite of the fact that 1776, 1812, 1837, 1851, 1876, 1906, 1914, 1932, and 1939 have all brought periods of war or depression or other hardships, people have kept right on marrying and having all kinds of family relationships, good and bad. Marriages and family affairs seem to go on, regardless of the state in which the world finds itself.

The three basic problems in wartime are the same as in any other time, viz.:

1. Are the two people who marry well mated to begin with?
2. Once married, will the couple utilize the resources available which may contribute to the solution of many of their problems, born of ignorance?
3. Is the way of life called marriage important enough to

cause each sufficiently to forego his own ego-centric nature as to be able to make the necessary adjustments which marriage demands?

In the past the average couple, living in a large industrial city like Detroit, had two chances out of three of their marriage's not ending in divorce, and, for the country as a whole, about four chances out of five. Their chance of success is greater if they live on a farm or in a small rural community and less the larger the city they live in. So we must be careful not to blame the war for events that happen all the time anyway. People do not get married and live happily ever after. They never do. They are happy some of the time and unhappy some of the time, married, single, widowed, or divorced, with one's spouse or away from him.

The number of marriages tends always to increase just before and at the beginning of war, to decrease during the period of the war, and increase following a war. Marriages also tend to increase in number when times are good and to decrease in hard times.

While our divorce rate has been on the increase for seventy-five years, it also tends to decrease during depression and increase as jobs and income are on the increase.

The birth rate also follows these other trends. As marriages increase, a year later we begin to get a bigger crop of babies, but over a long period of time we have been decreasing the size of the American family. In 1720 there were nearly six persons per family, whereas at present there are less than four.

Three Crises in Twenty-five Years

World War No. I was followed by a number of significant events which affected marriage and family life.

1. There was, for several years, an unprecedented financial boom. This spurt of so-called "good times" resulted in more marriages, more divorces, and more sex experimentation than we had ever known.

2. There was a general breakdown in the mores. That is, every heretofore accepted code of moral conduct between the sexes, before and after marriage, was held up to critical judgment. There was a flood of books on sex, companionate marriage, love in the machine age, birth control and similar topics. Sex experimentation was rampant. Everyone, young and old alike, thought they must try out this new idea of freedom. There was a revolution in thinking about marriage and the family. Every traditional concept was brought into question:

    a. The relation and authority of parents to children, and

    b. The child's responsibility to his parents.

3. Sex purity before and after marriage was questioned.
4. Husband-wife relationships were altered.
5. The importance of sex in marriage was emphasized.
6. Demand for more effective contraceptives arose.

The prevailing tenor of public opinion was that marriage and family life had outlived their usefulness and that the home was of questionable value to civilization. Along with all this there was a flood of articles and books on and about sex, marriage, family relationships, and home life.

As to the relationship of World War I to marriage, it is difficult to separate those results due to changing economic conditions and those arising from the war itself.

The Depression of 1933 was a more sudden blow to most city dwellers than to the farmers. The serious depression for farmers began about 1919 but the urban population enjoyed abounding prosperity for ten years longer until the stock market crash of 1929. The full effects of this major financial crisis did not appear, however, until the time of the fall elections of 1932 and the closing of the banks throughout the country a few weeks later. The so-called New Deal brought the N.R.A., the N.Y.A., W.P.A. and many emergency measures of alleviation. Millions of people for the first time in their lives were on public relief rolls. Young people were unable to finish school or find jobs. Thus, again, a major calamity had its effect upon marriage and family life.

1. Young people of marriageable age were raising questions about subsidized marriages, wives' working and supporting unemployed husbands, what to do with their thwarted sex urge, and whether life held anything for them in the years to come. Youth was pessimistic and unrestful. The economic system came in for much critical analysis. There was the lowest marriage rate in our history.

2. There was increased stress and strain on already established families. The weak personalities cracked up and the stronger ones survived, as is always the case.

3. There was a swing back to the idea of the importance of the family as a basic "cornerstone" of democratic society.

4. A new emphasis was given education and counseling along family lines. Nursery schools, marriage courses, family counseling services, and research on marriage and family life took on new vigor.

World War II presented an entirely different picture compared to 1919 and 1933:

1. Jobs were plentiful. Manpower short. Wages were the highest ever paid to wage earners and tax burdens the heaviest.

2. We had another spurt in marriages. Over 1,800,000 marriages took place in 1942. Many were "war marriages," and many were usual marriages in wartime.

3. The shortage of manpower caused millions of women of all ages to take gainful employment for the first time in years or in their lives. New fields of work and avenues of training were opened to women. The WAC and WAVES and SPARS became new terms and fields of female endeavor.

4. The cost of living increased rapidly in spite of govern-

ment attempts at price control and rationing. Young people in high school made wages higher than many of their fathers ever earned.

5. Millions of young men were inducted into the army.

These and other factors resulted in many problems for families — hours of work for both husband and wife were irregular; mothers and family members were separated more often; there were more absentee husbands; children had less adequate care and supervision; homes were crowded, and abnormal living arrangements existed in many places; certain areas became centers of abnormal and unstable community and family life due to trailer camps and the mushroom growth of communities with few of the usual health facilities.

Advantages and Disadvantages of Wartime Marriage

Marriages at present have all the advantages and disadvantages of marriage in wartime or at other times of national stress. In addition, there are certain ones which seem important to emphasize as far as the question of whether to marry or not to marry is concerned.

ADVANTAGES OF WARTIME MARRIAGES:

1. It brings a sense of security to both man and woman. Each has his mate, and that anxiety is over.
2. It gives each a sense of responsibility which stabilizes the individual.
3. Women, even though a husband is called to service, can work at a useful and important war industry.
4. It gives each person something to look forward to when the war is over.
5. If the couple is well mated and plans to marry anyway, there is usually no reason for postponement.
6. As one gets older, chances for marriage are less, and childbearing is better if done at an earlier age.

DISADVANTAGES OF WARTIME MARRIAGES:

1. To many men it brings a sense of insecurity and worry about their wives back home.
2. Responsibility for a family makes a man worry more and perhaps detracts from his value as a soldier.
3. People may change during long absences and under war conditions.
4. Wives may become economically dependent on family or in-laws.
5. Pregnancy may handicap wives' economic security.
6. The social and recreational life of each will be handicapped for the duration.
7. Many girls will be faced with widowhood at a very early age. This and having children born of the union will make another marriage less easily attainable.
8. There is no possibility of establishing a real family life.
9. The process of adjustment will be to do without, rather than to live with, the other person.

Parents and Children in Wartime

The basic difference between the peacetime relationship of parents to their children and their wartime relationship is the increased need in the latter period for parents themselves to be as stable and unemotional as possible. The child has always reflected in his attitudes, emotions, and behavior the atmosphere of the home and the kind of training he has received. The job of parents is that of trying to carry out what good practice in child rearing has always taught. Let us review some of these principles:

1. Parents need to be consistent in their management of the children.
2. Parents determine the rhythm and quality of home surroundings. It is important that the rhythm be calm and the quality be wholesome.
3. Parents should decide what they wish their children to be in terms of physical, mental, emotional, social, and

spiritual development, and the kind of attitude they want them to have toward race, politics, the rich, the poor, and the many other questions which go to make up the individual's philosophy of life.

4. Discipline should be consistently firm but not harsh nor severe.

5. Children should be given a sense of affectional security in the home relationships.

6. Parents need to study the individual child and plan their relationships with him in terms of his capacity and character, thus attempting to understand the child's needs and characteristics at each period of his development. We sometimes confuse love with understanding. They are different. One can love a child but fail miserably in understanding him.

Fear, anxiety, hostility, love, conflict, overprotection, dependence, immaturity, domination, and hate have always been a part of family relationships. Today, more than ever, it is important that the socially and personally destructive elements in human associations together be minimized and the solidifying and uplifting sentiments fostered. War and war's aftermath tend, for young children and adolescents alike, to create uncertainty, frustration, fear and anxiety, ideas of hate, hostility, and intolerance — conditions and attitudes that for generations we have been trying to eliminate. This fact emphasizes all the more the need for adults to stabilize themselves, to provide a sense of perspective for themselves and their children and to teach this love of right principles and of tolerance. The degree of instability and the extent of adolescent unhappiness can be affected by the kind of affection and stability which homes provide.

Youth Faces a Changing World

The young person from twelve to eighteen years of age normally lives a life full of physical, emotional, social, and intellectual change and conflict. He is developing rapidly from a boy or girl into an adult. These changes, associated with the attainment of full biological maturity, in and of themselves create many problems for him. Along with these radical changes come attendant emotional feelings and the need to acquire a set of social techniques useful in his hetero-sexual associations. He is rapidly expanding intellectually, beginning to emancipate himself from overly protective family control, is developing some economic independence, is expanding his leisure time and social and recreational in-terests and, throughout it all, is mentally grappling with many questions of life and achieving his first basic and con-scious philosophy of life. All of these things happen in the short span of six years. This goes on with young people, boys and girls, rural and urban, Catholic or Protestant, Negro, White, Chinese, or Hungarian, and rich or poor.

All of these growth changes require, for successful results, that the individual have the kind of family and home rela-tionships which will be sympathetic and understanding of his needs and help give him a sense of security.

War and the prospect of war brings to this already turbu-lent period added frustration, tension, excitement, fear, worry, and anxiety. The bombardment of radio, press, etc. needs to be offset by living in calm, reassuring surroundings.

Young people need parents, teachers, youth leaders, and other adults as friends and examples — adults who them-selves are secure and stable. They need adults who can be patient and who can help them achieve confidence in their own growing ability. They need some emancipation from the authority of their family, but they also need some new authority which they find in out-family groups or in society itself. They achieve a working relationship with authority slowly and gradually with some resistance. At a time when we are expecting young people to grow up in a hurry, we must remember that for generations we have fostered de-pendency and the lack of assumption of adult responsibility. Growth can take place just so fast. When pushed too hard, failure or other forms of personal maladjustment result.

Individual differences need to be recognized in the rate of maturing and the degree of security of each person.

Every young person needs to find ways of:

1. Becoming a part of adult life in so far as his time and maturity will allow, at all times safeguarding his physical health and normal social development.

2. Joining and becoming active in groups, clubs, or teams of various kinds. This gives one a sense of solidarity, security, and belonging in a world of confusion and uncertainty.

3. Finding activities which allow us to express rather than repress our thoughts and feelings. The democratic process is a stabilizing influence for the individual as well as the group. All kinds of creative activities, hobbies, etc. are more valuable than ever.

4. Getting a perspective on life as a seventy-five-year project and not just a matter of immediate concern.

5. Maintaining high moral standards, and having faith in the principles and practice of democracy.

6. Finding a religious faith which meets one's needs and helps to give one a bolstering faith in himself and in humanity.

War brings many disruptive influences to society as a whole:

1. It tends, biologically, to prune off a disproportionately large number of those whom the race can least afford to lose.

2. It tends to speed up the courtship process, resulting in great increases of hasty marriages.

3. It increases the amount of husband-wife and parent-child separation, resulting in an increase in many forms of personal and family demoralization.

4. It tends to reduce rational social controls, and the mores become an individual rather than a social matter. This results in sex freedom and promiscuity,

heartache and disappointment, increased illegitimacy and spread of venereal disease, to say nothing of the more important generally lowered moral standard.

5. It creates unusual living conditions due to housing shortages and twenty-four-hour and seven-day-week work schedules.

6. It creates an acute problem of social and recreational outlets for the population.

7. It creates large scale problems of desertion, orphanhood, widowhood, mental disease, handicaps, and other forms of demoralization due to shock.

8. It leads to inflationary tendencies and poverty for the masses.

9. It sows the seed for future wars, thus usually achieving few, if any, positive results in terms of lasting peace.

10. It may, because of its catastrophic nature:
    a. Result in improved education.
    b. Emphasize the importance of human and spiritual values as against material things.
    c. Lead to the discovery of new leaders who will be an asset to the country after the war.
    d. Lead to fundamental changes in governmental policy and working relationships between capital and labor and urban and farm interests.

CHAPTER XVII

THE UNMARRIED

For the average normal young person of eighteen or twenty years of age, about nine out of every ten can expect to marry. This leaves approximately 10 per cent of the population who never marry. In addition to these, there are about 500,000 married women widowed each year and a small percentage of the married population divorced. This brings the percentage of the population who live their lives as unmarried to a fairly high proportion of the total, if the figure is taken at any one time. But of course a goodly number of the widowed and divorced remarry. Let us consider the three classes of the unmarried in terms of their family life.

The Single Who Never Marry

It is absurd to speak of any group or individual as permanently unmarried. Every single, widowed, or divorced person has a chance of possible marriage, although as one grows older there is a decreasing chance of marriage.

In talking of the single who never marry, one is speaking of an undefined group. Nearly every young woman looks forward to and hopes that she will marry and have a home and children of her own. Yet each one is confronted with uncertainty as to when the right man will come along. Often she must be prepared to improve herself for the eventuality of a permanent career.

Figure 2 presents a diagrammatic sketch which indicates the alternative possibilities for which every woman must prepare herself. Some girls go through school, work a little, marry, and never again enter a gainful occupation. Others may finish school, take a job, and live the rest of their lives hoping they will marry and never doing much to equip themselves for occupational advancement. Still others work, marry, then, because of death or other crises, have to retrain themselves for gainful employment and soon after may again marry. Woman's role is indeed a much more complicated one than that of man.

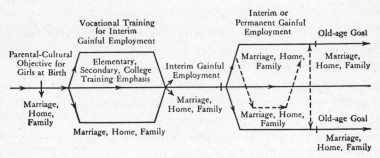

Fig. 2. Direction of women's life realistically conceived.

A man's life has a much more consistent trend. His entire drive is toward achieving vocational success. Marriage, for him, is a matter of choice and is probably secondary in importance, even though it may be a great convenience and an asset to his personal, social, and economic development. Yet there are many men who never marry.

There are many and complex reasons why individuals remain single. No one actually knows how much personality factors are responsible for nonmarriage. Certainly there are, no doubt, many superficial reasons given for nonmarriage which, if investigated further, would be found to be basic personality reasons. These reasons are not only unstudied, but are even more unknown to the individual himself. Since marriage is a paired relationship, the finding of a mate complement is even more difficult. We have a hint as to one major cause in the way in which we acquire friendliness patterns in the course of our development, as discussed in the earlier chapters of this book.

In many localities the sex distribution is disproportionate and, as a consequence, in some cases there are too many women for the available men, or too many men for the available women. Congested areas where many women are employed is probably a poor place for a young woman to take a position, if she is interested in meeting eligible men and wants to marry. It would be equally undesirable for a young man to go west to any one of the many mining, cattle raising, or logging communities where men predominate. One's occupation and the type of community in which one is situated are important factors. The occupations which seem to have the lowest marriage opportunity for women are medicine, social work, library work, dietetics, teaching, law, and nursing. In large cities it is often difficult to make desirable contacts, and there are few opportunities for living in other than sex segregated groups. In small and rural communities, the professionally trained women must often choose between nonmarriage or accepting a man of lower educational and often cultural standards than her own. Going to college may doom some young women to spinsterhood because of the scarcity of eligible men of her age as she grows older, as well as of the emphasis often placed by institutions upon vocational achievement.

Family reasons are valid ones. Sometimes one will need to assume the support of younger children or invalid parents. In other instances, parental influence or disapproval prevents one from marrying the person of his choice. There are some young men and women who never are able to emancipate themselves from a mother or father. A young man always must make a distinction between his devotion to his mother and the love he professes for his sweetheart. If he has too strong a parental fixation he should probably not marry. A wife has one role to perform and a mother has another, both before and after marriage. If we could recognize each person's contribution to the newly established set of relationships, much unnecessary conflict might be avoided.

One's ideas about men, marriage, and the kind of person

or home one wants may interfere with getting married. If one's personal ambitions and desires are unrelated to marriage, that person will often avoid matrimony. Others may have peculiar attitudes toward men or women due to early training or a single unfortunate experience or from having grown up in an unhappy or broken home. Still others fail to marry because they have built up an ideal for a mate, the like of which does not exist in reality. One may have been disillusioned or disappointed in a love affair, may be in chronic poor health, or may have many conscious or unconscious fears of marriage. These fears may be general or specific. One may have a general fear of taking a risk, of which marriage has many. One may be vaguely afraid that he will not be able to fulfill what he thinks are the expectations of the other person. On the other hand, he may fear sex, pregnancy, being responsible for children if and when they come, or that marriage will cramp his style and interfere with the satisfactions of his personal pleasures. This latter, not too uncommonly held view is the one based upon the premise that one has fun while single, but when one marries, fun in life is over.

What to Do About Singleness

If one wants to marry, most of the reasons for nonmarriage just discussed can be overcome. The individual who works in an area where there are too few of the opposite sex can usually move to another section of the country, if he can stand pulling up stakes and leaving the security of his family. One who has an overly developed sense of devotion to his parents will no doubt continue that devotion and forego marriage, but he may get help from a trained counselor which may help him to emancipate himself. Very often we get more satisfaction out of what we are doing than we anticipate we would get from the thing we are always talking about wanting to do and therefore we do not make much effort in the other direction. Many of the personal handicaps to mating and marriage can be overcome. Here again it may take the help of an understanding counselor to give the added push, but if the urge is there, and a person truly wants to marry, he can usually overcome most obstacles.

The war has created a temporary and unusual situation for a portion of the population, especially the girl who has just graduated from college. Men older than she, and desirable, are either already married to younger girls or are away. Her younger sisters in later high school and early college are having many more opportunities to marry and with some possibility of selective choice.

If One Does Not Marry

If, because of circumstances or choice, one does not marry, it need not be a crisis in one's life. Concentrate upon preparing yourself for a useful and successful career, not shutting out the possibility of marriage but, nevertheless, having some kind of interesting and useful work that has a future. Maintain a wide set of contacts with friends of both sexes and with married people. Develop interests in sports, cultural and social activities, as well as other forms of recreation. Be the kind of person others would like to know. Friends are just other people like yourself who want to be friendly but are afraid you will not be. Establish for yourself a home where, either alone or with another person, you can have most of the satisfactions which home life offers, your own furniture, your own fireplace, your own garden, pets, etc. Become a part of the institutional life of your community, church, school, YMCA or YWCA, youth activities, and many others. Recognize the fact that marriage is no cure-all for one's difficulties but often adds problems and responsibilities which the single person does not have to meet. Realize that sex unawakened is easier to deal with than it is after one has engaged in unconventional affairs. Be and act normal. Do not go through life feeling sorry for yourself, rejecting your feminine role, hating men or life in general. These all defeat both prospect for marriage and family, and maximum happiness if one never marries.

CHAPTER XVIII

THE INDIVIDUAL AND SOCIETY

Just as marriage is a negation of individualism, so is society a restrictive force in what individuals and family groups may do or become.

At the outset of our civilization we had biological matings which probably resulted in the formulation of certain rules or restrictions (taboos) on human relationships, particularly between the sexes. The regulation of the sexes before marriage and the establishment of marriage as a religious and state sanctioned institution came into being. Thus, from the very beginning and among all peoples, marriage and the family have been a concern of the state. There is a great body of common law as well as statutory law which rules on practically every aspect of marriage and family relationships. The variety of forms of human association is almost limitless. What seems to us right and proper may be a grievous violation of some rule in another culture, and vice versa. We may say, therefore, that society creates the sanctions and restrictions which govern human association. Every aspect of effort devoted toward self-maintenance, protection, and government, self-gratification and religion influences individuals and hence their relationships to each other. The economic organization of human affairs alone affects marriage in several ways: first, it may form the basis for a polygamous or monogamous form of family life; second, it may offset the degree to which family life is largely patriarchal, matriarchal or other pattern; third, it may create conditions which provide a reasonably adequate standard of living for all, a poverty for the masses and riches for the few; fourth, these conditions may in time affect marriage rates, divorce and desertion rates, sex delinquency, illegitimacy, prostitution, crime, birth rates, *et al.*; fifth, it may create conditions which actuate inflationary poverty and depressionary wealth; sixth, it may foster such attitudes of competitive individualism as to be destructive to the democratic, social, and religious philosophy in our culture; seventh, it may be so geared to social welfare motives as to make for the maximum of economic wellbeing for every class of the population; and, eighth, it may foster such practices in advertising, selling, and deception in the quantities and qualities of products produced, as to contribute to family poverty and personal attitudes of hostility and resentment that are the seeds of economic revolution.

In the attempt of every society to provide means for the satisfaction of individual needs for play, recreation, and other social activities, some forms become commercialized and others remain in the nature of individual and folk experiences. These opportunities may be fostered by the public policy of a society or be made restrictive by them. Where they are left entirely to commercial endeavor, there is a tendency for them to be at such cost or of such quality as to eliminate many from their enjoyment.

The Family's Social Function Today

In spite of the fact that society does many things which tend to disrupt family life and few basically to conserve and promote its successful functioning, the family still performs many useful functions for both the individual and society. Any classification of these functions tends to break down because family life is both changing and complex. The best way to evaluate the functions performed by the present day family is to look at families and see, in so far as possible, what they do.

Marriage provides, for a young man and woman, a home where privacy, companionship, and socially approved sex relations may occur. This home-giving form of economic cooperation and psycho-sexual companionship has always been one of the basic contributions of marriage to the adults of the population. While changing conditions may alter the form, the basic function remains.

Marriage has still a certain status-giving value for men and particularly for women and children. This function is especially important for the child as he grows to maturity.

Home ownership gives a place basis for family solidarity. For any social group to have a place basis adds to its solidarity and persistence, whereas insecurity of place or too frequent mobility, with no intermediary fixed place of abode, tends to disorganize and disrupt the life of the family. We still have millions of families for whom stability is given their daily life through having a home place of residence.

The family is still an economic division of labor between men and women. It serves economic advantages for each. Even though, as Ogburn puts it, the woman no longer makes her own bread or does her own sewing or laundry (but many still do), and the man is at the shop or office a few miles away instead of in the adjoining room or field, the economic function of mutual aid and specific contribution of this form of life persists. The child also, while no longer an apprentice to his father, except perhaps on farms, must be inducted into a pecuniary capitalistic system, and the responsibility for this is no easy one for the average family.

The family still provides protection for the child, his care and nurture, his concepts of right and wrong in his relations to the outside world, and cultural guidance in protecting him from influences and conditions that are to his disadvantage. For these functions the family still is held legally responsible.

As an educational and social, emotional conditioning influence, the family has always been important. Besides the actual physical care and help in attaining proper physical development, the family educates the child in every area of his life and reinforces the formal education he receives from outside agencies, including the school. This functtion is just as important today as it ever was.

The reproductive function has remained one of the basic functions of the family. True, the number of children per family has decreased considerably, but this is more the result of technological development, our economic system, and public policy than a fault of the family.

Actual religious institutions and practices have lost considerable ground in present day family life. This is more true in urban centers than in rural areas. The basic philosophy of life, including such things as respect for personality, human social attitudes, social, religious, economic, political, and other prejudices, etc., is still fundamentally one which the individual acquires as a result of family experience. The function needs to be improved so that the quality of outcome is better, but the function still remains an important one.

The recreational function is now largely a commercial or extrafamilial one with children and adults, except in the earlier years of the child's life. Here, literature, constructive play, music, art, parties, trips, vacations with family members, and other forms of recreation constitute a part of what families do together. This function has lost in what it does but not in its directive responsibility of guiding the child's selection of outside social and recreational participation, as well as the selection of his own forms of recreation.

Companionship, affection, a sense of importance, of being wanted, of belonging, are basically functions which the family still provides for husbands, wives, and children. It is also a progressive function which exists throughout the entire span of each family generation. No social substitute in the community has been evolved which provides for individuals the same satisfactions in this area as do successful marriage and family relationships of a high quality.

The by-products of planned activities are ofttimes as important as the activities themselves. Some say that it is not important that the family commune together frequently in order that it be a happy relationship with a high degree of solidarity. While this may be true in many cases, in the long run I believe that many common relationships, shared by the members of the household, make for a degree of appreciation of and respect for the interests, ambitions, problems, and needs of each other that can be attained in no other way.

"To be emotionally and sexually compatible, to supplement each other and to be a stimulus to each other, so that each one reaches a higher level of development because of marriage, to find with each other the satisfying companionship which means that pleasures are at hand and burdens lightened by sharing them, all these make marriage an experience which one supremely desires may be a lasting one. It would seem that a marriage based on love which had in it not only mutual attraction and sex urge, but also elements of unselfishness and willingness to adapt to another, as well as elements which make for truly satisfactory companionship, had in it those elements which modern marriage requires. If, in addition to the mutual satisfaction found in each other, the husband and wife desire children and are prepared to assume an intelligent responsibility toward helping those children attain satisfactory growth, we have a marriage which has laid the cornerstone for a successful family life." (22)

The Family and the Individual

The importance of the family should not be underestimated in what it does to and for the individual, both constructively and destructively. *First*, the human matings of a family determine the hereditary potentialities of the offspring. There are certain physical characteristics, such as stature, hair, and eye color, which can be definitely predicted. But the more important aspects of heredity are less well known. We know with a fair degree of certainty that certain diseases, such as asthma, hay fever, diabetes, and some types of deafness and blindness have real gene inheritance, whereas others, such as syphilis, heart disease, and alcoholism, do not.

Thus it is clear that the family is important because it gives its offspring the potential possibility of good or bad heredity which can be passed on from generation to generation. These diseases may not always be a ban on marriage but may point to the need for consideration with reference to childbearing.

Second, family experience is an almost universal human experience. Only about 1 per cent of children under ten years of age are being cared for in homes or institutions apart from their natural parents. If we begin with one hundred thousand babies at birth, some will die, some will be of such low grade mentality as never to live outside an institution, and others will have peculiarities which, for some reason, prevent their normal development. But 78 per cent of them will grow up and marry, and about 85 per cent of those who marry will become parents. Looking at it another way, 57 per cent of the one hundred and thirty million persons in our population spend most of their time in home activities, for 23 per cent are homemakers, 19 per cent are young people, 11 per cent are children under school age, and 4 per cent are feeble or aged.

Third, the family is an interpreter, modifier, and transmitter of the sanctions and restrictions of the culture into which their children are born. Thus, parental attitudes toward what our democratic society believes and is striving for are passed on early in life to the children.

Fourth, family experience is perhaps the most potent one in the formation of the individual's physical, social, emotional, and personality patterns. His prejudices and biases, beliefs and feelings about matters of economics, politics, race, religion, education, work, social values, and so on, as well as his personality structure, are early formed from his family experience. His basic personality structure is probably a matter of heredity, whereas his manifestations of personality characteristics are a matter of learned experience.

Fifth, prolonged infancy is largely a human characteristic. The young of other forms of animal life grow into maturity more rapidly and are, therefore, dependent upon the care of parents a shorter period of time. The effects of prolonged infancy have numerous implications for the child and parent.

1. This long period of dependency facilitates learning and results in intellectual and cultural progress.

2. The growth of parental attitudes is inspired by the child's helplessness, trust, and affection.

3. These newly created parental attitudes give rise to altruistic, as contrasted with sexual, love. These in turn are transmitted as attitudes to children. The home becomes the center for nurturing altruistic, democratic, and spiritual ideals.

4. Prolongation of dependency provides a longer period of training and education, thus emphasizing the importance of the family as an educational experience.

5. Prolonged infancy also offers the possibility that the child will be kept infantile beyond the chronological age when he should have become socially and emotionally mature and independent of his family. It makes it possible for the parent to do great damage to the individual's development and maturity.

6. The parent may also, however, be a great aid to him in maturing and becoming a part of the adult world.

We come into the family helpless. Our parents are in a sense dictators. They make all the decisions and set the stage for our normal or abnormal development. They should gradually relinquish this authoritarian position so that we, as infants, the objects of their love or hate or indifference, can gradually become not only competitors for family goods, services, and affections but democratic participants in the decisions and affairs of family life. The family does everything to us that is important in shaping our tendencies toward maturity or immaturity, success or failure, happiness or unhappiness.

CHAPTER XIX

WHAT LIES AHEAD

Your babies, the babies who are born this year and next will run the new world. Now is the time to plan how you are going to live the coming years, for personal happiness and in order to rear, train, and educate your children for the future, for Today is the Future.

In one way marriage is like a trip. If one is enthusiastic about traveling, goes to the first station or dock at hand and sets out for no particular destination, he is likely to arrive at no place in particular. Likewise, if, when a couple marry, they are not looking and planning far ahead, they are likely to live aimlessly and ineffectually. Love alone is not enough. Of course, on your wedding day you hope and almost know for certain that you will be happy. But for how long? Have you taken full measure of what a happy life or a happy marriage means? It means good health, economic self-sufficiency, good home management, satisfactory relationship with one's husband, relatives, in-laws, friends, and the institutions of one's community. It means living each day fully, while at the same time planning for the future, for children, a home owned, economic security in later years, participation in the cultural and civic enterprises of one's home town, and constant education and improvement of one's self in order both to enjoy life and to advance in one's vocation.

One couple, at the time of marriage, made a simple, long time plan; after twenty-five years of married life, though they had not attained all the goals set for themselves, they felt it had given a long look ahead to their marriage. To them it was a permanent venture with goals to be worked and strived for. It is included here so that you may share in it.

"TWENTY–FIVE–YEAR PLAN FOR OUR MARRIAGE"

"It is hoped that we will be able to achieve the following goals by 1940:

"1. To own our own home.

"2. To have four children.

"3. To be successfully established in a profession.

"4. To be a regular and active member of a church and to try to live what Christian teaching means to us.

"5. To take an active part throughout the years in educational, religious, and civic affairs of our community.

"6. To have acquired a sufficient amount of life insurance adequately to provide protection for the family and assure us a retirement income for our old age.

"7. To celebrate our Golden Wedding together."

These seven items made up the entire document, but it helped, without any doubt, to give a sense of stability to this marriage.

Now let us look at what happened to this long time plan after twenty-five years:

1. They have owned and sold their houses in different places where they have lived and own their present residence.

2. They have two, instead of four, children.

3. They are successfully established in a vocation.

4. They have been intermittently active in the church.

5. They have usually been active in some community enterprise.

6. They have acquired an unusual insurance program which, to date, has served their purpose. If they can hold on to most of it, their goal on this point will have been attained.

7. It is, of course, too early to know whether they will live to celebrate their Golden Wedding Anniversary.

Sometimes we get discouraged if our relationships are not 100 per cent perfect. That is foolish. Nothing in life is as efficient as that.

It is our job to find out what our capacity is and to try to manage our lives so as to live up to our maximum efficiency. It may be 80 per cent or it may be 90 per cent, but never will it be 100 per cent.

What is happening to family life makes living as a husband, wife, or parent none too easy. But people are meeting unheard of crises with fortitude and success every day. The letter from Mary F. which follows should be an inspiration to any couple who reads it. It is a marriage that has endured, — two personalities, different, but made of the stuff of which successful marriages are made — tolerance, understanding, intelligence, industry, and adaptability.

"I wanted to have a part in this war. In World War I, I was the mother of a vigorous five-year-old boy — paying half of my husband's salary for rent alone and practicing all the economies, now new discoveries, that help to make ends meet. I wanted to get into this war. My older son is now a captain in the medical corps of the army and the younger boy left in May for year-round work in a midwest university. For the first time in my married life, I could go through a whole week without hearing: 'Mother, where is . . .?' No, this idea didn't sprout and burst into full bloom in a day or a week. At first it was a sickly and puny plant; at times the lower leaves would turn yellow and then it would wilt like an unwatered geranium in a summer sun. At first I played around with the idea. I casually mentioned it to my husband as though it were just a product of the moment. He looked up from his reading to remark, 'It might work.' He thought it was one of these brain storms that men are always expecting from our sex. I went shopping and studied the clerks, looked over their shoulder while they filled out the sales slip. I barged into the doctor's office to see what the 'white starched girls' were doing. Stenographic work was out. While I could knock off a creditable letter on a typewriter with the 'hunt and peck' system, the 'pot-hooks' vocabulary was entirely beyond me. My courage was rising. One day I walked right into the employment office of a big department store and asked for an employment blank, tucked it into my handbag and walked out. That was a personal triumph!

"A friend casually mentioned that her daughter was returning to college and that they were planning to employ more statistical workers in the defense office she was leaving. Here was a hot trail. What was statistical work? Would my old 'math' training come back? I recalled that I had coached two adolescent sons through high-school mathematics. Maybe I could bluff along until I could learn. The personnel supervisor had a kindly face and that helped. When he produced the 'blank' my courage deserted me. Cold beads of sweat stood out on my temple. My response was quick and high pitched. My writing was — well, say jerky at least. There was no use trying to hide it. I was upset and the personnel director knew it. He pushed the papers aside and began to inquire about my boys. Who wouldn't come back with a bang? A doctor son, a captain in the army, and a younger son in college, knocking off four A's and three B's this year? When I had got the tongue of this proud mother under control, I was ready for the toughest blank. In fact, I was ready for three or four of them. My writing was normal, and if I do say it myself — legible. The few simple test problems were quickly and correctly done. Oh, yes, my diplomas. Did I have them? Only then I remembered that they had disappeared with a box of household junk in one of the movings twenty years ago. My statement was accepted as fact and in a kindly voice that fine personnel director said, 'We believe you will be able to do the work. You can start to work tomorrow.' I moved out of the office — 'floated' I believe is the word. I hadn't worked in thirty years and I was starting in tomorrow. I was in the seventh heaven in the front row. I was ready to say goodbye to bridge luncheons, war rallies, lectures, matinees. I was a war worker. I got the car under control as I approached home and letdown set in. What would friend husband say? Could I do the work? How could I manage the house without a maid? Would I be forgotten by all my friends? Eight forty-five every morning was the dead line and I intended to be at work on time.

"At dinner that evening we talked about the war and the need for men and women in the new war industry and in a most casual way, I mentioned that I had a job. It didn't happen at all as the story books tell. Husband missed one puff on his pipe and said, 'That's fine. When do you start?' I was over the worst hurdle, but Old Man Worry pursued me to bed and long into the night I was planning meals and dusting and searching for a maid. The first day was a triumphal march. I knew what I was doing. My mathematics were accurate and I left in the evening feeling that my output would be equal to the average in three or four days.

"My husband was one of those big helpless men who wanted to be waited upon and I enjoyed doing it. I was not sure that I could carry the work in the office and operate the house. Maids were impossible to hire but I intended to push myself to the limit to keep both shops working. Marketing and laundry were something that would have to be worked out. I thought I knew 'friend husband,' having lived with him for thirty-three years except for the trips that he took on business that accounted for almost fifteen years. He could distribute more clothes about the house between bedtime and leaving for the office than a good husband should. He would live on his hump rather than get a meal and dust about the house never entered his consciousness. He could repair an electric fixture cord and leave more tools around him than a woman would use in house cleaning. He could get himself an evening snack and leave the icebox door open. In filling his pipe he would spread tobacco and ashes with a wide and lavish gesture. But he had a good time at home and it didn't bother me. What would you do with a husband like that if you got a job after thirty years as a homemaker? I didn't have to solve it. My first day at the office, he was up at 6:00 A.M. and before I could drag myself out he had the breakfast ready. Yes, and we did the dishes before we left. He makes his own bed. And once a week he gets home from the office and, clad in tennis shoes and track pants, he vacuums, cleans every rug in the house while I get dinner. How I envy muscles that can drive a Hoover with the energy that he puts into it! He never knew we owned a dust mop before I went to work, but he now manipulates it with a fine art. He seems to get a lot of fun out of these jobs he has taken over and in fact we are both getting a little more out of life.

"No, I haven't worked in thirty years. Last week I came home with my second pay envelope filled with cash and a complimentary comment from my supervisor. More, all act as if they were proud of me. I've learned that you can never tell what a family will do. I'm going to work until this mess is over and then I hope that I can settle down to the job of enjoying a few grandchildren." (25)

In the light of this story it should be clear to those many young people who think there is no fun in marriage that they are mistaken. Their delusion is born of inexperience and observation of their own or other families where conflict has predominated, and perhaps they have studied too many courses in abnormal psychology and social pathology.

The Case for Optimism

Many people are pessimistic. It is possible, however, to take an optimistic view of the future of marriage. Let us not overlook the fact that the war babies of 1918 were the fine, patriotic, high spirited, intelligent young men and women who fought and won the last war. While everyone recognizes the increasingly serious need for more adequate planning to meet our social needs on the home front, and the inevitable failures and heartaches which lie ahead for those who have been unfortunate in the conduct of their personal lives, we must also realize that the keenest insight, soundest judgment, and most effective learning results when experience is a part of the educative process.

We have never had, in the lifetime of most of us, a situation more completely filled with opportunity to participate in experiences which are as socially useful as at the present time.

The problems of today can be helped, *first*, by seeing both the effects of immediate crises upon the lives of individuals and gaining a long term perspective with reference to the basic and fundamental values in life.

Second, in order to attack the basic social needs which underlie many present day difficulties, it is important that both educational and social agencies cooperate in providing the kind of social and recreational opportunities which meet our needs for release. We can no longer assume that commercial institutions will provide socially constructive means, whereby we will be able, through the period of emergency, to find proper ways of getting relief from frustration and fatigue. We must not let the almighty dollar stand in the way of providing, in every community, those facilities which are needed.

Some of it will have to be done at public expense. One of the main purposes of education is to reduce personal and social disorganization to a minimum. Community programs, including education, should be the means of reducing the need for remedial agents and institutions.

The *third* means of meeting the present problem lies in seeing that the democratic process is utilized and carried out in all matters of social and educational planning. There may be too much of someone in Washington saying what should be done, which, in turn, is reinterpreted and passed on by someone in the state, which, in turn, is reinterpreted and passed on by a city official, a school principal, or someone else; and, in too many cases, the teacher is told to eliminate this subject, or add another, without having had any opportunity to participate in planning with administrative officers.

Administrators and teachers must stabilize themselves through the process of cooperative planning. They will then be better able to guide students to think through their problems and find means of meeting them. There are opportunities for this in every public school. Youth conferences, involving all public high schools, should be a continuous part of education during the next few years. So far as I know there is no one in Washington, London, Moscow, or Chungking, who has enough wisdom to make decisions for the whole of organized society. This very process of democratic group thinking and planning will be one of the most valuable stabilizing influences we can provide.

Fourth, war has been considered an inevitable concomitant of modern civilization. Our whole emphasis has been upon the idea that each war is different from other wars. This is true as far as method of fighting the fray is concerned, but basically it is human warfare — as warfare has always been a human affair and has grown out of human greed, human suspicion, human struggle for power, and humanly engendered racial, religious, and nationalistic hatreds.

The biggest problem confronting us today, therefore, as it affects home and family life, is the recognition of this basic underlying cause of human conflict and a recognition of the fact that much of human conflict grows out of the kind of family life in which we grow up, and the philosophy surrounding business enterprise and politics to which we are exposed.

The Study of Man

We need, therefore, to concentrate our attention on the human being for a few centuries, even if it is necessary to give technological development a short vacation. We need better to understand the factors which motivate and enhance the growth and development of man himself.

We need to be concerned in education, not so much with courses which prepare for college and courses which prepare for earning a living, as with education which equips people, not only with the ability to earn their own livelihood, but the ability to live with one another cooperatively, democratically, and happily. The school curriculum must increase tenfold its emphasis on human values. Every young man and woman who passes through our school system must, in the future, be well educated in the field of human development and human relationships. His education must include experience which deals specifically with premarriage education; he must be better equipped to play his role as benedict and parent.

The school must move into the community and provide educational opportunities for the newly married on problems of adult relationships and the care and development of children. This program must extend to, and in turn be extended by, churches, settlement houses, business firms, and youth organizations of all kinds. (24)

Preparation for marriage begins in infancy and early childhood. It continues until the knot is tied and thus on throughout one's married life. Marriage is different today only because certain problems make life harder for some people to live than for others. The extra work of these times adds to our problems of adjustment to others. We cannot run away from responsibility, nor always be taking out our frustrations, irritations, and disappointments on some other person. The generals and the armies may win the war, but they can never win the peace. A lasting peace will have to be won on the home front by the kind of family and other social relationships which emerge from the experiences of the present crisis.

There is no perfect solution to these problems of marriage today. If you would make a good mate at any time, and if you think you can work out the financial, social, and personal aspects of adjustments to marriage under present conditions, get married. If you are not a good risk as a prospective husband or wife and cannot work out the personal, social, and economic problems of the present day, do not marry. It is probably better to wait than to marry, if you are not fit to marry.

The Future Is Now

Tomorrow is the day after today for most of us. Planning for after the war and postwar readjustments is a good and profitable pastime for the "oldster," but young people are concerned with life right now. Today many of you are in school, concerned largely with yourselves, your acceptance by other young people, your popularity, your looks, your relationships with other boys and girls, how to get through much of the uninteresting, unrealistic material of the school curriculum, how to get a job so you can get married and begin living life on your own. Today is the future! That should be the motto for everyone. The best preparation for the future is to be sure we are enlightened on things which concern us now, to see to it that we actually know what is going on in the world of the present.

There are two problems which confront us; one is that of understanding the world today and being able to interpret it, the other is to work out for ourselves a program based on sound mental hygiene and an adequate social philosophy.

We should understand that the world today is, in most essentials, no different from the world of yesterday or the world of tomorrow. It is still a world in which the major responsibility and decisions of life, be they economic, political, social, or personal, revolve ultimately upon human beings with intelligence, insight, judgment, and vision.

Since you are concerned with yourself, the best preparation which you can make for meeting the world of today and the world of tomorrow is by having an opportunity thoroughly to investigate all the ramifications of your own selves, biologically, psychologically, and culturally; how you came to be, what you are, the factors which have entered into your conditioning, your growth, your attitudes, your emotions, your feelings, your prejudices, etc. When you leave the portals of high school or college you should understand yourself and be able to say, "I know my potentialities, I know something of my strengths and weaknesses as a person. I know what I can do without help or assistance."

You need to understand the economics of everyday life. This knowledge begins with an understanding of how to get spending money and how to earn and supplement what we may inveigle out of our parents. We sometimes fail to realize that economics is a subject which confronts us from our earliest years throughout our entire lives. We assume very often that a three-point course on economic theory as a sophomore in college does the job of economic education. We sometimes assume that we can understand the problems of the world of today, even though we do little else to supplement that college training, which is available only to the few, either prior to their sophomore college year or subsequent thereto. Our exposure to money early in life, our assumption of responsibility for it in relation to purchasing our own things is the beginning of our understanding of our economic system.

There is need for an ever widening introduction into the mechanics and devices which our society has set up for handling the problems of production and distribution. This is one of our chief concerns and forms an interest around which motivation and desire for learning is ripe. How can we become interested in the major problems of international life which center around the distribution of the goods of the world among the people of the world; how can we understand that this is all tied up with international trade, inter-

national finance, and with the banking policies which lead
to war or peace, unless, throughout our whole course of
development, we have been helped to have a realistic touch
with the economics of everyday life?

We need to understand that government is not a myth nor
a mysterious mechanism by which somebody, quite apart
from ourselves, runs the society of which we are a part. Yet
when, as is so often the case, we grow up in a family in
which there is no democracy, in which there is absolute
dominance and authoritative control throughout our early
years, and when we attend a school in which there is a continuation of this same autocratic procedure, and, finally,
when we get into a business or profession and find the same
kind of relationship with our superiors, how can we conceive
of a practical, working democracy from a political point of
view? Democracy begins at home — political democracy,
if you please.

We need to understand that, quite regardless of the complicated problems of the economic organization of life, the
kind of economics we have ultimately depends upon the
social viewpoint and social philosophy of the individuals who
make up that society. Our first questions in high-school life
have to do with social etiquette and social ethics, with our
relationships with other boys and other girls. We must find
the way to carry out a social life that is related to achievement of personal satisfaction and the social welfare of the
group of which we are a part.

We need to understand that wherever we live there are
certain sanctions and restrictions within which every individual must live his life. Some of these we may not like, and
our choice may be to break them and accept the consequences of social disapproval or to move to some other
society. If we choose the latter, no matter where we go we
will find different sanctions or restrictions, but we will
always have to face the problem of conforming to certain
group regulations. All through life we often rebel against
restrictions because they are imposed upon us by a parent

or teacher and are not tied up with our own experience or with any insight we may have as to the reasons for such restrictions.

We must understand that there is a moral basis for personal and social living; that there is an almost organic relatedness to all of life which works out ultimately within the individual's own conceptions of himself, his relationships to other people, and his philosophy and goal in life; that we live in an economic system which we call capitalistic, which is competitive and allows for a maximum of individual effort, except in so far as that is restricted by monopoly or governmental regulations; that there are conflicting points of view with reference to the organization of our economic life, each of which, theoretically at least, is concerned with the welfare of the whole of society; that we have conflicting political philosophies which are tenable within the framework of our constitution, and that an understanding of these and their implications as they affect individual and social welfare is important for an intelligent citizen; that we have conflicting religious philosophies, since we are a nation in which the freedom of individual worship is allowed; that there are points of conflict between our political theory, our economic philosophy, and, many times, our social and religious philosophies. All of these things we can understand in terms of our own immediate interests in the world of today. We can understand them in such a way that they present for us a challenge rather than a stone wall that blocks progress or leads to an attitude of defeatism.

We all need to understand that the individual is a product of group experience and that his own family and the family he will establish are the two most important influences in determining the ultimate outcome of civilization. We need further to realize and understand that family life is a universal human experience; that it is the most potent factor in the development of personality; that home is the place where most of us acquire our basic behavior patterns, our religious sentiments, our moral and ethical precepts, our

political and economic philosophy, our attitude toward
people, and our unique personality; that the family does
interpret and transmit to us the basic and ultimate attitudes
which we have and which we, in turn, will no doubt be
instrumental in transmitting to our own family; and that
life is a continuation of intermittent crises, none of which
to date have wiped out civilization. We only need to go
back 100 years and compare the change from 1842 to 1942
and look at the catastrophies, so to speak, which have
threatened our American way of life; we need to become
acquainted with those individuals who have assumed leadership and who have directed the forces of our common life
toward new and better achievements; we need to recognize,
even more than we do, the importance of an education which
is closely tied in with our life experiences and which helps us
to live that life more successfully and more adequately.

Finally, we need to understand that nations fought World
War II, not primarily to obliterate Hitler and his type of
leadership from the face of the globe, but because there were
many social and economic inequities within nations and between nations; and that the world was in a state of
social upheaval because these many conflicting philosophies
came into impact with each other, each striving to dominate and organize a world for better living according to its
own particular philosophy. We need to know and understand the truth about history and government and politics
and nations, as well as the truth about science and our
personal way of life. We need to be helped to think through
much more objectively the issues of industry, of labor, of
agriculture, of social affairs, and of religion. We need to
recognize that, in the immediate future, our families are
likely to be faced with greatly reduced income due to rising
cost of living and increase in taxes; that many of the privileges which we have enjoyed heretofore may not, in the
future, be forthcoming, but the satisfactions of life will be
those which we are able to derive as a result of our own
effort; and, finally, that out of this present turmoil we will

not arrive at any static condition because life itself is in the process of constant change, and everyone needs to acquire for himself a pattern of adaptability to new experiences and changed conditions. This is the essence of keeping up with progress, in science and in other fields.

There are six things about which a young person graduating from high school, entering college, or going to work for the first time should want as complete an understanding as possible in order to meet life as it has to be met. He should want, in so far as possible, to understand himself and the factors related to his success in working with and getting along with other people. He should want some knowledge of practical economic affairs as they involve earning a living and spending an income intelligently; he should want to understand the relationship of his economic function in life to the total economic problems on a large scale. He should want a socially tolerant and understanding attitude about society. He should want a conviction that all civilization is based upon the strength of the moral stamina of its citizenry. IIe should want to have arrived at a belief in political democracy and a zeal to make it work at home, at school, and in all other phases of public life. And, finally, he should want some knowledge of, and some passion for, the task which lies ahead — that of working out all of the interrelated and seemingly conflicting viewpoints about individual, social, economic, and political life. The future is now. We who live in 1950, especially those of college age, will be responsible for what little progress civilization makes between now and the year 2000. Today is the future! (26)

Appendix

APPENDIX A

REFERENCES FOR SUPPLEMENTARY READING

PART I. PERSONAL DEVELOPMENT IN RELATION TO MARRIAGE

CHAPTER I. UNDERSTANDING ONE'S SELF AND OTHERS

Bowman, Henry A., *Marriage for Moderns*. McGraw-Hill Book Company, Inc., New York, 1948. Chap. 1.

Cole, Luella M., *Psychology of Adolescence*. Farrar and Rinehart, Inc., New York, 1948. Chap. 1.

Hill, Ruben and Evelyn Duvall, *When You Marry*. Association Press, New York, 1945. Chap. 1.

Landis, Paul H., *Your Marriage and Family Living*. McGraw-Hill Book Company, Inc., New York, 1946. Chap. 5.

Langer, Walter C., *Psychology and Human Living*. D. Appleton-Century Company, Inc., New York, 1943. Chaps. 1, 3–6, 9–11.

Menninger, William C. and Monroe Leaf, *You and Psychiatry*. Charles Scribner's Sons, New York, 1948.

Moore, Bernice Milburn and Dorothy M. Leahy, *You and Your Family*. D. C. Heath and Company, Boston, 1948. Chaps. 1, 4–8.

Travis, Lee Edwards and Dorothy W. Baruch, *Personal Problems of Everyday Life*. D. Appleton-Century Company, Inc., New York, 1941. Chaps. 1–6.

Wood, Mildred Wigley, *Living Together in the Family*. American Home Economics Association, Washington, D. C. Chap. 2.

CHAPTER II. BASIC NEEDS AND HUMAN BEHAVIOR

Coon, Beulah and Bess Goodykoontz, *Family Living and Our Schools*. D. Appleton-Century Company, Inc., New York, 1941. Chap. 3.

Prescott, Daniel A., *Emotion and the Educative Process*. American Council on Education, Washington, D. C., 1938.

CHAPTER III. THE EVOLUTION OF FRIENDLINESS PATTERNS IN
RELATION TO MARRIAGE

Breckenridge, Miriam and E. Lee Vincent, *Child Development.*
W. B. Saunders Company, Philadelphia, 1948. Chaps. 1, 2.

Bullis, H. Edmund and Emily E. O'Malley, *Human Relations
in the Classroom. Course I.* 1947.

Bullis, H. Edmund. *Human Relations in the Classroom. Course
II.* 1948. Delaware State Society for Mental Hygiene,
1404 Franklin St., Wilmington, Del.

PART II. THE IMMEDIATE PRELUDE TO MARRIAGE

CHAPTER IV. DATING AND COURTSHIP

Bowman, Henry A., *Marriage for Moderns.* McGraw-Hill
Book Company, Inc., New York, 1948. Chaps. 2, 5, 8.

Fedder, Ruth, *A Girl Grows Up.* McGraw-Hill Book Company, Inc., New York, 1948.

Fisher, Frederick C., *How to Get Married and Stay That Way.*
Rayart Publishing Company, Detroit, 1938.

Hill, Ruben and Evelyn Duvall, *When You Marry.* Association Press, New York, 1945. Chaps. 2-4.

Landis, Judson T. and Mary G., *Building a Successful Marriage.* Prentice Hall, Inc., New York, 1948. Chap. 4.

McKown, Harry E. and Marion LeBron, *A Boy Grows Up.*
McGraw-Hill Book Company, Inc., New York, 1948.

Moore, Bernice Milburn and Dorothy M. Leahy, *You and
Your Family.* D. C. Heath and Company, Boston, 1948.
Chaps. 10-11.

CHAPTER V. MATE SELECTION

Becker, Howard and Ruben Hill, *Family, Marriage and Parenthood.* D. C. Heath and Company, Boston, 1948. Chap. 8.

Binkley, R. C. and F. W., *What Is Right with Marriage.* D.
Appleton-Century Company, Inc., New York, 1929.
Chaps. 2, 4, 5.

Bowman, Henry A., *Marriage for Moderns.* McGraw-Hill
Book Company, Inc., New York, 1948. Chaps. 6, 7.

Cavan, Ruth, *The Family.* Thomas Y. Crowell Company,
New York, 1942. Chap. 4.

Folsom, Joseph K., *Plan for Marriage.* Harper and Brothers,
New York, 1938. Chaps. 1-4.

Goldstein, Sidney, *Meaning of Marriage — A Jewish Interpretation.* The Bloch Publishing Company, New York, 1940.

Groves, Gladys H., *Marriage and Family Life*. Reynal and Hitchcock, Inc., New York, 1942. Chaps. 9, 10, 12, 13.

Himes, Norman, *Your Marriage*. Farrar and Rinehart, Inc., New York, 1940. Chaps. 1–10.

Jordan, Ruth, *You and Marriage*. John Wiley and Sons, Inc., New York, 1942. Chaps. 2, 3.

Landis, Judson T. and Mary G., *Building a Successful Marriage*. Prentice Hall, Inc., New York, 1948. Chaps. 6, 7.

Lord, Danial A., *Questions I'm Asked about Marriage — A Catholic Interpretation*. The Queen's Work, St. Louis, 1938.

Magoun, F. Alexander, *Love and Marriage*. Harper and Brothers, New York, 1948. Chaps. 1, 5, 6.

Popenoe, Paul, *Modern Marriage*. The Macmillan Company, New York, 1940.

Schmeidler, Edgar, *Marriage and the Family*. McGraw-Hill Book Company, Inc., New York, 1946.

Travis, Lee E. and Dorothy W. Baruch, *Personal Problems of Everyday Life*. D. Appleton-Century Company, Inc., New York, 1941. Chap. 9.

Waller, Willard, *The Family*. The Dryden Press, New York, 1938.

PART III.   EVOLVING A SATISFACTORY FAMILY LIFE

CHAPTER VI. LOOKING FORWARD TO MARRIAGE

Becker, Howard and Ruben Hill, *Family, Marriage and Parenthood*. D. C. Heath and Company, Boston, 1948. Chap. 9.

Bowman, Henry A., *Marriage for Moderns*. McGraw-Hill Book Company, Inc., New York, 1948. Chap. 9.

Folsom, Joseph K., *The Family*. John Wiley and Sons, Inc., New York, 1943. Chaps. 11, 12, 15.

Hill, Ruben and Evelyn Duvall, *When You Marry*. Association Press, New York, 1945. Chap. 5.

Landis, Judson T. and Mary G., *Building a Successful Marriage*. Prentice Hall, Inc., New York, 1948. Chaps. 8, 9.

Magoun, F. Alexander, *Love and Marriage*. Harper and Brothers, New York, 1948. Chaps. 7, 8.

CHAPTER VII. THE FIRST YEAR OF MARRIAGE

Folsom, Joseph K., *The Family*. John Wiley and Sons, Inc., New York, 1943. Chap. 13.

Hill, Ruben and Evelyn Duvall, *When You Marry*. Association Press, New York, 1945. Chap. 9.

Landis, Judson T. and Mary G., *Building a Successful Marriage*. Prentice Hall, Inc., New York, 1948. Chap. 10.

Moore, Bernice Milburn and Dorothy M. Leahy, *You and Your Family*. D. C. Heath and Company, Boston, 1948. Chaps. 12, 13.

CHAPTER VIII. PERSONALITY FACTORS IN RELATIONSHIPS

Bowman, Henry A., *Marriage for Moderns*. McGraw-Hill Book Company, Inc., New York, 1948. Chaps. 10, 11.

Burgess, E. W. and Leonard Cattrell, *Predicting Success and Failure in Marriage*. Prentice Hall, Inc., New York, 1939.

Foster, Robert G. and Pauline P. Wilson, *Women After College*. Columbia University Press, New York, 1942. Chap. 2.

Himes, Norman, *Your Marriage*. Farrar and Rinehart, Inc., New York, 1940. Chaps. 6, 19–21.

Levy, John and Ruth Monroe, *The Happy Family*. Alfred A. Knopf, New York, 1938. Chaps. 1–3.

Travis, Lee E. and Dorothy W. Baruch, *Personal Problems of Everyday Life*. D. Appleton-Century Company, Inc., New York, 1941. Chap. 9.

CHAPTER IX. SEX AS A FACTOR IN FAMILY LIFE

Bowman, Henry A., *Marriage for Moderns*. McGraw-Hill Book Company, Inc., New York, 1948. Chap. 14.

Butterfield, Elmer M., *Sex Life in Marriage*. Emerson Books, Inc., New York, 1937.

Fishbein, Morris and E. W. Burgess, *Successful Marriage*. Doubleday and Company, Inc., Garden City, N. Y., 1947. Part I, chap. 5; Part II, chaps. 1–3, 9, 10; Part V, chaps. 3, 5, 6.

Hill, Ruben and Evelyn Duvall, *When You Marry*. Association Press, New York, 1945. Chaps. 7, 8.

Himes, Norman, *Your Marriage*. Farrar and Rinehart, Inc., New York, 1940. Chaps. 22–25.

Kimber, C. D., Carolyn Gray and Coraline E. Stakepole, *Textbook of Anatomy and Physiology*. The Macmillan Company, New York, 1937, 11th ed. Chap. 24.

Levy, John and Ruth Monroe, *The Happy Family*. Alfred A. Knopf, New York, 1938. Chap. 4.

Scheinfeld, Amram, *You and Heredity*. Garden City Publishing Co., Garden City, N. Y., 1939.

Strain, Frances Bruce, *Love at the Threshold*. D. Appleton-Century Company, Inc., New York, 1939.

——, *Being Born*. D. Appleton-Century Company, Inc., New York, 1936.

CHAPTER X.   PARENTS AND IN-LAW RELATIONSHIPS

Landis, Judson T. and Mary G., *Building a Successful Marriage*. Prentice Hall, Inc., New York, 1948. Chap. 12.

Strecker, Edward A., *Their Mothers' Sons*. J. B. Lippincott Company, Philadelphia, 1946.

CHAPTER XI.   RELATIONSHIPS INVOLVING MONEY

Biglow, Howard F., *Family Finance*. J. B. Lippincott Company, Philadelphia, 1936.

Hill, Ruben and Evelyn Duvall, *When You Marry*. Association Press, New York, 1945. Chap. 11.

Himes, Norman, *Your Marriage*. Farrar and Rinehart, Inc., New York, 1940. Chaps. 12–18.

Jordan, David F. and Edward F. Willett, *Managing Personal Finances*. Prentice Hall, Inc., New York, 1945.

Moore, Bernice Milburn and Dorothy M. Leahy, *You and Your Family*. D. C. Heath and Company, Boston, 1948. Chap. 15.

Public Affairs Pamphlets. Public Affairs Committee, Inc., New York.

No. 5, *Credit for Consumers*.

No. 18, *How We Spend Our Money*.

No. 61, *Installment Selling*.

No. 62, *How To Buy Insurance*.

No. 63, *More for Your Money*.

CHAPTER XII.   MANAGING THE HOME AND HOME RELATIONSHIPS

Bonde, Ruth L., *Management in Daily Living*. The Macmillan Company, New York, 1944.

Cushman, Ella M., *Management in Homes*. The Macmillan Company, New York, 1945.

Nickell, Paulena and Jean Muir Dorsey, *Management in Family Living*. John Wiley and Sons, Inc., New York, 1942.

United States Department of Agriculture, *Guiding Family Spending*. Miscellaneous Publication 661, 1949.

——, *Helping Families Plan Food Budgets*. Miscellaneous Publication 662, 1948.

CHAPTER XIII. SOME OTHER FACTORS IN FAMILY RELATIONSHIPS

Fosdick, Harry Emerson, *On Being a Real Person*. Harper and Brothers, New York, 1943.

Groves, Ernest R., *Christianity and the Family*. The Macmillan Company, New York, 1943.

Groves, Ernest R. and Catherine, *Dynamic Mental Hygiene*. Stackpole Sons, Harrisburg, Pa., 1946. Chaps. 1, 10.

CHAPTER XIV. THE COMING OF CHILDREN

Aldrich, C. A. and Mary, *Babies Are Human Beings*. The Macmillan Company, New York, 1938.

Binkley, R. C. and F. W., *What Is Right with Marriage*. D. Appleton-Century Company, Inc., New York, 1929. Chaps. 10–13, 15, 17.

Breckenridge, Miriam and E. Lee Vincent, *Child Development*. W. B. Saunders Company, Philadelphia, 1948.

Corbin, Hazel, *Getting Ready To Be a Father*. The Macmillan Company, New York, 1939.

Hollingshead, A. B. *Elmtown's Youth*. John Wiley & Sons, Inc. New York, 1949.

Schulz, Lois R. and Mollie S. Smart, *Understanding Your Baby*. The Sun Dial Press, New York, 1942.

Smart, R. C. and Mollie S., *It's a Wise Parent*. Charles Scribner's Sons, New York, 1944.

Spock, Benjamin, *A Pocket Book of Baby and Child Care*. Pocket Books, Inc., New York, 1946.

Taylor, K. W., *Do Adolescents Need Parents?* D. Appleton-Century Company, Inc., New York, 1938.

PART IV. THE FAMILY AND DEMOCRATIC SOCIETY

CHAPTER XV. SUCCESS OR FAILURE IN FAMILY DEVELOPMENT

Bernard, Jessie, *American Family Behavior*. Harper and Brothers, New York, 1942. Chaps. 20–21.

Burgess, E. W. and Leonard Cottrell, *Predicting Success and Failure in Marriage*. Prentice Hall, Inc., New York, 1939.

Terman, Lewis *et al.*, *Psychological Factors in Marital Happiness*. McGraw-Hill Book Company, Inc., New York, 1938.

CHAPTER XVI. CRISES AND HUMAN RELATIONSHIPS

Angell, Robert C., *The Family in the Depression*. Charles Scribner's Sons, New York, 1936.

Becker, Howard and Ruben Hill, *Family, Marriage and Parenthood.* D. C. Heath and Company, Boston, 1948. Chaps. 21–24.

Bergler, Edmund, *Divorce Won't Help.* Harper and Brothers, New York, 1948.

Groves, Ernest R., *Conserving Marriage and the Family.* The Macmillan Company, New York, 1944.

The Annals of the American Academy of Political and Social Science, March, 1932; November, 1936; November, 1940; September, 1943.

CHAPTER XVII. THE UNMARRIED

Bowman, Henry A., *Marriage for Moderns.* McGraw-Hill Book Company, Inc., New York, 1948. Chap. 3.

Foster, Robert G. and Pauline P. Wilson, *Women After College.* Columbia University Press, New York, 1942.

Groves, Ernest R., *Marriage.* Henry Holt and Company, Inc., New York, 1941. Chaps. 29, 30.

CHAPTER XVIII. THE INDIVIDUAL AND SOCIETY

CHAPTER XIX. WHAT LIES AHEAD

Anshen, Ruth Wanda, *The Family: Its Function and Destiny.* Harper and Brothers, New York, 1948.

Becker, Howard and Ruben Hill, *Family, Marriage and Parenthood.* D. C. Heath and Company, Boston, 1948.

Burgess, E. R. and Harvey Locke, *The Family.* Ginn and Company, New York, 1945.

Folsom, Joseph K., *The Family and Democratic Society.* John Wiley and Sons, Inc., New York, 1943.

Frank, Laurie K., *Society as the Patient.* Rutgers University Press, New Brunswick, N. J., 1948.

Frank, Lawrence K., *Yes, Families Are Changing.* Survey, Dec. 1949.

Groves, Ernest R., *Marriage.* Henry Holt and Company, Inc., New York, 1941.

Hill, Ruben, *Families under Stress.* Harper and Brothers, New York, 1949.

Mead, Margaret, *Male and Female.* Wm. Morrow & Co., New York, 1949.

Truxal, Andrew G. and Frances E. Merrill, *The Family and American Culture.* Prentice Hall, Inc., New York, 1947.

APPENDIX B

QUESTIONS AND EXERCISES FOR STUDENTS TO ACCOMPANY STUDY OF THE TEXT

PART I. PERSONAL DEVELOPMENT IN RELATION TO MARRIAGE

CHAPTER I. UNDERSTANDING ONE'S SELF AND OTHERS

1. What is meant when you say a person has a good personality? A poor personality?
2. What is the difference between saying John Smith has a personality and John Smith is a personality?
3. Write a short two- or three-page description of the kind of person you feel yourself to be. After you finish, list the characteristics you feel to be desirable and those you feel to be undesirable. Does this help you to see yourself more objectively?
4. Describe the characteristics of a person whom you do not like. List the characteristics which annoy you most. Why do these particular characteristics irritate you?
5. What is the difference between your conception of the kind of a person you are, the kind of a person you think others think you are, and what some other person actually thinks of you?
6. See if you can account for your favorable or unfavorable feeling toward the physical appearance, complexion, style of dress, or mannerisms of some other person?
7. A high-school senior girl asks for help in overcoming her inability to make and keep friends. What suggestions would you make to her?

CHAPTER II. BASIC NEEDS AND HUMAN BEHAVIOR

1. What is the difference between our basic needs and our desires and ambitions?

2. When you cannot have or achieve something you want very much, what do you usually do? Do you react the same way when you cannot satisfy some basic need such as food, or warmth in cold weather?

3. After reading Beulah Coon and Bess Goodykoontz, *Family Living in Our Schools*, Chap. III, try and outline your own basic needs which are adequately, partially, or not in any sense being satisfied. Can you pick out any kinds of undesirable behavior on your part that may be associated with this lack of basic need satisfaction?

4. A professor made the statement that "adjustment was doing what someone else wanted done at a time when you did not want to do it." Do you agree?

5. Give an example of an instance where you have met a difficult situation by (1) running away or evading it; (2) attacking it and trying to change the other person or situation; (3) altering your own attitude toward it.

CHAPTER III. FRIENDLINESS PATTERNS IN RELATION TO MARRIAGE

1. Trace your relationships with your mother and father from your earliest recollection to the present. Does it follow the general outline of psychological development briefly discussed in this chapter?

2. Can you discern ways in which your relationships with boys or girls have been affected by your own kind of friendliness feelings?

3. What seem to you to be the characteristics of a normal person at three years of age? Twelve years of age? Your own age?

4. Trace your own relationships to family, friends, and teachers in elementary school, in high school, and, at present, in school, socially or on your job. Have they been the same or have they changed as you have grown older?

5. What is the relationship of one's friendship patterns to one's past relationship to authority, to his reality experiences with the external world about him, and to his sense of security in his family relationships?

6. What role do such emotions as fear, anger, hate, and jealousy play in the kind of friendships we form and particularly in our dating, courtship, and engagement relationships?

PART II. THE IMMEDIATE PRELUDE TO MARRIAGE

CHAPTER IV. DATING AND COURTSHIP

1. Why do some girls have many dates while other equally attractive girls have none?
2. What are the advantages and disadvantages of going "steady" with one's first "crush" throughout college, as against dating several persons?
3. What suggestions do you have to help young people solve the perplexing questions which arise in the process of dating?
4. When a person says to you, "I love you," what does he really mean? How can you tell when you are truly "in love"? (See Bowman, pp. 31–42. Agree or disagree? See Jordan, *You and Marriage*, Chap. III, Psychology of Attraction. Agree or disagree?)
5. What satisfactions are students seeking when they date?
6. What justification, if any, is there for a double standard of morals?
7. In your observation, to what extent does the popularity of a girl depend upon her willingness to "pet"? What specific forms of activity do you believe most helpful in sublimating one's sexual desires? What are the best ways for diverting this energy into constructive action?
8. What are some of the best ways in which young people can be helped in developing their own codes of sex morality?
9. From your observation and experience, what have been the actual effects of attempts at sex education by Y.M.C.A.'s, Y.W.C.A.'s, ministers and special lecturers in schools?
10. For what activities, if any, should young people of marriageable age be required to secure permission of their parents?

CHAPTER V. MATE SELECTION

1. What is the family's legitimate responsibility for the proper mating of its children?
2. Do coeducational schools and jobs tend to increase one's marriageable chances? What types of organizations for women tend to have the highest and the lowest marriage possibilities?

3. Do you think many girls do not marry because there are no available men or because they do not know how to meet and act in their relationships with men?

4. Check yourself on the Marriage Prediction Scale in Himes, Chap. VI. Do you think it considers all the most important factors?

5. What do Burgess and Cottrell and Terman find to be the most important factors basic to successful mating?

6. Do you think the generally acceptable ideas about length of engagement hold true in wartime? Justify your answer.

7. What factors seem to you to carry most weight in considering differences between couples contemplating marriage — age, education, economic status, religion, race or nationality, and health?

8. Dr. Paul Popenoe, Director of the American Institute of Family Relations, says that men invited to a sorority dance are, by convention, almost arbitrarily limited to fraternity members. These men are not, at the most critical time, the most prospective husbands. The sororities would do better to issue invitations to the members of the 20–30 Club and the Junior Chamber of Commerce. Discuss the wisdom of this statement.

9. What advantages or disadvantages would there be in reducing the proportion of people who do not have the opportunity to marry by allowing women more initiative and freedom in selecting their mates?

10. What would be the advantage of modifying our American plan of individual choice of a mate and allowing parents more leeway in arranging marriages? This seems to work satisfactorily in certain other societies.

CHAPTER VI. LOOKING FORWARD TO MARRIAGE

1. Should engaged persons tell each other everything about their past experience? Why?

2. What is the most satisfactory way to break an engagement when the other person is still in love with you?

3. What do you think are the limits of one's intimacies during engagement? Why?

4. What do you think are the things which contribute to the best preparation for marriage? Does your answer apply equally to men and women?

5. Talk with several young married women and see if they feel there has been any "slump" in romance during the first year of marriage?

6. Why is there more emphasis placed on preparation for marriage for women than for men? What kind of pre-marriage education do men need?

7. Do you think long separation during engagement and before marriage has any advantage in testing or proving the sincerity of one's love?

8. What are justifiable reasons for breaking an engagement?

9. What conditions make it advisable or inadvisable for a couple to postpone their marriage until after the war?

10. What relationship would you expect promiscuity in the unmarried to have in their attitude toward the family after marriage?

11. If possible, talk with a young woman and a young man engaged to be married and try to find out what each expects from marriage. Take this information and see if you can find where their expectancies are similar or in opposition to each other. Ask yourself the question, "Does each know what he expects from marriage, and does each person know what the other expects to get from their marriage?"

PART III.   EVOLVING A SATISFACTORY FAMILY LIFE

CHAPTER VII.   THE FIRST YEAR OF MARRIAGE

1. Could you justify the statement that 75 per cent of young men and 50 per cent of young women are not fit to marry?

2. What types of problems, if any, do couples as a rule not have to meet during the first year of marriage?

3. Why is the first year the most crucial year?

4. What are the advantages and disadvantages of living in a family? Is the family the best and only basis for society? Why or why not?

CHAPTER VIII.   PERSONALITY FACTORS IN RELATIONSHIPS

1. Bill Jones and his wife are in conflict over his sending money to his brother who is in college. His wife has to forego certain things for herself, buy less expensive gifts for Christmas, and cannot continue in a bowling league she belongs to. Analyze this situation. To what extent is it a money problem, an in-law problem, a recreational problem, or a personality conflict problem?

2. Contrast the role of husband and wife and of parent and child in the colonial period and today. What changes do you find? What further changes do you see ahead?

3. Should husband or wife have the final word about such questions as what the income is to be spent for, the frequency of marital relations, how often each person's parents should be visited, the kind and amount of entertaining to be done, and the management of children?

4. Harry Emerson Fosdick says, "It is not marriages that fail, it is people who fail. All marriage does is show people up." Discuss. How does this compare with Plant's statement that our basic personality patterns never change, we just redirect our behavior along different lines in order to make a better adaptation to new situations as they arise.

5. If the best golf courses are those with many hazards, would you say that having many difficulties to overcome would tend to increase or decrease family solidarity?

CHAPTER IX.   SEX AS A FACTOR IN FAMILY LIFE

1. List the things you think men and women should know about each other, as a helpful guide to better premarital as well as marital relationships.

2. Name at least ten differences you observe in the daily activities of men and women. Are these mainly differences due to habit training or biological in their origin?

3. What differences, if any, exist between men and women in cell structure, metabolic rate, blood temperature, heart rate, and glandular secretions? Do these facts have any bearing on understanding each other?

4. Do you think adequate sex education has any bearing upon how moral or immoral a person may be? Why? What would you consider to be adequate sex education?

5. When, in their development, do young people become markedly sex conscious? Do you attribute this to social factors, biological development, or attitudes resulting from early training at home?

6. Why do you think there is not more early adolescent sex play between the sexes? Parental vigilance, psychological timidity, or some other cause?

7. Human reproduction is a physical function belonging to the field of biology without reference to mental, societal, or ethical considerations. If this is true, why do many people always think sex sinful or immoral?

CHAPTER X.   PARENTS AND IN-LAW RELATIONSHIPS

1. For what legitimate reasons should parents interfere with the family life of a son or daughter?

2. Discuss the statement frequently made by parents, "I have given my children a good education, and it is their duty to support me when I get old."

3. Read the novel by Josephine Lawrence entitled *Years Are So Long* and show how you would have handled the situations presented.

4. What is a grown child's responsibility to his parents? How is the best way to get parents to recognize this?

5. Why are so many young married persons still afraid of their parents?

6. How can parents live up to high ideals without giving their children the impression that they are old-fashioned?

CHAPTER XI. RELATIONSHIPS INVOLVING MONEY

1. If every married couple in the United States had an income of $100 a week, would all their financial problems be settled? Why?

2. Why are budgets so unpopular? What is the real purpose of budgeting?

3. What periods in the life history of a family bring the most acute financial problems?

4. Work out a sound financial plan for an individual getting married today. What, if any, differences does our being at war make in this plan?

CHAPTER XII. MANAGING THE HOME AND HOME RELATIONSHIPS

1. A young woman college instructor said, "Home economics has no place in a college curriculum. A girl can learn to cook and run a house after she is married." Discuss.

2. What household skills, if any, should a man be expected to perform? Why?

3. If a young couple have money enough to have all their household work done by hired help, is it necessary for the wife to have had training in home economics? Why?

4. Talk with two or three homemakers and see what kind of daily and weekly schedule for managing their homes they follow, if any? Which person interviewed seemed to be the most mature and happiest in her home relationships and general outlook on life?

CHAPTER XIII. SOME OTHER FACTORS IN FAMILY RELATIONSHIPS

1. Talk with a couple married less than a year and find out what their social and recreational activities are, both together and separately, at home and outside. Do the same

for a couple who have school-age children. Do the same for a couple whose children are grown. Contrast and discuss the differences found.

2. How can young people be taught the importance of practicing what they know about good physical and mental health habits since what they do in their early development may only show up as they reach middle life?

3. In what ways is continuing education available in large cities? In rural areas?

4. What is the role of the church in religious education of parents?

5. What do Burgess and Cottrell and Terman find to be the importance of religion in marital happiness? Do you agree with their findings? Why?

CHAPTER XIV. THE COMING OF CHILDREN

1. What are the advantages and disadvantages of postponing childbearing for several years after marriage?

2. Talk with a mother who has a baby under a year old and find out in what ways the coming of the child affected their household routines, their social activities and personal relationships.

3. What might ideally be a father's role in relation to the care and training of the infant and young child?

4. Observe young children in a nursery school and look for individual differences particularly signs of fear, aggressiveness, withdrawal from the group, and sharing equipment with others.

5. Do you think the nursery school provides a substitute for the home in the early training of children? What are its advantages and disadvantages?

6. What is the importance of making a distinction between loving a child and understanding him?

PART IV. THE FAMILY AND DEMOCRATIC SOCIETY

CHAPTER XV. SUCCESS OR FAILURE IN FAMILY DEVELOPMENT

1. Describe a successful family. Write up your own criteria for judging a successful family.

2. Ask ten married people what factors they would include in judging whether a family was successful.

3. Ask ten unmarried young people the same question as above and compare the results of each group.

4. What evidences would you accept to show whether married couples really are or are not happily married?

CHAPTER XVI. CRISES AND HUMAN RELATIONSHIPS

1. Talk with a family case worker and get her observation of how families who had never before been on welfare reacted to unemployment during the depression of 1933.

2. Discuss the generalizations on the effect of the depression on family relationships (made by Lazarsfeld in Social Science Research Council Monograph — *The Family and the Depression*).

3. Discuss in class the contrasting ways in which different families met the depression in Robert Angell, *The Family in the Depression.*

4. What does the evidence seem to show as to the effect of divorce upon children? "Divorce creates as many problems for the individuals concerned as it solves." Discuss.

5. "War has its origin in home training. It is essentially a personality problem." Do you agree? Why?

6. If one should never marry, formulate a plan of living which you think would bring to him the maximum of satisfaction and fulfillment in life.

7. "Fear of death is evidence of immaturity." Do you agree? Why?

8. How may the church aid those persons who for some reason do not marry? What other agencies should share this function?

9. To what extent does the divorce rate accurately measure the success or failure of marriage? Would marriage benefit if divorce laws were uniform and more strict? Would this be better than having marriage laws uniform and more strict?

10. Farnsworth Crowder, in *McCall's* magazine for February, 1936, lists the following code to follow if one would avoid divorce: stay out of the west; do not live in a metropolis; do not be childless; own things; do not scorn to do the things your grandparents did; avoid being bossy; be physically up to par; do not be a matrimonial idiot; love your mate. From your readings in this field, what reliable bases, if any, do you find for these statements?

11. What are the best methods of being helpful to persons who have lost members of their family through death?

CHAPTER XVII. THE UNMARRIED

1. What percentage of the total marriageable population are unmarried?

2. What special attention needs to be paid to a girl's education, as different from the education of boys?

3. Interview several people over 35 years of age, who are not married, and see if you can discover why they are not married.

4. In what ways do unmarried men and women make their life rich and satisfying?

5. What substitutes are there for the unmarried, to take the place of not being able to have children of their own?

6. Why do unmarried people die at an earlier age than married people? Why do married women tend to live longer than their husbands?

7. Does the desire to follow a career exclude marriage for most girls? Why?

CHAPTER XVIII. THE INDIVIDUAL AND SOCIETY

1. What are the responsibilities of government toward private efforts which tend to be disruptive influences in family life, e.g., certain types of movies, commercialized recreation, false advertising, high pressure sales propaganda, etc.?

2. What do you think are the important functions of the modern family?

3. What implications do you see in this chapter for the kind of home training and education one should have to succeed in the modern world?

CHAPTER XIX. WHAT LIES AHEAD

1. Compare the following articles on the future of marriage, as to differences in point of view:
   a. Baber, Roy, "Marriage and the Family After the War." *The Annals*, Sept., 1942.
   b. Hill, Reuben, "The Future of the Family." In Becker, Howard, and Hill, Reuben, *Marriage and Family Life*, Chap. XXVI.
   c. Folsom, Joseph K., *The Family* (1943 edition), Chap. XVIII, "Men and Women in a Democracy."

2. What practical things can an individual do to improve the conditions in community life which are detrimental to individual and family welfare?

3. What is the role of the church, of government, and of business and industry in social progress and welfare? Are their aims and philosophies compatible?

4. Many people say it is not the function of the school to provide courses in preparation for marriage but that this should be done by parents. Since many parents do not feel equipped so to educate their children, whose job is it to educate the parents?

5. What kinds of economic and industrial changes are likely to affect marriage and family life during the next ten years? What effects do you think these changes will have on the family?

6. In view of the fact that there has been a decline in the feminist movement since about 1928, does this mean that women do not want to be on an equal plane with men, are not physically able to keep up with them, are not intelligent enough for this competition, or what?

7. How important is the population problem in relation to world peace?

8. How can proper family experience contribute to a democratic society and world peace?

APPENDIX C

ADDITIONAL QUESTIONS FOR CLASS OR GROUP DISCUSSION OR FOR INDIVIDUAL REPORTS BASED UPON INTERESTS OF COLLEGE FRESH-MEN (27)

QUESTIONS ABOUT MARRIAGE AND FAMILY LIFE ASKED BY FRESHMAN COLLEGE STUDENTS

I. THE FAMILY AS A SOCIAL INSTITUTION (PART IV OF TEXT)

1. Has the purpose of marriage changed within the last 100 years?
2. Would a study of the average American family bring about desirable changes in many homes now and in the future?
3. Should not the study of eugenics and heredity be placed in the curriculum of every college student?

II. TWO AND THREE GENERATION ADJUSTMENTS (THESE QUESTIONS APPLY AT DIFFERENT LEVELS. PARTS I, II, AND III OF TEXT)

1. Up until what age should parents "lord it" over their children? Or in other words, when is a boy or girl usually capable of choosing his own friends, hours, and actions? Is it possible for parents to be too strict with their children in social life?
2. To what extent should your parents tell you what to do, and name specific examples with explanations where you should be on your own feet?
3. Should children do as parents say even though they know it to be stupid and wrong?
4. "Just what is the extent of my independence of my parents? As a student of less than voting age, yet assum-

287

edly on an equal plane of intelligence with my parents, who have had less education, am I justified in making my own decisions as to habits and pursuits?"

5. How can parents draw their children closer to them instead of driving them away?

6. "My parents and I don't mix together as well as I should like us to. We have good times together but at the dinner table, for example, we do not joke and have as much fun as we should have. Each one of us sometimes thinks of his own problems and there is not enough cheerful and uplifting conversation although there is some. How can this be remedied?"

7. What can be done to narrow the gap found between son or daughter and his or her own parents?

8. What relation exists between the student's parents in the way of happiness and family harmony? What type parents does he have — nagging or reassuring?

9. "I believe one of the greatest problems of family life to be the temperament of the parents. This can make or break family life. If one of the parents is to become irritated by his or her work, or by some petty thing concerning only himself, if he has a bad temper he can spoil the family relations for many days at a time. My ideal in family life is one in which the mother and father are two pals with their children and do not treat them as if they were younger but as if they were old friends. How can this be brought about?"

10. Are your parents alert and interested in all that surrounds them, or are they staid and settled and reluctant to change their ideas and mode of living?

11. A student is sometimes placed in embarrassing situations in his town because of actions of a parent. Should he "stick it out" in that town or move where he is not known?

12. Should your parents choose your friends?

13. Have the parents a natural right to choose mates for their sons and daughters?

14. How much should one's family be considered when one thinks of getting married?

15. Should a parent intervene on a question of the marriage of a member of the family to the point where they will absolutely stop a prospective marriage?

16. Should any member of a family consider his own happiness in preference to the welfare, or at the expense, of other members of his immediate family?

17. Just how much does one's family mean to a college student and what things does he owe to that family?

18. When the child has reached the college age, just what privileges can he expect to receive from the family, and, in turn, what duties is he responsible for?

19. The question is often asked, "Am I depriving my family of many pleasures and necessities by going to college?" Perhaps this course should take such problems into consideration.

20. Should parents deprive themselves of bare necessities to send their children to college?

21. Should the children be expected to follow in their parents' footsteps as far as a career is concerned?

22. Should parents plan their children's lives for them and expect them to carry out the plans?

23. "How can I get my parents to allow me to take the right course, the one I am most interested in?"

24. Should parents be allowed to choose a vocation for their son or daughter?

25. What ways are there to improve family relationships with the maternal and paternal relations?

26. How may a young couple successfully and without hard feelings break away from their respective parents-in-law? Or would it be possible to get the laissez-faire idea across to the parents? Must we marry orphans?

27. Should a married man help support his parents?

28. Should "in-laws" depend on their children for financial aid?

29. Should a young married couple live with the husband's or wife's family for a short time until they get a start?

III. PREMARRIAGE PROBLEMS (PART II OF TEXT)

1. What type of person is usually able to carry on a successful marriage?

2. How should one choose a good wife? What qualities should she possess and what should she be capable of doing?

3. In relation to choosing a mate what is the:
   a. Role of heredity, health, and physical qualifications.
   b. Role of education and intellectual level.
   c. Role of social status and background.
   d. Role of likes and dislikes, interests.
   e. Role of personality.
   f. Role of religion, race, and nationality.

    g. Role of age differential.
    h. Role of love.
    i. Role of infatuation.
    j. Best way of knowing if choice is right one.

4. What types of men and women should or should not marry to produce the most intelligent and healthiest families?
5. Personal health: should it be considered before people marry?
6. Should a girl marry if she knows definitely she cannot have children?
7. If you know you have active tuberculosis and are in love, should you break off the affair?
8. Should a person marry when his family are all inclined to be tubercular?
9. Should the man and woman be equally well educated or should the man be superior in this respect?
10. Is it advisable for a college graduate to marry a person who is not a college graduate?
11. Are college love affairs usually successful?
12. If the woman is of superior intelligence, will that tend to produce an unhappy state?
13. Should a person refrain from marriage because his would-be partner has a poor background?
14. Should a girl look for a man who has plenty of money and no background, or one she really loves? One cannot be happy on love alone.
15. Should the background of one's wife be considered before marriage?
16. Is it well to marry above or below one's station in life?
17. Can two people with widely different cultural tastes ever "make a go" of marriage?
18. Should a couple marry when each one has lived under different economic conditions or in different social and spiritual fields?
19. What degree of similarity of interests of husband and wife are necessary to insure successful marriage?
20. Should a couple whose likes differ marry?
21. How much discrepancy in interests can exist between two parties to a marriage contract and yet have the experiment successful?
22. Is it possible for two people of opposite temperaments to be happy together?
23. Is it wise to marry a girl of different nationality or religion?

24. How can religious differences be overcome?
25. Are religious differences sufficient reason to refuse to marry? What proportion of such marriages succeed?
26. Should a man marry an older woman?
27. How much difference between the age of man and wife should there be for a happy marriage?
28. How great a difference in age should there be at the time of marriage?
29. Is love on the part of both individuals necessary for a successful marriage?
30. Should couples marry if they do not experience a true love but only a need for companionship.
31. How can one differentiate between infatuation and love before it is too late?
32. How can you tell whether you are really enough in love to make your marriage successful?
33. How can you tell whether your love for a person is not just passion? Even if you stay in love for two or three years before marrying, it can die quickly after marriage. Why is that? How can you determine before marriage whether your partner is the right one?
34. How can you be sure you are choosing the right mate for a life of marriage?
35. What is the best age for marriage from the viewpoint of both physical and mental maturity?
36. It seems that many who want to enter into matrimony have, because of economic conditions, to wait so long that much happiness is denied them for an extended period or lost altogether. What chances are there for happiness if a couple marries when young but does not enter into housekeeping until financially able? Should students marry? What advantages are there, if any, and what are the disadvantages?
37. How long should a courtship, ending in marriage, last?
38. How long should persons be engaged, and what does this engagement mean?
39. Should college graduates marry as soon as they graduate, depending upon their education to secure them a job, or wait until they are settled and are earning enough to support a partner in marriage?
40. How should young couples intending to get married arrive at the point and discuss children, beliefs, etc.?
41. What are the proper relationships during the period of courtship?

42. Does a girl have to "neck" to be popular in college?
43. How much of the student's time should be occupied with social and recreational activities as compared with study?
44. Can a boy or girl work his way through college and still get the most out of it?
45. Should you run around with sons of rich families even though your father says he cannot afford it? How can you refuse their invitations politely?

IV. SEX (APPLY AT DIFFERENT STAGES OF DEVELOPMENT — PARTS I, II, AND III OF TEXT)

1. Might more adequate sex education be effective in improving family relations as well as other relations?
2. Give some information regarding the problem of thoroughly understanding the underlying and fundamental motives of sex?
3. Why do we not have more instruction on the biological functions, especially those pertaining to the physical relationship?
4. How can parents inform their children on sex and its problems efficiently, sensibly, and in a way that they can understand?
5. At what age should sex instruction for children start, how much should they be told, and what particular aspects should be explained to them?
6. Basic courses in the psychology of marriage should also be offered. Men and women are essentially different in most of their attitudes toward life, and methods should be devised which would make these attitudes harmonize more nearly. A great many marriages have failed because men do not understand women as personalities and vice versa. How remedy this?
7. What is the psychology of a suitable sex life after marriage and how should it be treated?
8. What to do, or not do, in courtship for best results and happiness in marriage later on.
9. How can two average young people who are in love and cannot be married for a few years keep from, or at least control, satisfaction of sexual impulses?
10. If marriage is not financially possible, what is the substitute, if any?
11. Would not a frank treatment of sexual desires and emotions as well as ways of satisfying them be welcomed?

12. How can sexual intercourse be indulged in so as to give maximum satisfaction, benefit, and enjoyment?

13. What will be the result of any intimate relations with men or women outside of marriage?

14. Is the much heralded sex as great a factor in a successful marriage as it is said to be?

15. What are the best methods of contraception, and what are the virtues?

16. "I am a Roman Catholic, and I find it hard to reconcile the view of the Church on sex, birth control, etc., with the prevalent worldly and seemingly logical views of today. Therefore, I'd like a little clear-headed thinking done for me on this problem. Naturally a wife and a husband would have to hold the same views on this problem, and I'm wondering how we'd straighten it out if I, with the worldly masculine viewpoint on sexual relations, should marry a girl who had been reared a strict Catholic and held exactly opposite views to mine."

17. Is it possible to plan when to have children so that neither career nor finances will be in the way?

18. Is it possible to limit the number of children? How?

19. Are occasional visits to disorderly houses really as detrimental as is said?

20. Is not companionate marriage a wise thing — that is to live with a man for a certain length of time to make sure you are willing to live with him the rest of your life?

V. ACCORD IN FAMILY ADJUSTMENT (EXCLUDING SEX) (PART III OF TEXT)

1. When a man and woman get married, there are many changes they must make in their lives. Could they be taught how to accustom themselves to married life?

2. What can we do to make ourselves sufficiently interesting so that we may be able to keep the interest of our mate, husband, or wife?

3. How can love grow deeper through the years?

4. Is frankness and truth always to be desired in marriage?

5. Does love exist for years after a couple is married, and how can it be retained and treasured?

6. What form of recreation can the family as a whole participate in?

7. In order to have a satisfying family and successful marriage, people should be taught to live together and

appreciate one another. The reason for a great many unsuccessful marriages is that either one of the persons or probably both are too interested in worldly activities. If this is the case, there will be little or no family life. This could be eliminated if the husband and wife would share their social responsibilities with those of their family. How can this be promoted?

8. Is it right for a wife to expect her husband to give up recreations, such as fishing or hunting, because she wants him to? Should not she try to learn them instead?

9. What are the probable effects of married life on character?

10. Students should be given an idea what life is about, what constitutes happiness, what to strive for, and what not to strive for. What are the important things in the end?

11. One of the primary difficulties of early marital life is the lack of consideration which college graduates show for their partners. Primarily, marriage is a partnership. College graduates are usually self-centered individuals whose foremost considerations are for the ego. This inflated ego often leads to the destruction of an otherwise successful marriage. The refusal to consider your partner's viewpoint leads to difficulties which become more and more serious and end in disastrous results. How can this situation be remedied?

12. How can one live his life to the fullest so that not only he, but also his family, may benefit from the results of his living?

13. How can one learn to analyze a person's mind in order to be able to get along with that certain person?

14. Is it essential that either husband or wife predominate in household affairs?

15. How should the institution of marriage be managed? Should it be a fifty-fifty proposition, or should there be one boss of the family?

16. How much "say" should husband and wife have over each other?

17. In a successful marriage should not the husband and wife do everything fifty-fifty, each admit the other's equal intelligence, each have a share in the finances, etc.?

18. What should be the attitude of a husband toward the arrival of a child? Should he be pushed into the background or are there things for him to do? To what extent does the coming of children create or help to eliminate family conflict?

VI. DISCORD (EXCLUDING SEX) (PART IV OF TEXT)

1. What does all this incompatibility mentioned so often in divorce cases include? How can divorces be obtained for this?
2. What is lacking in a family that breaks up in divorce courts?
3. How can one make one's home life happy and successful when one's parents are divorced, and not allow divorce to spoil one's conception of marriage?
4. Should families in which there are children consider divorce?
5. How is it possible for children to get along and lead a normal life when their parents are divorced?
6. What are the common causes and probable cures for the breaking down of homes?
7. Should financial matters rule family discord?
8. Is lack of control and selfish desire an important cause of unhappy marriage?
9. How can family disagreements, if and when they arise, be corrected? Can family disagreements be avoided?

VII. FAMILY ECONOMICS (PRIMARILY PART III OF TEXT — SOME QUESTIONS APPLY TO PART II ALSO)

1. How does one go about making a complete budget of the family income?
2. Should instruction be given on how to make and maintain an adequate budget?
3. How can the budget be well balanced?
4. Is too careful budgeting detrimental to the family?
5. What should the factor concerning money be if both the wife and husband work? Should the money be controlled jointly, or one or the other have the balance of power?
6. Who should control the purse strings in a family where both husband and wife work?
7. What is better and works for a more harmonious household — pooling incomes or separate bank accounts?
8. How is it possible for those unable to pay for competent medical care during pregnancy to obtain it?
9. Is it advisable to have children if you are without definite financial security?
10. How should one save for the future?
11. What is the proper way to spend, and yet save enough money to get through "hard times"?

12. How can financial affairs be properly taken care of in the home?

13. What are the chances of a successful marriage when only a subsistence wage is earned by the husband?

14. Is it right for a boy or girl to come to college at the extreme sacrifice of the parents? There are a number of students of parents from the laboring classes who are troubled by this problem. This is a mental handicap to the student, who never enjoys "college life" (social activities, etc.) because he is struck with the idea that he must labor unceasingly so as not to fail his parents. From still another point of view this gives the boy or girl a sense of obligation to his or her parents. Thus he will not marry unless his parents are "well fixed" financially. Discuss!

15. If one or more members of the same family are going to college and if funds are low, should the youngest one be allowed to sacrifice his place so that the older one may finish his course?

16. Why are not expenses of college looked upon as the earnings of the students rather than luxury?

17. Is it true that when the "bill collector rings at the front door, love goes out the back"? Give three reasons in support of your answer.

18. Children should know where the family income goes and how much of it is spent on them. Is it necessary to have allowances for this? This point is mentioned because much of the family trouble which has arisen, has been over money matters. Discuss.

19. Should the wife be allowed to work if the husband can support the family? How does the war situation affect your answer?

20. Should the wife be allowed to work if it eases the financial burden of the husband?

21. Can one have a successful career and marriage?

22. What are the chances of combining a career and marriage? Can a woman be successful in both? Will she find enough happiness in a career, such as that of a lawyer or doctor, to give up marriage? Can you give us examples of such women and suggestions?

23. What is the minimum income that would be necessary for marriage? To support a family?

24. Should a young man, who has gone through college on borrowed money, delay his marriage until he has repaid his debt? Should he deprive himself of certain things

immediately after graduation and make an effort to return the money immediately?

25. Should two people very decidedly in love refuse to marry because their yearly income is not enough to meet their usual expenditures, but is adequate if they reduce their style of living?

VIII. CHILDREN (PART III OF TEXT)

1. One of the most important family matters that should be taken care of in such an instruction course is the care and training of children. Many people of today do not realize the value of knowing how to raise their children. Why is this not a part of every college curriculum for women? Men?

2. What are the most prevalent child diseases, and what are the best means of, primarily, prevention, and secondly, cure?

3. "My parents and others have told of mistakes they have made in raising their children and realized these mistakes only too late. I would eagerly elect in my course some subject pertaining to the development of the intellect and character of children from the very beginning of their lives." Is this possible in every college? Why?

4. Just what attitudes or relationships should be maintained between parents and children on the problem of discipline?

5. How should the task of rearing the children be divided?

6. How many children can the average woman have in the average home without destroying her vitality and the savings of the family?

7. Is there a tendency for childless married couples to break up more easily than married couples having children?

8. Is it possible to have a modern, successful marriage without having a child for a "binding" influence?

9. Can two married people live a full and happy life without children?

IX. RELIGION AND ETHICS (PART III OF TEXT)

1. Do you think it is a good thing for a child to have too much to say in respect to its choice of a religion?

2. How avoid complications of differences in religious beliefs in raising children?

3. After marriage should the husband go with the wife to her church or vice versa? Or should this problem be decided upon before marriage?

4. Where should the children go if each parent goes to a different church?
5. What is the part of religion in family life and marriage?
6. What should be the religious participation of the family as a unit?
7. Can a marriage be really successful without a spiritual background? How important is similarity of spiritual background, i.e. Catholic vs. Protestant?

APPENDIX D

A PREMARITAL CONTRAST INTERVIEW BLANK

By Robert G. Foster

The Premarital Contrast Blank is not to be used as a questionnaire. Its main purpose is as a guide in interviewing. It offers many items, some of which are more important than others, but all of which, at some time or another, and in different situations, may prove to be the points at which definite help needs to be given to the person or persons seeking advice. It is for the use of the counsellor and to be filled out by him.

Person Interviewed_____

Interviewer_____Date_____

Item	Yourself	Your Fiance	Notes
1. Age			
2. Length of engagement			
3. How and where did you meet			
4. Education			
5. Major in college			
6. College debts			
7. Nationality — Father / Mother			
8. Religious views			
9. Religion of parents — Father / Mother			
10. Club Affiliations — In College / Present			
11. Physical vigor (If no exam)			
12. Eugenic history			
13. Mental level (Test or scholastic grade average)			
14. Emotional stability and mental health (From interview)			

Item	Yourself	Your Fiance	Notes
15. Occupational history (Home and outside)			
16. Occupation of parents			
17. Family living together			
18. Knowledge of family of fiance			
19. Attitude toward fiance's family			
20. Number brothers and sisters			
21. Rank among children			
22. Parental attachments			
23. Sibling attachments			
24. Agreement as to having children			
25. Agreement as to number of children			
26. Where do parents live			
27. Where will you live after marriage			
28. What is your income			
29. Years worked			
30. What savings have you			
31. Born and reared in city, village, farm			
32. Mobility of parental group			
33. Money pattern of parents			
34. Your plans for money handling			
35. Economic responsibility			
36. When do you plan to marry			
37. Reasons for date above			
38. Personal habits you dislike			
39. Do you smoke			
40. Do you drink			
41. Personal appearance of individual			
42. What recreational interests have you			
43. What are your hobbies			
44. Interest in art, music, drama, etc.			
45. Primary interest — people or things			
46. Primary interest — country or city			
47. Will wife work after marriage			
48. Background of sex attitudes and relations			
49. Attitudes and relations with opposite sex during engagement			
50. Attitudes and relations with opposite sex after marriage			
51. What ultimate aims have you for your married life?			
52. What do you like most about your fiance?			

Item	Yourself	Your Fiance	Notes
53. What do you like least about your fiance?			
54. Premarital Relations			
55. What is your greatest ambition in life?			
56. What have you read in preparation for marriage?			
57. Unusual crises in life to date			
58. Type of wedding planned			

59. Test and examination reports
   a. Physical premarital Examination
   b. Bernreuter Personality
   c. Detroit Advanced Intelligence Test
   d. Values test (Allport-Vernon)			

APPENDIX E

WHERE TO GO FOR HELP

CALIFORNIA

The American Institute of Family Relations
Paul Popenoe, Director
5287 Sunset Boulevard
Los Angeles, 27, California.

Family Counseling Center
Evelyn Berger, Director
315 14th Street
Oakland, California.

Family Service Association of San Diego
Nevin Wiley, Executive Secretary
645 A Street, Room 200
San Diego, California.

Family Relations Center
Henry M. Grant, Executive Secretary
2504 Jackson Street
San Francisco, California.

ILLINOIS

The Association for Family Living
28 East Jackson Boulevard
Chicago, 4, Illinois.

KANSAS

The Menninger Foundation
Robert G. Foster, Counsellor
Topeka, Kansas.

Shawnee County Guidance Center
Robert G. Foster, Counsellor
Topeka, Kansas.

MASSACHUSETTS

Counseling Service
Lester W. Dearborn, Chief Consultant
316 Huntington Avenue
Boston, 16, Massachusetts.

MINNESOTA

Marriage Counseling Service
Mrs. Irving Simos, Marriage Counselor
223 Walker Building
803 Hennepin Avenue
Minneapolis, 3, Minnesota.

NEW YORK

Family Guidance and Consultation Service.
Child Study Association of America
Sidonie M. Gruenberg, Director
221 West Fifty-seventh Street
New York, 19, New York.

Jewish Institute on Marriage and the Family
Sidney E. Goldstein, Chairman

302

Synagogue House
40 West 68th Street
New York, New York.

Marriage Consultation Center
The Community Church
40 East 35th Street
New York, New York.

NORTH CAROLINA

Marriage and Family Council,
Inc.
Galdys Hoagland Groves,
Director
Chapel Hill, North Carolina.

OHIO

Family Service
Anna Budd Ware, Executive
Director
312 West Ninth Street
Cincinnati, 2, Ohio.

Cincinnati Social Hygiene
Society
Roy E. Dickerson, Executive
Secretary
312 West Ninth Street
Cincinnati, 2, Ohio.

Consultation Service
Hazel Jackson, Director

2101 Adelbert Road
Cleveland, Ohio.

PENNSYLVANIA

Marriage Council
Emily B. H. Mudd, Director
1930 Chestnut Street
Philadelphia, Pennsylvania.

UTAH

Utah State College Marriage
Counseling Service
Lawrence S. Bee, Director
Logan, Utah.

VIRGINIA

Pre Marital and Marriage
Counseling Service
Beatrice V. Marion, Director
421 West Grace Street
Richmond, Virginia.

DISTRICT OF COLUMBIA

Social Hygiene Society
Ray H. Everett, Director
927 Fifteenth Street N. W.
Washington, D. C.

If you do not know of a counseling service near you, write to one
of the following organizations:

American Association of Mar-
riage Counselors
Robert W. Laidlaw, M.D.,
Secretary
563 Park Avenue
New York, 21, New York.

Family Service Association of
America
Frank J. Hertel, General Di-
rector
122 East 22nd Street
New York, 10, New York.

National Council on Family Relations
1126 East Fifty-ninth Street
Chicago, Ill.

SOURCE MATERIALS

FILMS AND FILM STRIPS*

Association Films, Y.M.C.A. Motion Picture Bureau, 291 Broadway, New York 7, N. Y.

Bell and Howell Co., 1801 Larchmont Avenue, Chicago 13, Illinois.

British Information Services, 30 Rockefeller Plaza, New York 20, N. Y.

Educational Film Guide, N. W. Wilson Co., 950 University Avenue, New York 52, N. Y.

McGraw-Hill Book Company, Inc., Text-Film Dept., 330 West 42 Street, New York 18, N. Y.

Methodist Publishing House, Visual Aids Dept., 740 Rush Street, Chicago 11, Illinois.

Metropolitan Life Insurance Company, 1 Madison Avenue, New York 10, N. Y.

New York State Department of Health, 18 Dove Street, Albany 6, New York.

New York University Film Library, 26 Washington Square, New York 3, N. Y.

United States Department of Agriculture, Films available from United World Films, 30 Rockefeller Plaza, New York 20, N. Y.

United World Films, 30 Rockefeller Plaza, New York 20, N. Y.

Vocational Guidance Films, 2708 Beaver Avenue, Des Moines 10, Iowa.

PAMPHLETS

American Institute of Family Relations, 5287 Sunset Blvd., Los Angeles 27, California.

American Medical Association, 535 North Dearborn St., Chicago 10, Illinois.

American Social Hygiene Association, 1790 Broadway, New York 19, N. Y.

* Most State Departments of Health and State Universities or Agricultural Colleges have limited visual aid services available for small rental fee.

Association for Family Living, 28 East Jackson Blvd., Chicago 4, Illinois.

Association Press, 291 Broadway, New York 7, N. Y.

Better Homes and Gardens, 1716 Locust Street, Des Moines 3, Iowa.

Child Study Association of America, 132 East 74 Street, New York 21, N. Y.

Children's Bureau, United States Dept. of Labor, Washington 25, D. C.

Cincinnati Social Hygiene Society, 312 West 9 Street, Cincinnati 2, Ohio.

Commission on Marriage and the Home, Federal Council of Churches of Christ in America, 297 Fourth Avenue, New York 10, N. Y.

Emmerson Books, Inc., 251 West 19 Street, New York 11, N. Y.

Family Life Bureau, National Catholic Welfare Conference, 1312 Massachusetts Avenue, N. W., Washington, D. C.

The Macmillan Company, 60 Fifth Avenue, New York 11, N. Y. and 2459 Prairie Avenue, Chicago 16, Illinois.

National Committee for Mental Hygiene, 1790 Broadway, New York 19, N. Y.

National Congress of Parents and Teachers, 600 South Michigan Blvd., Chicago 5, Illinois.

National Council on Family Relations, 1126 East 59 Street, Chicago 37, Illinois.

New York Tuberculosis and Health Association, 386 Fourth Avenue, New York 16, N. Y.

Planned Parenthood Federation of America, 501 Madison Avenue, New York, N. Y.

Public Affairs Committee, 22 East 38 Street, New York 16, N. Y.

Science Research Associates, 228 South Wabash Avenue, Chicago 4, Illinois.

United States Government Printing Office, Washington 25, D. C.

University Extension Services, State Health Departments and Agricultural and Home Economics Extension Services in each state have helpful resource materials.

PROFESSIONAL JOURNALS

American Journal of Orthopsychiatry. 1790 Broadway, New York 19, N. Y., organ of the American Orthopsychiatric Association.

American Journal of Psychiatry. Published by the American Psychiatric Association, 9 Rockefeller Plaza, New York 20, N. Y.

American Journal of Sociology. University of Chicago Press, Chicago 37, Illinois.

Annals of American Academy of Political and Social Science. Published by the American Academy of Political and Social Science, 3457 Walnut Street, Philadelphia 4, Pennsylvania.

(The) Child. Monthly news summary published by the Children's Bureau, United States Dept. of Labor, Washington, D. C.

Child Development Abstracts and Bibliography. Publication of the society for Research in Child Development. National Research Council, 2101 Constitution Ave., Washington 25, D. C.

Child Study. Published by the Child Study Association, 221 W. 57 Street, New York, N. Y.

Family Life. Published by The American Institute of Family Relations, 5287 Sunset Blvd., Los Angeles 27, California.

Geriatrics (Old Age). Official journal of the American Geriatric Society, 84 South 10 St., Minneapolis 2, Minnesota.

Journal of Child Psychiatry (new). Published by Child Care Publication, 30 W. 58 St., New York, N. Y.

Journal of Educational Sociology. 26 Washington Place, New York 3, N. Y. Editorial office, New York University.

Journal of Home Economics. 620 Mills Bldg., Washington, D. C., organ of the American Home Economics Association.

Journal of Social Case Work (formerly titled *The Family*). Official organ of the Family Welfare Association, 122 E. 22 St., New York 10, N. Y.

Journal of Social Hygiene. 1790 Broadway, New York 19, N. Y., organ of the American Social Hygiene Association.

Journal of Social Psychology. Journal Press, Provincetown, Massachusetts.

Marriage and Family Living. Published by the National Council on Family Relations, 1126 East 59 Street, Chicago, Illinois.

Mental Hygiene. Published by the National Committee for Mental Hygiene, 50 W. 50 Street, New York 20, N. Y.

(The) National Parent-Teacher. Published by National Parent-Teacher, Inc., 600 S. Michigan Blvd., Chicago, Illinois.

(The) Parents' Magazine. Published by The Parents' Magazine, 52 Vanderbilt Ave., New York 17, N. Y.

Psychological Abstracts. Published by the American Psychological Association, Northwestern University, Evanston, Illinois.

Smith College Studies in Social Work. Northampton, Massachusetts.

Social Forces.   Williams and Wilkins Co., Baltimore, Maryland, Editorial office, University of North Carolina, Chapel Hill, North Carolina.

Survey.   112 East 19 Street, New York 3, N. Y.

Understanding the Child.   Published by National Committee for Mental Hygiene, 1790 Broadway, New York 19, N. Y.

APPENDIX G

REFERENCES CITED IN THE TEXT

1. Plant, James S., *Personality and the Cultural Pattern*. Commonwealth Fund. Division of Publications, New York, 1937.
2. May, Mark, *Proceedings 2nd Colloquium on Personality Investigation*. Held under auspices of the Amer. Psychiatric Association Committee on Relations of Psychiatry and the Social Sciences. Nov. 29–30, 1929, New York.
3. Thomas, W. I., *The Person and His Wishes*. A restatement by Jennings, Watson, Meyer and Thomas in *Suggestions of Modern Science Concerning Education*. The Macmillan Company, New York, 1917.
4. Prescott, Daniel A., *Emotion and the Educative Process*. American Council on Education, Washington, D.C., 1938.
5. Burgess, E. W., and Cottrell, Leonard, *Predicting Success or Failure in Marriage*. Prentice-Hall, Inc., New York, 1939.
6. *Ibid.*
7. Terman, Lewis M., *Psychological Factors in Marital Happiness*. McGraw-Hill Book Company, Inc., New York, 1938.
8. Popenoe, Paul, "Should College Students Marry?" *Parents' Magazine*, vol. 13, p. 18, July, 1938.
9. Anonymous, "I Have Been Married a Year." *Ladies' Home Journal*, p. 31, Apr., 1937. Copyright. Quoted by special permission.
10. Foster, R. G., and Wilson, Pauline P., *Women After College*. Columbia University Press, New York, 1942. P. 27.
11. *Ibid.*, pp. 80–84.
12. Frank, L. K., "The Needs of the Child." *The National Parent Teacher Magazine*, Dec., 1938. The National Parent Teacher, Inc., 600 St. Mary Ave., Chicago S, Ill.
13. Anonymous, "I Have Been Married a Year." *Ladies' Home Journal*, p. 31, Apr., 1937. Copyright. Quoted by special permission.
14. Foster, R. G., "Democracy in The Family." *Forecast*, p. 470, Dec., 1938. Quoted by permission.

15. Foster, R. G., "Democracy in The Family." *Forecast*, p. 470, Dec., 1938. Quoted by permission.

16. *Ibid.*

17. *Ibid.*

18. Crowell, Grace Noll, *Good Housekeeping*, New York. Oct. 1936. Quoted by special permission.

19. Donne, John, *Devotion Upon Emergent Occasions. Meditation No. 17.* As quoted in Hemingway, Ernest, *For Whom the Bell Tolls.* Charles Scribner's Sons, New York, 1940.

20. Terman, Lewis W., *Psychological Factors in Marital Happiness.* McGraw-Hill Book Company, Inc., New York, 1938.

21. Becker, Carl, and Hill, Reuben, *Marriage and the Family.* D. C. Heath and Company, Boston, 1943.

22. Rand, W., Sweeny, M., and Vincent, E. Lee, *Growth and Development of the Young Child.* W. B. Saunders Company, Philadelphia, 1940.

23. Lindeman, Eduard, "The Importance of the Family in the Democratic Process." *Parent Education*, p. 36, Dec., 1937.

24. Foster, Robert G., adaptation with permission from "Marriage During Crisis." *Journal of Home Economics*, June, 1943.

25. Farrell, Mary F., "After Thirty Years." *What's New in Home Economics*, March, 1941.

26. Foster, Robert G., adaptation from "Today Is the Future." *What's New in Home Economics*, Feb., 1942.

27. Drummond, Laura, *Youth and Instruction in Marriage and Family Living.* Contributions to Education No. 856. Bureau of Publications, Teachers College, Columbia University, New York, 1942. Quoted by special permission.

INDEX

311